The
BEAUVOIR SISTERS

BY CLAUDINE MONTEIL

Translated from the
French by Marjolijn de Jager

D0249975

SEAL PRESS

THE BEAUVOIR SISTERS: AN INTIMATE LOOK AT HOW SIMONE AND HÉLÈNE INFLUENCED EACH OTHER AND THE WORLD

Published by
Seal Press
An Imprint of Avalon Publishing Group Incorporated
1400 65th Street, Suite 250
Emeryville, CA 94608

Published with the cooperation of the French Ministry of Culture—National Center of the Book. Ouvrage publié avec le concours du Ministère de la Culture—Centre National du Livre.

ISBN 1-58005-110-3

9 8 7 6 5 4 3 2 1

Cover Design: Diane Rigoli
Interior Design: Amber Pirker
Printed in the United States of America by Worzalla
Distributed by Publishers Group West

For Marie and for Bernard.

This story, which is theirs as well, is for Chantal, Catherine, Monique, and Sandro.

For Annick, Cecelia, Liliane, Michèle, Patrick, Thérèse, Victor, and Yolanda.

Also by Claudine Monteil:

Les Amants de la liberté, l'aventure de Jean-Paul Sartre et Simone de Beauvoir dans le siècle, Paris, Editions 1, 1999.

Les Amants des temps modernes, Charles et Oona Chaplin, Paris, Editions 1, 2002.

Simone de Beauvoir, le mouvement des femmes. Mémoires d'une jeune fille rebelle, Montréal, Alain Stanké, 1995, Paris, Editions du Rocher, 1996.

CONTENTS

ACKNOWLEDGMENTS

I owe a great debt to Hélène Monties, the first reader of this book, who patiently and delicately gave me her opinion—both critical and benevolent—of the text. I wish to express my feelings of friendship for her.

My deep thanks go to Marjolijn de Jager who beautifully translated this book from the French and gave me the joy of becoming an exquisite friend. Our collaboration was pure delight. My gratitude also goes to Christina Henry de Tessan, my editor, who took the time to read my book in French and who supported this project with great kindness and cheer from the very beginning.

The following individuals encouraged me to write this biography, which is also a testimony: Annick Dain, Liliane Lazar, Michèle Clément, Michèle Mazier, Thérèse Ponthieu, Rebecca Chalker, Yolanda Astarita Patterson, Patrick Pommier, Victor Koshkin-Youritzin, and Cecelia Yoder. Their support has been invaluable to me. Jean-Pierre Pouget, the associate director of the French Cultural Center in Turin, was kind enough to help me gather information on the life of Lionel de Roulet and Hélène de Beauvoir in Milan. Andrée Rizzuto, former research librarian of the French Cultural Center in Milan, was very helpful as well.

A Togolese family, Mr. and Mrs. Ametepee and their five children, two of whom are the godchildren of Hélène de Beauvoir and Lionel de Roulet, give their unfailing loyalty to both. I wish to express my friendship and affection to them.

My sincere appreciation also goes to Jeanne Fayard, a specialist in the lives of Camille Claudel and Auguste Rodin, who was kind enough to share the results of her research on the two artists.

Finally, I wish to express my gratitude to Anne Strasser-Weinhard, who defended her doctoral thesis in French Language and Literature at the

University of Nancy-II on the topic "Les Figures féminines dans les auto-biographies de Simone de Beauvoir" ("Female figures in Simone de Beau-voir's autobiographies") in December 2001. She was generous enough to confirm for me—as she mentions in her thesis—that Simone de Beau-voir herself had made substantial cuts in the letters that Sartre had written to her before they were published under the title *Lettres à Castor.*

Simone de Beauvoir had specifically eliminated all the passages Sartre had written that were critical of Hélène de Beauvoir, thereby indicating that she did not wish that anything hurtful to her sister be published.

This book also owes a great deal to my conversations with Simone de Beauvoir, Hélène de Beauvoir, and Lionel de Roulet over the many years of our friendship.

Readers wanting to obtain further information should consult the different volumes of Simone de Beauvoir's memoirs, the *Souvenirs* of Hélène de Beauvoir, as well as the book by Patricia Niedzwiecki on the artwork of the latter.

In conclusion, I would like to say that I am confident that Simone and Hélène de Beauvoir would have very much appreciated the fact that their story is being published in the United States by a publisher of women's books. Thank you very much to Seal Press. I wish them luck with their pub-lications, which help promote women's arts and women's rights.

Claudine Monteil

TRANSLATOR'S
ACKNOWLEDGMENTS

My profound gratitude goes to Claudine Monteil for her patience and invaluable help in answering questions, both linguistic and factual, during the process of translating her book.

For me, as for so many women of my generation, Simone de Beauvoir was and remains a figure of enormous influence. "Meeting" her sister Hélène de Beauvoir has been an experience I will always treasure, and for this, too, I thank the author and her generosity in sharing such an extraordinary friendship with all of us.

Finally, my deep appreciation goes to Christina Henry de Tessan, who entrusted me with this exceptional personal testimony.

Marjolijn de Jager

The
BEAUVOIR
SISTERS

PROLOGUE

In 1970, in front of the art academy, the École des Beaux-Arts, near the church of Saint-Germain-des-Prés, I saw a poster that announced a meeting of the Women's Liberation Movement.[1] Who were they? As I was trying to get some information, I heard a lot of noisy protest around me. Indeed, the reputation they had was appalling—lesbians, hysterics, and those who couldn't get laid! Still, I decided to go to the meeting, and what I found instead were scintillating women, intelligent and funny, who welcomed me as an equal. So I left the post-1968 Maoist movement to join the women's cause.

In my circle this choice was interpreted as a veritable betrayal. I lost many of my friends. Associating with these "hysterics" often led to disgrace and exclusion. But I forged new friendships very quickly, and two of these would change my life.

One evening at a meeting of the Mouvement de Libération des Femmes (MLF), I was told that Simone de Beauvoir wanted to meet me. She had heard about my work as an activist with female factory workers. And so one Sunday in November 1970 I was expected to be at her house at five in the afternoon. The invitation really threw me. I thought of my mother, a chemist and an academic, who, thanks to her reading of *The Second Sex*, had found the strength to establish herself as a researcher. From the time I was an adolescent, she had been singing the praises of Simone's books. I had devoured them. Here I was, just twenty years old and about to meet my idol, who was now sixty-two.

I walked back and forth in front of 11bis, Rue Schoelcher, across from the Montparnasse Cemetery, waiting for it to be five o'clock. "Be on time!" Anne, one of the founders of the MLF, had warned me. "She insists on punctuality." So at the exact hour I rang the doorbell. "You're late!" Simone de Beauvoir told me reproachfully. Actually, I was not. On her desk a hideous alarm clock was seven minutes fast. I was later to learn that she and Sartre were in such demand with activists that, in order to be able to continue writing, they needed to observe a very strict schedule. Flustered and intimidated, I sat down. The conversation began immediately.

Sitting on one of her yellow sofas, Simone was beaming. In her painter's studio with its large bay windows were several women who were determined to change the world. The "girls" of 1968 had invaded her home.

Ideas were flying around, yet everyone agreed on one point: the first goal should be the abolishment of the law against abortion, which at the time was seen as a criminal offense. Under the Occupation, Marshall Pétain had a woman guillotined because she was guilty of helping her colleagues in trouble. We all knew too many examples of lives wrecked by these clandestine abortions. Practiced by people who more often than not lacked any medical knowledge, these acts sometimes turned into real tragedies. In their contempt for the health of French women, the authorities closed their eyes in false modesty and refused to tackle the question.

I was listening attentively when, to my great surprise, Simone asked for my opinion. I agreed wholeheartedly with the project and suggested we put together a campaign to break the taboo and attract the public's attention. Simone supported the idea that we needed the media. So we decided to publish a manifesto in favor of abortion. The list of signatories grew longer. "Add my sister's name," Simone said. The manifesto was published in the spring of 1971 in *Le Nouvel Observateur*[2] and caused one of the century's greatest scandals. The headline on the cover stood out in fiery red letters against a black background: the list of 343 women who declared "I have had an abortion!" The names were printed in alphabetical order on the first page of the magazine. The signatories came from every possible social class. Next to those of Catherine Deneuve, Françoise Sagan, and Régine Desforges were the names of unknown women. Even though I had never had an abortion, I had signed out of solidarity. The names of the two Beauvoir sisters appeared side by side.

CHAPTER ONE

Two Dutiful Daughters

In the classroom of a private Catholic school for young girls, called the Cours Désir, which was located on Rue Jacob, two little girls sat on low stools at a round table. In contrast to the children in public schools, the pupils were not allowed to have desks.

Their mothers had settled in behind them. Armed with their embroidery fabric and thread, they were doing a variety of needlework. The ladies had comments on their offspring's every word, and their judgment was brutal. Any hesitation, any clumsiness would be reported back to the family as a whole. In the higher grades one pupil crushed the others with her intelligence and eagerness. Her arrival at the Cours Désir had created a sensation. Young Simone de Beauvoir knew how to read, write, and count before any of her little classmates.

Setting itself apart from the state educational institutions, the Cours Désir did not hand out books as prizes at the end of the school year. It held a ceremony in Wagram Hall in March at which the bishop or archbishop was present and where medals were awarded to the best students. Eight and ten years old, consistently the first in their respective classes, the Beauvoir sisters easily obtained honorable mention with the silver medal. Yet they never claimed the supreme recognition of the gold medal, for in the eyes of the teaching staff neither one was a model of virtue.

Georges de Beauvoir boasted about the academic success of his older daughter. Hélène's achievements interested him less. After Simone's birth, the aristocratic Beauvoir family had hoped for a boy and were disappointed with the arrival of another girl. They instantly nicknamed Hélène "Poupette"—little doll—and Georges de Beauvoir paid far less attention to his younger daughter than to the older one. Besides, according to her own parents, Simone's character demanded exceptional treatment: "Oh, you shouldn't interfere with Simone or she's going to have a fit."[1] On the other hand, they could reprimand Hélène as much as they wanted. She wouldn't get angry, but often sought refuge in her sister's arms.

Françoise de Beauvoir kept a close eye on her youngest, over whom she had more influence. Having herself despised her younger sister, who had been the favorite, she transferred the jealousy she had felt as a child onto her second daughter, and so Hélène was constricted and deprived of the freedom Simone enjoyed. Nevertheless, there was a real rapport between the two little girls that Françoise found hard to take. When they would talk together in bed before they fell asleep she had her ear to the wall, eaten up with curiosity and, irritated that she couldn't hear anything, would yell at them to be quiet.

The amazing thing is that Hélène never resented her sister even though there were plenty of reasons for her to rebel. Not recognizing her merits, her parents were always holding her older sister up to her as an example. One evening at dinner, Françoise de Beauvoir was bragging to a cousin:

"Simone was first in her class again."

"But, Mother, I am first also!" Hélène protested.

"It's easier for you!"[2] she was told, although there wasn't any logic to the remark.

She remembered the snub for a long time. Fortunately Simone, her confidante and protector, was there. How could Hélène not love her?

"Comparing my lot to that of my sister is most revealing," Simone would write many years later in *Tout compte fait*. "Her road was far more arduous than mine because she had to overcome the handicap of her early years. In photographs of myself at age two and a half I look determined and self-assured, she has a frightened little face. . . . They certainly must have smiled at her less often and paid less attention to her. Worried and anxious even, she took a long time to set herself completely free of her childhood."[3]

An accomplished authoritarian from her earliest years, Simone would grasp her sister's hand and order her to sit down. It was time to study. She would be the teacher and Hélène the student. "What I most appreciated in our relationship is that I had a real influence over her. . . . Thanks to my sister— my accomplice, my subject, my pet—I was asserting my autonomy."[4]

"Repeat!" she'd cry out imperiously. Hélène, full of admiration and eager to please her gifted older sister, would comply. Once again she would recite the multiplication tables, try hard to decipher the letters in her beautifully illustrated books. Sometimes the reward would come: "Soon you'll be able to come to the library with Mother and me!" This last promise, enthusiastically uttered, was a dream of Hélène's. The Cardinale Library on the Place Saint-Sulpice was Simone's kingdom. She could choose what she wanted. The world was hers. Browsing through the shelves of books for young people, she would point at some of them and comment on the ones she had read.

■ ■ ■

"Hurry up, we're going to be late!"

On the narrow sidewalk of Rue de Varenne, Simone was pulling her sister by the hand, impatient to get to her new friend. Hélène was reluctant to keep moving. Elisabeth Mabille, whose nickname was "Zaza," was in Simone's class. From a bourgeois Catholic family and an excellent student, she could have become a rival but affection had supplanted jealousy between the two little girls. At Désir, Zaza was generally thought of as a special character because of an accident she had suffered: "In the country, she had set fire to her dress while she was cooking potatoes; because her thigh had sustained third-degree burns she had screamed for nights on end and had to stay in bed for a whole year. . . . She immediately seemed like a special person to me."[5]

When the door of the Mabille's apartment opened, the Beauvoir sisters had a shock. Zaza's eight brothers and sisters were running around in every direction creating an indescribable uproar. To be able to talk quietly, Zaza and her two guests found refuge in the study. Poupette soon felt she was in the way. A feeling of anguish tightened her throat and prevented her from taking part in the conversation, the laughter, and the games. For Hélène it was a terrible afternoon. She felt that her older sister only had eyes for Zaza and she trembled with fear of losing her love. Back at home that evening, in the small room they shared, she asked Simone with tears in her voice:

"Don't you love me anymore?"

"Of course I love you."

"You won't leave me?"

"Of course not!"

They turned out the light. In the dark Hélène couldn't get to sleep. Since the new school year had begun her sister had lost interest in her and she felt defeated. The little girls her mother forced upon her as friends were stupid and silly, a thousand miles removed from Simone and her intelligence. She cried noiselessly until morning.

Simone got up early, impatient to get back to the Cours Désir. She didn't see or she pretended not to notice Poupette's red eyes. From that time on, Simone's world and happiness depended on just two things: "to be herself and to love Zaza."[6]

■   ■   ■

The years went by. At lunch on Sundays, Georges de Beauvoir cursed the institution for young ladies of a good background that was costing him a great deal of money and where his children were learning so little. Since a friend of his had praised the merits of the *lycée*[7] and the fact that it was tuition free, he said loudly:

"These women are absolute idiots! I would really like to put you in the *lycée.*"

As she couldn't imagine being separated from Zaza, Simone protested. Then Georges de Beauvoir asked Hélène what she wanted to do.

"If Simone is staying I'm staying," the little one answered adamantly. Hélène felt herself blush. Her sister had abandoned her for that Zaza whom she hated. Simone no longer confided in her at all. Sure, they would still talk at bedtime, they still giggled together sometimes, but all Simone could talk about was Zaza. Jealousy ate away at Hélène.

In the school playground Simone and Zaza would isolate themselves and talk in hushed tones. When Hélène approached, Zaza made fun of her. Back home, Hélène would finally have her sister to herself again. But there, too, privacy didn't last long. Françoise de Beauvoir, indiscreet and troublesome, interfered: "What are you talking about?" Hélène lived with her sadness in secret, oppressed and without any real friends.

While Simone impressed with her grades and her ease at learning, Hélène made some timid first attempts at being unruly. She was sometimes called into the principal's office. A wind of rebellion was blowing across the Cours Désir.

Hélène created the *Echo of the School Désir*, a satirical paper for which she did the drawings and which Zaza, amused by her irreverence, duplicated. In it, she made fun of the courses and teachers, and imparted innocent gossip. Still, the whole thing showed proof of a certain daring. Had she been caught she would most certainly have been immediately expelled. The result went beyond her wildest dreams: Simone was impressed. Zaza, the copycat, laid down her arms. The "little one" was amazing. But the consequences were not long in coming—the following semester, Georges de Beauvoir flew into a violent rage when he discovered Hélène's notebook just when she had lost her standing as the first in her class. In resignation she stopped writing her beloved *Echo* and focused on her studies. A month later, she was back in first place again, like Simone, and the honor of the Beauvoirs was saved.

❚   ❚   ❚

The war of 1914–1918 had transformed Georges de Beauvoir into a bitter and unhappy man. He had stopped believing in happiness and held it against his milieu. Like so many others, he had returned from the trenches sickened by the spectacle of suffering, death, and barbarity. A failed lawyer, he sought to forget his bitterness in gambling and society parties, and soon preferred the company of actors to quiet evenings at home with his family. He was a theater lover and liked to recite poems and declaim lines of verse. His knowledge of literature fascinated his attentive listeners, something that did not escape his daughters, who were suddenly full of admiration. He would have liked to be on stage in front of a real audience— his true dream was to be an actor. Sometimes he would sit in the living room with his wife and daughters by his side and read a play from his library. Simone and Hélène would feed him the responses and soon Molière, Labiche, Corneille, and Racine were like old friends to them. Whether he played the tragedian or comedian, they marveled at their father. His joy in acting was obvious. The taste for literature Simone was later to express may well have been born during those happy evenings.

Unfortunately, they became more and more infrequent. In fact, when he went out to his society gatherings Georges de Beauvoir had a tendency to seek comfort from other women, and this upset his wife. Amid arguments, tears, and recriminations, the family atmosphere deteriorated and quarrels gradually replaced the hours of shared reading.

■   ■   ■

"Quickly, girls!"

Hélène and Simone dashed into the train. They had been waiting for this moment for months, since summer vacations on the family properties brought them the freedom they dreamed of all year long. Happy days were in sight: July in Meyrignac in the Corrèze and August in La Grillère in Haute-Vienne.

At a run the sisters arrived at La Grillère, the realm that would finally bring them together. The château had a huge library that held the works of Jules Verne and an immense fireplace. The girls played cricket in the park and spent hours walking in the woods. The adults paid them no mind. Their mother seemed to forget the worries of Parisian life and slackened her supervision. Simone and Hélène were only obliged to be present at mealtime. How far away Paris was now!

One summer, Georges de Beauvoir wanted to give them bicycles but ran into the opposition of Françoise, who categorically refused. Simone and Hélène begged and threw their arms around their parents' necks, clapping their hands, but their charming offensive did not soften their mother. That the little ones roamed around the woods by themselves was one thing, but bicycles were an excess of freedom. And besides, she herself had never had one.

Georges de Beauvoir didn't insist. The girls had to make do with walking, reading, and playing with the cricket mallet. In the end, the games they invented and nature's treasures were more than sufficient for them. In one of the château's bedrooms, just before they fell asleep, they would whisper and make fun of the adults and their harebrained ideas, and dream of the next day and the pleasures it would bring.

"Early in the morning my first joy was to catch the field in its awakening; with a book in my hand, I would leave the sleeping house. . . . I read as I walked, feeling the coolness of the air melting against my skin. . . . I was by myself to wear the world's beauty and God's glory and in the pit of my stomach lay a dream of hot chocolate and toast."[8]

Young Simone wrote her first feelings down in her notebooks. She was discovering the magic and power of words. Thanks to them she felt she existed. She was not yet aware that such happiness could lead to the writer's profession. Once she had copied her secrets down in ink she'd go running back to the château. Hélène and a solid breakfast awaited her in the kitchen. Hélène, too, was radiant—with the exception of her solitary escapades early in the morning, throughout the summer Simone was all hers. The rivalry with Zaza was temporarily resolved.

■ ■ ■

At the Cours Désir, the adolescents were talking about love. Zaza and Simone compared their dreams and thoughts about the ideal couple. Simone remained cautious on the subject—her parents' dissension, her father's boorish behavior, her mother's melancholy and ennui offered her a negative view of marriage. If it led to bitterness and regrets, what was the point of marrying anyone?

Georges de Beauvoir, once radiant and tender, no longer spoke a word to his wife unless it was to make fun of her or abuse her. Simone promised herself that her life would be different. She wanted a man she could admire, with whom she could share and exchange ideas, someone to whom she could confide even the smallest thought: "I'll be glad for the day when a man will overpower me with his intelligence, his culture, and his authority."

▪   ▪   ▪

Next to the stove on the carpet, Simone opened her notebook and began to write as she did every day. The contact of the pen on paper calmed her and dispelled her frustrations. In spite of the comings and goings of her ever curious mother, Simone concentrated on her work.

Next to her, Hélène was discovering the books by the Comtesse de Ségur, which were a revelation to her. The younger sister also had the *Contes de Perrault*—fairy tales—illustrated by Gustave Doré that her godfather had given her. Simone raised her head and watched her.

With her pretty blond braids and her light blue eyes Poupette looked like the proverbial good little girl. With her pencils in front of her she was drawing, copying the illustrations. Her gestures seemed sure and quick. Simone thought of her own clumsiness, and how little painting appealed to her. She appreciated museums, but they bored her after a short while. It was all for the best. Her younger sister was no longer imitating her.

Later on their tastes would meet each other, nurture each other. The sisters invented a new game: Simone wrote novels that she would read to her captivated sister, one chapter at a time, and Hélène would then make the appropriate illustrations. At the same time she started to immerse herself in the history of the great painters. She felt a growing fascination for them, admiring their talent, spirit, and determination.

▪   ▪   ▪

"Miracles in Lourdes! And what else, pray tell?" Even in front of his children, Georges de Beauvoir scoffed at his wife's religious beliefs. Simone and

Hélène lowered their heads in silence. Their father always reacted violently to any questions of religion, which stood in such sharp contrast to the pious teachings at the Cours Désir. It was a kind of tradition—for some mysterious reason the men in the family never went to mass. In Meyrignac only the women attended church. Georges de Beauvoir eagerly reminded them that the greatest writers shared his agnosticism. Simone listened; personally, she had trouble believing in miracles and was astonished at the world's injustice.

"One evening in Meyrignac, I was leaning out the window on my elbow, as I did so often. . . . 'I don't believe in God anymore,' I said to myself without any great surprise. . . . Suddenly everything grew quiet. What silence! . . . It was now my turn to feel like the black sheep. What made it worse in my case was that I was pretending: I would go to mass, I took communion . . . but how could I have dared admit it. They would have pointed their finger at me, expelled me, and I would have lost Zaza's friendship."[9]

Simone imagined the scandal and her mother's distress were she to discover her terrible secret. Every one of her gestures now required a bit of acting. She observed Poupette in the Church of Saint-Sulpice, so pretty in her first communion dress that she looked like an angel. Simone couldn't divulge anything to her either, as she would have felt disoriented and uncomfortable with such knowledge. Hereafter her conversations with Zaza rested on deception, as her friend was deeply religious. Their exchanges began to lose authenticity. Her cheeks on fire, Simone wondered whether there would ever be a day when she could share this truth with someone who understood her.

On the other hand, Hélène felt tremendous disappointment during her solemn communion. In spite of the prayers, the vows of piety, and the oaths of obedience, God refused to inhabit her. During the ceremony, as she sang hymns and carried a candle before her parents and Simone, nothing happened. The organ resounded in the church. Ready to enter into a mystical union, she felt only fatigue. No miracle, no communion with God. Where was He? She didn't dare talk about it with her sister.

■ ■ ■

Sitting in her father's study, Simone concentrated on her work. Night had just fallen and, as on every other evening, Georges de Beauvoir had gone out to play bridge in Versailles. Her mother and Hélène had gone to bed, and she was studying—she wanted to obtain her *lycée* diploma, the *bachot*. The possibility of becoming a university student held a thousand promises of freedom. Between writing an essay and a Latin translation, areas in which she excelled effortlessly, she devoted herself to scientific subjects. "I used to love material that was resistant: I liked math."[10]

The exam was given in June 1924 on the premises of the Sorbonne. Despite the mediocre quality of the teaching at Cours Désir, Simone brilliantly passed two separate *baccalauréats*, one in science and one in philosophy, and even obtained a commendation. The news caused quite a stir in the family and everyone was very proud. While preparing, Simone had been pondering her future. Philosophy appealed to her. Fellow students had spoken to her about the Ecole Normale Supérieure de Jeunes Filles in Sèvres, the finest teacher training college for young women. The institution was widely recognized and had no equal, but Françoise de Beauvoir was vehemently against it. The students lived away from home, which allowed them to become dangerously autonomous. No discussion was possible. Beyond her mother's control, Simone risked running into bad company. As the Sorbonne was also not recommended for a Catholic girl from a good family, it was decided that Simone would prepare for a certificate in general mathematics at the Catholic Institute and would study philosophy at the Institut Sainte-Marie of Neuilly.

CHAPTER TWO

Freedom

In the classroom at the Institut Sainte-Marie in Neuilly, Simone impatiently awaited the arrival of Professor Garric. An enlightened and generous Christian, this man lived an ascetic life in Belleville. He asked for nothing for himself and had given up a career at the university level in order to devote himself to the young whom he inspired, as he believed that solidarity and fraternity between people could overcome social barriers.

"Garric showed up; I forgot everything else, myself included, the authority of his voice subdued me. . . . Everybody has a right to culture. . . . The earth was but one immense community, all of whose members were my brothers. Denying every limitation, every separation, moving beyond my social class, leaving my skin: that slogan electrified me. . . . I went home, ecstatic . . . . Above me I heard a higher voice: 'My life must serve a purpose! Everything in my life must serve a purpose!'"[1]

At dinner Simone suddenly realized she was looking at her family with different eyes. Obsessed with the sufferings of the Great War, what could they possibly understand of this speech, this revelation? Even Hélène, sitting beside her, was not anything more than a well-bred adolescent, far removed from this ennobling quest. Perhaps Zaza could grasp Simone's upheaval. And

Jacques, too, a cousin who had recently come into her life and shared her liking for literature and reflection. He brought her forbidden magazines and books. Simone was spilling over with enthusiasm: everywhere she went, whether the Luxembourg Gardens or the library of the Catholic Institute, she devoured one book after another.

Jacques pried her away from Anatole France (whom her father loved) and introduced her to Gide, Claudel, Paul Valéry, Proust, and Baudelaire. The world around her exploded and the Sainte-Geneviève Library became her kingdom. After obtaining a Certificate in Literature, Simone, who had stopped writing for a time, started a new notebook. She needed this journal, her confidant, to transcribe her feelings and thoughts. Soon she would begin a novel. More necessary than ever before, writing allowed her to fight loneliness.

Simone was, in fact, quite lonely. Zaza was smothering in the fetters of her family and its religious mold. But instead of thinking about escaping or rebelling, she submitted and gradually languished. These sad circumstances ate away at the prized friendship that had meant so much to Simone. Every day the gap grew wider. How could she admit to Zaza that she no longer believed in God? How could she share her discoveries? Spontaneity, a fundamental element in their relationship, vanished.

Hélène was finishing the next to the last year of the *lycée*. In her father's study, the only heated room in the apartment, she secretly began to write as well. She started by telling the little events of her daily life. With humor and sarcastic asides, she described the innocent realities of her childhood. "The definition of friends: little girls you like even less than the others but whom you are forced to see more often. Friendship is a distressing invention."[2] After a few facetious remarks such as this one, she went on to more serious notions: "If I were a great painter, I would like to make humorous paintings that would be comical only to me. . . . A painter should show each person what he wants to see and always keep a small corner for himself alone so he can laugh quietly."[3]

After spending hours at the Louvre, an inner fire urged her toward paints and brushes. Yet she didn't dare imagine a future such as this. Later on, she confided to me that she had lacked self-confidence—a small voice kept repeating that she wouldn't make it. Besides, she was a woman, and art history focused primarily on male painters. Museums that overflowed with paintings hardly ever showed any work by women. Seeking inspiration and models to emulate, Hélène deeply regretted this absence.

Meanwhile, Simone continued to write in her journal. Her ideas about where her writing would take her were still rather abstract. If she were to write a book, she needed a subject. On the threshold of their adult life, the two sisters were full of hope for the future, but it was a future that still seemed uncertain and elusive to them.

■   ■   ■

Since her solemn communion, Hélène went to Sunday mass with her mother. In the large, cold, and sterile building, she would listen to the choir. It made the time go by more quickly. The same questions that Simone had were haunting her as well. She thought of her father's scorn and agnosticism. Not too long before she received her diploma, she noticed without any real surprise that she no longer believed in God. It was a simple observation. Then Simone asked her a liberating question:

"And you, are you a believer?"

Hélène hesitated.

"If I really think about it, why would I have any faith? Religion is poisoning my life. Actually, I know I no longer believe in it."[4]

Simone felt huge relief. Once again she would be able to confide in her sister completely. But this had to remain absolutely secret. Françoise de Beauvoir would have been too deeply hurt by it. The two dutiful daughters had turned their backs on the house of God.

■   ■   ■

"It's not fair!"

Standing face to face with her mother in the living room at home, Hélène's cheeks flushed with rage and indignation. So many reasons for exasperation had accumulated over the years—this time it was too much. In her pearl gray suit, Françoise de Beauvoir explained her viewpoint once more to her daughter:

"There's no need whatsoever for you to take your *baccaulauréat* exams! It would be of no use to you."

It was more than enough for her to have one daughter running after degrees. She tolerated the success of her oldest because she was bright and precocious. Sometimes she even boasted about it. The younger one, however, should continue to be a normal girl, perhaps as a kind of compensation. All those ungodly writers, those dangerous readings, ran the risk of turning her away from religion and real values. Under no circumstances should Hélène go to the university. That way her mother would save her. In her gentle voice, the young girl answered:

"My dear Mama, I can assure you that nothing will be able to stop me from taking the *baccalauréat* exams!"

Her eyes suddenly grew hard and adamant. She turned on her heels and left the room, slamming the door. Five minutes later, she walked up Rue de Rennes. On Boulevard Montparnasse, she turned off and headed to Avenue Denfert-Rochereau. Her sister had always encouraged and protected her. At this hour of the morning, Simone was bound to be at home in the room she rented from their grandmother. Hélène envied her sister's freedom; one day, she thought, she too would be allowed to be free. The door opened. Violently shaking, Poupette collapsed in Simone's arms.

"Don't worry, I'll talk to Mother today."

Simone got dressed, had coffee, and prepared for the confrontation. With Hélène right behind her, she went to their parental home. Simone went up by herself. On the verge of tears and short of arguments, Françoise de Beauvoir gave in. It was either the *baccalauréat* or the loss of her daughters' love. Besides, the diploma really was not a handicap for marriage anymore. The daughters had won out over their mother's inflexibility.

The was just one of many obstacles they faced. A few months earlier, another incident had erupted. Françoise de Beauvoir was still opening the letters that Simone, now nineteen years old, wrote to Hélène. One day, she read some passages out loud, sniggering at them. Furious, Hélène stood up to her:

"I will never talk to you again!" Simone had intervened that time, too, protesting the intrusion into their privacy. At nineteen, she certainly expected to be able to have a private correspondence. A private life! Françoise had beaten a retreat. Her youngest daughter's disdainful words had petrified her. She wanted so much to insulate and protect her girls. She certainly didn't do it well, but their love was all she had, and she didn't want to lose them. Her face swollen in distress, she had accepted Simone's demands.

Holding her own and fighting were things to which Simone had become accustomed. First against her mother, then against her father's sarcasm. Georges de Beauvoir constantly reminded his daughters that they had no dowry whatsoever and would therefore have to work. Professional work was limited for women; teaching was one of the few possible career options and offered only a meager salary. For a daughter to become a civil servant would be a disgrace. As a true aristocrat, Georges de Beauvoir couldn't imagine such degradation—it would put his family to shame.

■   ■   ■

Between the courses at Sainte-Marie of Neuilly and her studies at the Sainte-Geneviève Library, the months flew by. Simone heard that her cousin Jacques was getting married. The young man had set his heart on the daughter of a wealthy industrialist. Simone felt somewhat saddened but, fortunately, that didn't last long. She had other things on her mind. She had just passed her exams in math and philosophy. A mentor at Sainte-Marie advised her to present herself for the *agrégation*—the highest qualification available for teachers at the secondary level—in philosophy. She felt up to the challenge.

While preparing for this competitive exam she met Simone Weil, another *agrégation* candidate, also well known for her intelligence and especially for her fierce sense of solidarity. Their first conversation was brief. Simone Weil stated curtly that only one thing mattered anymore and that was the Revolution, which would feed everyone. The other Simone replied that the problem wasn't one of making all people happy but of giving meaning to their lives. Simone Weil eyed her scornfully: "It's obvious that you have never been hungry."[5] In her journal Simone made a note of this judgment. Such humiliation! They were taking her for a *petite-bourgeoise.*

Having passed her final exams as well, Hélène had joined an art studio run by the City of Paris, but they only taught decorative arts there. Her parents had prohibited her from attending the Beaux-Arts academy because of the bad reputation of its students. They then heard about the school for art and advertising on Rue de Fleurus just a few hundred yards from home. It was lucky for Françoise de Beauvoir, who wanted to keep an eye on her daughter. Here Hélène would learn a variety of artistic skills. She began with woodcuts and then moved on to etching.

One evening she met Simone in the bar of the Hotel Lutétia. The sisters blew their savings and treated each other to a couple of glasses of punch. "Oil painting is my drug, I love working with it, I love its fluidity, the flexibility of its technique, and I love the smell of turpentine."[6] Laughingly they clinked glasses: Hélène had finally found her purpose in life. "If our parents only knew I was drawing nude men!" Hélène told her that on Sundays she was gorging herself on paintings at the Louvre instead of piously going to church. She would stand motionlessly before the canvases of Corot and Delacroix and the cubists whom she loved: "The Louvre is my mass!" she confided to her sister. She wanted to understand the techniques of these painters, fully intending to make this her profession.

"To our future!" the older sister said, raising her glass.

■   ■   ■

The time for the *agrégation* exams was fast approaching. Simone absolutely had to pass, for freedom and financial independence awaited her if she did. She dreamed of receiving a salary. Sometimes she would meet her friends at the Ecole Normale Supérieure, where a group of supercilious and indifferent students intrigued her: "The only group that remained impenetrable to me was the clan of Sartre, Nizan, and Herbaud; they mixed with nobody. . . . Sartre didn't have an unpleasant face but they said he was the worst of them all and they even accused him of being a drinker."[7]

Nevertheless, the three men were stealthily watching Simone. Her eyes the color of forget-me-nots and her fine features had not escaped Sartre. He didn't say a word but promised himself he'd find a way to meet her. One day at the Bibliothèque Nationale she was surprised to run into Herbaud. He sat down beside her and shared a sandwich with her. He complimented her cheerfully on her new outfit (which was bound to have been unpretentious). Thanks to him, she discovered the power of her own charms and that she could hope to seduce a student who had passed the institution's difficult and highly prestigious competitive exam. Teasingly, he called her "mademoiselle," undoubtedly as a reference to her last name preceded by the noble "de." Then he concocted a nickname for her, "Castor." In big letters he wrote on her notebook: BEAUVOIR = BEAVER. "You are a *castor*—a beaver," he told her. "They travel in groups and have a constructive spirit."[8] Amused, Simone listened to him. It wasn't exactly a flattering name but when all was said and done it was certainly appropriate.

A few days later, young Jean-Paul Sartre approached her and asked her to have a drink with him in a tearoom close to the Odéon. Surprised and flustered, Simone accepted the invitation. It didn't take her long to regret it: a young girl from a good family didn't speak to a man she didn't know. Besides, Herbaud would be furious, as he was eager to introduce them to each other himself. Thus she felt she couldn't keep the appointment. She called Hélène to the rescue and begged her to take her place.

"What does he look like?"

"A very ugly man with glasses. You won't be disappointed. He is supposed to have a fine sense of humor."

Hélène rolled her eyes and then agreed. For the occasion she wore a black dress that flattered her looks. A necklace of Japanese pearls enhanced her graceful chest, and she had put her blond hair up in a chignon.

Elegant and young, she apprehensively entered the tearoom, where an aroma of chocolate floated through the air. Suddenly she had a shock: there were two unattractive men wearing glasses at two neighboring tables. She introduced herself: "I am Simone's sister." The smaller one stood up, looking grim, and offered her a seat. Hélène's heart sank. Following her sister's instructions she spouted the formulated lie.

Sartre looked at her dubiously and didn't hide his disappointment.

The younger sister certainly was gorgeous, but he felt cheated. Did Simone refuse to meet him because he was ugly? Out of courtesy, he took Hélène to see a film with the suggestive title *Une Fille dans chaque port*—A Girl in Every Port—and did not grace her with a smile all afternoon. Very ill at ease, Hélène went home as soon as she could. Simone was waiting for her, impatient to hear the verdict, which came out before she could ask for it: "He really is ugly and nowhere near as funny as they say."

Simone thought this over. There was no disputing Sartre's ugliness, but they said that his sharp intelligence amply made up for it. At any rate, she was happy he had seemed disappointed, and she was looking forward to a later opportunity to speak to him.

Not long thereafter Herbaud finally suggested she come and study with them for a philosophy exam at the Ecole Normale. In the presence of Sartre, Nizan, and Herbaud, Simone excitedly though in a halting tone set forth her viewpoint on Leibniz. Sartre looked as if he was listening to her attentively but actually he was watching her, fascinated by the pretty girl and her subtle mind. When she left them that evening he already wanted to see her again. They soon became inseparable, and both passed their *agrégation* exams. To everyone's astonishment, Sartre had failed them the previous year. This time around he couldn't possibly flunk, as one of the topics to be discussed seemed made for the existentialist-to-be: liberty and contingency. How could he not pass with such an important theme? In front of the bulletin board where the results were posted, Sartre gave a sigh of relief. "Now I shall take you in hand," he said to Simone, reminding her in his protective tone that he was three years her senior. At the oral exam, Simone dazzled the jury. The examiners hesitated for a long time over the ranking but felt they had to bolster that poor but brilliant student who had been forced to take his exams again. Sartre took first place, ahead of Simone, who at twenty-two was one of the youngest women to obtain her *agrégation* in philosophy. Georges de Beauvoir didn't say a word when he heard the news. His daughter had passed a difficult and competitive exam and he would no longer have to provide for her. She had become independent and was now frequenting the bars in Montparnasse. He doubted she would ever marry and grumbled that the family now included a civil servant. The impoverished aristocrat could not have imagined the other surprises his older daughter had in store for him.

Simone and Sartre celebrated their success with champagne, and Hélène joined them, amusing Sartre with her presence. Her freshness and enthusiasm appealed to him, and the attention he paid her showed his concern for the people close to Simone.

■   ■   ■

Summer vacation in La Grillère and Meyrignac arrived, and Hélène was impatient to return to the country. Simone, on the other hand, was upset. How would she be able to bear a separation of two long months? Sartre asked if he could write to her, and she accepted immediately. Since her argument with her mother about the mail she knew that her letters wouldn't be opened, although her comings and goings were no less closely watched.

One hot morning Simone and Hélène were having breakfast in the garden of La Grillère when suddenly their cousin Madeleine appeared, panting. She whispered in Simone's ear that a young man, who had arrived from Paris without notice, was waiting for her in a field nearby. Simone ran to meet him and they talked for hours.

As soon as Simone had left, Paris seemed like a desert to him and thus Sartre had taken a train and rented a hotel room in a village with a prophetic name: Saint-Germain-les-Belles.[9] To arrive at La Grillère he had had to walk two miles on foot—a real feat for someone who hated all physical exertion and undoubtedly a sign of love. In order to avoid any problem with her parents, Simone asked Madeleine and then Poupette to bring him food on the sly. Shortly thereafter their mother discovered that a piece of meat was missing, so Simone had to make do with preparing him sandwiches. She would leave in the morning with a basket filled with food and disappear for the day. The secrecy and the romantic aspect of her clandestine meetings with Sartre strengthened their relationship. The hours she spent with him enthralled her. He listened to her intently and reacted vividly to what she had to say. There was no doubt about the young man's intelligence. The way he understood her overwhelmed her, as did their shared fondness for writing. The days held a sweet perfume of lavender mixed with the fragrance of the forbidden. It was no longer merely a question of intellectual understanding; in a field, hidden by an old Medieval tower, they made love.

A few days later, the two lovers were taken by surprise by Georges de Beauvoir, with his wife in tow. He urged Sartre to leave the area, as his presence there jeopardized Simone's reputation and also that of one of her cousins who had just become engaged. Sartre was not intimidated. In his deep, strong voice he replied that the bond he had with Mademoiselle de Beauvoir was very strong and that he intended to continue meeting her every day near La Grillère.

Georges de Beauvoir had not expected such audacity. Crushed, he left with Françoise in tears. Simone looked at Sartre—her adult life was beginning; soon she would receive her first paycheck and not be dependent on anyone anymore. Hélène was fascinated by her sister's nerve. At the same time, her thoughts grew shrouded with sadness—she now had to face a gambling, drinking, and skirt-chasing father alone, and would be alone as well in facing the tyranny of a sour-tempered mother. "Don't worry," Simone reassured her, "I won't be far away."

▮   ▮   ▮

It was chilly on the riverbanks in Paris that evening, and Simone gave Poupette her shawl. Since the academic year had begun, the young teacher was harvesting the fruits of her labor: "Earning money, going out, having people in, writing, being free; life really was opening up. . . . I drew my sister along with me into this adventure. On the banks of the Seine just after nightfall, we would tell each other about our future triumphs until we had no breath left: my books, her paintings, our travels, the world."[10]

What a contrast with Zaza! Every time they met she seemed thinner and more defeated. She had fallen madly in love with a young man whom her family had forbidden her to marry. Having checked him out, her parents had actually discovered that he was the illegitimate child of an adulterous relationship. In order not to hurt her mother or humiliate her father and to avoid ruining their reputation, Zaza had once again submitted to their decision.

She agreed to forswear the man she loved and to go to Berlin and study there for a year. Her mother thought the distance would help her lick her wounds. Astounded, the Beauvoir sisters saw the impudent Zaza weaken, exhausted by a life filled with obstacles. She never even made it to Germany. She was hospitalized with a high fever at a clinic in Saint-Cloud, where the doctors thought she might have meningitis. She begged to see Simone, but in vain. Using the possibility of contagion as a pretext, the Mabille family would not let her friend visit her; it is more likely that the freedom Simone now enjoyed was the real reason. They suspected her of having a detrimental influence on Zaza. In resignation, Simone waited impatiently for her close friend to recover so that she could admonish her to live her own life. It was not to be: Zaza died a few days later, saying: "Don't be sad, dear Mama. Every family has its failure: I am the failure here."[11]

The news hit the Beauvoir sisters hard, especially since Simone had not been allowed to visit her during the last days of Zaza's life. Standing before Zaza's corpse in the chapel, Simone was overcome; her double was gone. She thought of their laughter, their hushed adolescent talks, their endless conversations. Brutally swallowed up, the past was vanishing. They had grown up together, had hopes together, and struggled against the destiny their families had wanted to impose on them.[12] Her heart constricted with feelings of guilt when Simone reflected on her own happiness. She then thought of the younger sibling she had neglected. Hélène was now the sole witness to her childhood.

■   ■   ■

The twelve hours by train in third class on wooden benches might as well have been a journey to the other end of the world. For her first job, Simone had been appointed a position as a philosophy teacher at a *lycée* in Marseille, while Sartre was posted in Le Havre. Since Zaza's death, Hélène had learned to share her sister with Sartre, but they still had never been physically separated. Simone's departure for the South left Hélène with a gap in her life that terrified her.

On the station platform both sisters tried to make the best of it. Hélène wondered anxiously who would protect her from now on. Sartre had already resolved the question, however—from this day onward he would spend his Sundays with Poupette.

Once in Marseille, Simone quickly found ways to occupy her days. Besides teaching, she explored the surrounding countryside on foot. At night, she filled page after page in her journals. She sent long epistles to Hélène, Sartre, and a few friends. Simone was twenty-three, and her love for the young philosopher made the distance unbearable. The mail saved her from her loneliness, as she recorded her every act and gesture in her letters.

On Sundays, Sartre would return from Le Havre and take Hélène for walks in Paris where he showed her the old houses and isolated nooks and crannies such as those in the Gobelins district. When he was with Hélène, Sartre talked about Simone, his work, or a book he was busy writing, doing his thinking out loud. In Simone's absence, he discussed his insecurities with her younger sister, his lack of self-confidence, and his insane desire to produce a piece of work that would survive history. He didn't know where to begin. Everything was such a blur in his mind. And his dear Castor was so far away. He missed the intensity of her remarks, as only Simone forced the best from him. Hélène was so lucky to be able to complete a painting relatively quickly; the anxiety of creation only lasted a few days, and gratification was almost instant. It had nothing in common with the torment of the writer, who works at his project for months on end.

In Marseille, Simone was going through the same ordeal as her lover. She, too, wanted to devote her life to writing, but what subject should she choose? She strung sentences together, wrote short stories. Politics were of no interest to her. Her main goal was to express freedom, as it was for Sartre, but she wanted to confront it only from a philosophical and individual viewpoint.

She would rush to the post office every day, hoping to find a letter, the quasi-carnal link that connected her to her chosen circle. In Paris, Hélène also went to the general delivery at Denfert-Rochereau on a regular basis, so that their mother couldn't intercept a single letter.

Hélène was able to visit her sister only once, in the winter. Simone took her walking on the paths of the rocky inlets, where Poupette, wearing espadrilles, had difficulty keeping up with her sister. She finally fell ill and had to stay home. As she felt a great need to be in nature, Simone left her tucked in under the covers and didn't even think of staying home to keep her company. Alone in bed, Hélène lay waiting for her sister's rare appearances. From her early childhood on, she had clung to her as to a guardian angel, a second mother who was more nurturing and protective than the one who had brought them into the world. She needed Simone to be present, and so her stay was infused with the bitter taste of failure. She tried to convince herself that her sister was right in acting this way and that she would have done the same thing in her place. A few days later the fever subsided and Hélène returned sadly to Paris.

■　■　■

"There you are at last!"

Hélène came into the dining room of the apartment on Boulevard Raspail, where her parents were about to have dinner. Dressed in his eternal frock coat, her father raised his eyes and gave a start.

"You're all red! Where have you been?"

"The Maison Grüber, of course!"

She sighed. With a small job as secretary in a gallery providing her only meager income, she was obligated to live at home. Her courses, drawing materials, paints, canvases, and traveling expenses were all entirely her own responsibility. She remembered Simone as a student, who had preferred to stave off her hunger and stay in the library rather than go home and have lunch at her parents' house. It was her mother's way of avenging their desire for freedom. But she hadn't counted on the degree of obstinacy of her daughters. In spite of the deprivations, Simone had passed her philosophy degree, and Hélène, too, was holding her own.

Light of step, she went to her chair. The aroma of the pot-au-feu hung in the room. She served herself generously, in silence. She was even hungrier than usual, but it was not because of her brushes and paints this time. Her cheeks crimson, thinking of her crazy day, she devoured her meal without daring to look up at her parents.

She still felt Jean Giraudoux's[13] caresses and passionate kisses on her skin. The writer had seemed interested in her painting and, pretending to want to see her canvases, had come to her studio. On the first visit, he had seduced her. Unable to resist such an experienced lover, she had let herself go in his arms, overcome by his attentions and drowning in new feelings. Hélène watched her parents' faces, their taut expressions and rigid bodies. Her mother's voice made her jump.

"Why do you look that way? Your hair is all tousled!"

Embarrassed, Hélène pushed her hand through her hair and then went back to her own reverie. My dear Mother, she thought, eating the dessert of cherry clafoutis, your two daughters have escaped you. I, too, have discovered love, forbidden love, passion.

She couldn't wait for the next day. She was going to have a drink at the Jockey[14] with Sartre. He would be her confidant and perhaps her advisor. She could be herself with him, and then she would write Simone and tell her everything. She was dying to let her sister know that she, too, had become a woman. Deep inside herself, she savored her secret. Nothing would stop her anymore. She was free. Work and pleasure would rule her life.

■   ■   ■

Sartre entered the classroom in Le Havre with confidence. Although he was wearing a dark brown velvet suit and a black tie he still seemed very young. Without further ado, he began to lay out the principles of Spinoza's philosophy. His deep voice and enthusiasm caught the students' attention. In spite of his ugliness and the strangeness of his heavy-lidded eyes, it took him only a few seconds to captivate his audience.

Seated in the first row, a svelte and elegant blond and blue-eyed young man drank in his every word. Thanks to Sartre, a breath of freedom had just come into his life, something Lionel de Roulet very much needed. Up to that point, his life had been a series of misfortunes. His wealthy parents had three children to whom they had barely paid any attention. Education was put on the back burner, far behind their primary interest—gambling—a passion that had brought the family to ruin. Lionel's parents had received a chalet in

Switzerland as a wedding present, and it had been gambled away in one night. The children were separated and farmed out to different relatives, where they grew up alone. Later, Lionel's sister Chantal told me that during her adolescence she had cried every night. The same sadness was part of Lionel de Roulet's history, in addition to a profound sense of isolation that followed him into secondary school.

It was in this context that his young philosophy teacher opened unexpected horizons for him. Contrary to other teachers and to the great dismay of the bourgeois families of Normandy, Sartre liked to talk with his students in a café after class. They would discuss the most recent detective novels together, get excited about boxing matches, and delight in the town gossip. Gradually Lionel felt less lonely. Now a smile was seen on his face. He loved to confide in the "little man," as the students had affectionately nicknamed him.

Sartre told him about his intimate relationship with a young philosophy teacher whose beauty and intelligence he admired and who would soon be coming to Rouen to teach. He could hardly wait to see her again and expected to introduce her to Lionel as soon as she arrived in Normandy. Chance would have it otherwise. In a compartment of the Paris-Rouen train, Simone and Hélène were listening to a blond young man talk excitedly about Agatha Christie's *The Murder of Roger Ackroyd* with his companion. Was he trying to show off his newly acquired knowledge? Looking important and mysterious, he said to his traveling companion: "Sartre recommended this book to me."

Simone was amused by his tone. "He must be a disciple of Sartre's!" she whispered to her sister. The two pretended not to be listening to the conversation and deliberately ignored the young men. The sisters behaved eccentrically, taking an iron rod from their luggage and then ingeniously using it as a nutcracker. Lionel watched them, dumbfounded at the bizarre manners of these young girls from such a refined family.

Upon arrival, the travelers went their separate ways. Simone hadn't uttered a word. She was waiting mischievously for the introductions to be made in Le Havre. When they were all finally formally introduced, Sartre made fun of Lionel. How could he possibly have thought he would impress the brilliant Mademoiselle de Beauvoir? Lionel defended himself and related the sisters' unusual behavior in the train. The young women decided to exact their revenge, saying they would like to visit the city of Rouen accompanied by Lionel. The trap was set—enthusiastic about art history, Hélène began to hold forth on architecture without sparing him a single detail. However, instead of being impatient, he heard her out and remained interested until the end. Hélène's grace and elegance had produced their desired result, and he fell under her spell.

Since Hélène rarely left Simone and Sartre during her stay, he saw her again on several occasions. His feelings for her grew more intense. Sadly, she would soon return to Paris. He had been preparing himself for an emotional goodbye and even imagined going so far as to declare his love. But the farewell on the station platform was far more disappointing than he had anticipated. She stopped him, told him dryly that she was thrilled to have met him, and offered him a chocolate bar! She boarded the train, which left almost immediately. Lionel was dumbfounded. What a rebuke for a young man! Hélène had treated him like a child. Hurt and angry, he complained about it to Sartre, who burst out laughing.

From then on, Simone and Sartre saw each other regularly. One of Simone's young students soon joined their circle. Olga Kosakievicz despised hard work. Under her spell, Simone thought that perhaps she had found someone who might replace her much-lamented Zaza in her heart. Their complicity was obvious, and they became inseparable. Sartre, too, was seduced by Olga's indefinable grace and, intrigued, he watched the birth of this unusual love. One evening he asked Simone if she would let him go out alone with Olga. Faithful to the principles they had established, Simone agreed. Thus began the love triangle which was to inspire the two writers later on. Under the duress of real life, this gift of absolute freedom they had given each other didn't last long. The pain that was the price of independence became unbearable and destroyed their arrangement. The trio soon split up and Olga went off to other loves. Nevertheless, their friendship remained intact.

A few months later, Lionel obtained his *baccalauréat* and began his university studies in Paris. Sartre asked Hélène to keep an eye on him.

Older than Lionel by a few years, she refused to go out with him—he was too young for her. Still, Lionel managed to see her and convinced Hélène, Simone, and Sartre to go skiing at Val-d'Isère. All that this small Alpine village possessed at the time was a church, some old gray stone houses, and a few ski lifts. They went up the peaks in sealskin and came down as best they could, intoxicated with the altitude, speed, and pure air.

■   ■   ■

In spite of Lionel's frantic courting, Hélène could think only of Jean Giraudoux, her wonderful lover in Paris. But her happiness didn't last long. Without a care for the pain he was causing Hélène, the writer soon ended their relationship, which was beginning to set tongues wagging. Now that she was a teacher in Rouen, Simone was too far away for Hélène to turn to in her distraught state. Lionel, on the other hand, was able to comfort her. Very quickly, she started seeing him regularly.

During school vacations, Simone and Sartre joined them in Paris. Hélène would prepare lovely meals for her sister. One day, as she unfolded her napkin, Simone came out with the pronouncement, "You'll see, Poupette, you too will be a good bourgeoise some day." Sartre remained silent.

Hélène put the cheese soufflé on the table and objected: one could be a fine cook and still be a liberated woman! However, it seemed the sentence was irrevocable. Simone was sure she was right—and left nothing on her plate.

Sartre had warned Simone—bourgeois marriage was not on their agenda. "Between us," he explained to her, "love is really imperative; but it is only right that we should experience unforeseen love."[15] She listened to him hold forth on his view of love. Liberty was essential, and this would guide their relationship. He maintained the right to see other women. She drew the obvious conclusion: she, too, would live freely and thus escape from the imprisonment her mother had known. Sartre had added a special clause to this non-marriage proposal; he demanded a sort of probation period of two years, for, in spite of his fondness of her, he could not exclude the possibility of changing his mind. Yet, the pact also rested on openness: they would tell each other everything. Between them there would be no deceit.

Carefully thought out, Sartre's proposal opened a path whose difficulties seemed negligeable in comparison to the enticing sense of independence she saw in it. This way she would escape that which had horrified her in her youth, the knowing smiles, the lies and hypocrisy, the bourgeois performance of marriage and its obligatory corollary: adultery. Instead of the conventional lies, one indestructible link would connect her to Sartre, and that was writing. And this would be their marriage contract.

■   ■   ■

A few weeks later, Hélène found a studio to rent in the fifth *arrondissement*, facing the leather market on Rue Santeuil. Despite the heady smells of skins, tannins, and leather, the fifteen-by-twenty-seven-foot space was a godsend for an artist looking for a place to work. But how was she to handle the rent? Having no resources, Hélène turned to Simone. Their little squabble about bourgeois living had had no serious consequences. In spite of her own low salary, the older sister promptly agreed to help with the rent, and Hélène saw her dream come true. The studio offered her the possibility of working for days on end, alone, in peace, and independently. The first time she came into the room permeated with smells, her eyes flooded with tears of happiness. She had waited for this moment for so long. With confidence, she placed her brushes and easel where she wanted them and prepared her canvases. Real life was beginning.

Solitude did not bother her. At noon, she'd quickly down a frugal lunch as she watched the children play hopscotch in the street or come home from school with a baguette under their arm. Then she would eagerly get back to work. The hours flew by easily.

■   ■   ■

Christmas was approaching. Laughing, Simone and Sartre uncorked a bottle. They looked at Hélène:

"Here's to your success, Poupette!"

She was the first of the three to be launched as an artist. At twenty-five,

Hélène was showing her paintings; it was her first taste of success. January 1936 would be a turning point in their lives. Admittedly, Sartre and Simone had not published anything yet. However, writing had become their inspiration and their sole objective. One day, perhaps, their names would be displayed in the window of a bookstore.

The evening before her exhibit opened, Hélène was alone with her paintings, which leaned against the wall before her. They represented her most private place. Soon they would be exposed to everyone's gaze. She would have to face up to critics, to half smiles. Her stomach was in knots. Had she managed to free herself from the influence of the masters she admired? She wasn't sure of anything anymore and went to bed very late. She couldn't find any sleep in the arms of Lionel, who was helping her forget her break-up with Jean Giraudoux. Simone had funded the exhibit. Her encouragement brought Hélène the comfort she needed in the face of her mother's criticism. Still, her self-assurance vacillated, and, more than anything else, she dreaded being a disappointment to her sister.

At the Bonjean Gallery, the chic cocktail party crowd rubbed shoulders with the circle of intellectuals who were flat broke. Sartre wore a tie for the occasion. Simone observed the elegant couples—affluent bourgeois who reminded her of her own world even if her family was now ruined. She despised these social gatherings where conversation was limited to a few sentences of deliberate triviality. But these men in suits and women covered in jewels were potential clients. And so she smiled for her sister's sake, mumbled a few words, and went into raptures over platitudes.

Suddenly, a tremor of excitement ran through the crowd. Sure of step and without so much as a glance at anyone there, Pablo Picasso entered the room. A regular of the gallery, he went straight to the young and elegant Hélène de Beauvoir. Was he struck by her beauty, as were so many others? Lionel would tell me later that men would fall all over themselves for her in those days. That particular evening, Hélène was wearing a blue outfit with a cameo of her mother's. While Picasso contemplated the paintings, her every nerve trembled. The crowd watched in silence, as in an arena. The intense eyes of the creator of *Les Demoiselles d'Avignon* went back and forth from canvas to canvas amid an anxious hush nobody dared to break. "Interesting, interesting," the master mumbled. He was not averse to blond women with blue eyes. At last he uttered his verdict: "Your painting is original."

Hélène was speechless. A murmur of approval ran through the room. Majestically, Picasso left, as mysteriously as he had arrived. While the last guests congratulated her, Hélène finally understood: "Every young painter, mostly of my generation, was copying him. I was one of the rare ones who didn't try to and was therefore an original. One doesn't copy a Picasso, it's useless. Copying talent means not having any."[16]

During the next few days, Hélène could think of nothing but the critics. Would there be any articles in the press? Reading her name in print would overwhelm her with happiness. Her heart pounding, she feverishly checked the newspapers and finally discovered what she was looking for: "Her talent is personal and forceful" (*Les Débats*); "In her work there is no influence to be seen other than that of a very classical tradition that gives her a certainty of style and compositional balance" (*L'Européen*).[17] Certainty of style and compositional balance. So she really did have talent, she was sure of it now and no one could make her doubt it any longer. She closed her eyes, thinking she would faint with joy.

When she showed the articles to Simone, she blushed. Her older sister seemed pleased and ordered a whiskey. Hélène cried out:

"Now it's your turn to become a writer!"

Simone drank in silence. Like Sartre, she found Poupette's painting too academic, but the master had spoken, and hurting her sister was out of the question. It was her role to support her. Was it not Hélène who was the first to make her dream come true? Their turn would come: Sartre and Simone had to persevere.

■   ■   ■

In Lionel's room at the Cité Universitaire,[18] Hélène did all she could to cover up her distress. The young man's health was failing. Lionel was sick again—a few months earlier he had caught scarlet fever, but this time the symptoms seemed more serious. The doctors had not yet diagnosed his case; still, it broke her heart to see Lionel so weak. Her anxiety made her understand that she loved him and would support him no matter what happened. Besides, she was the only one there for him: the memory of Lionel's last trip still troubled her. He had traveled to Lisbon to see his mother and her third husband, though they had barely paid any attention to him. When it was time for him to return to Paris, Lionel asked his mother for the savings he had entrusted to her when he arrived. With a big smile she told him there wasn't anything left. She had spent it all. And so Lionel had taken the train back without so much as a centime for a thirty-six-hour journey without food or drink.

Hélène seemed worried and Simone tried to reassure her. However, the problem was serious, as he had been diagnosed with tuberculosis of the bone, known as Pott's disease. It could paralyze him. He was immediately sent to a treatment center in Berck. Hélène collapsed in her sister's arms. What if he didn't come back? "You'll go and see him, I'll help you pay for the trip," Simone assured her. "Sartre and I will go with you."

So the three of them took the train to Berck. They were about to discover a whole different world. Immobilized on wooden boards, the patients lay in carts as they were walked through the streets of the small town. The sanatoria overflowed with young people, some of whom would be paralyzed for life. Lionel had read a book on the subject before he himself fell ill and had told Hélène: "It's horrible; it's impossible to live like that, it's just too awful! If I were in their position, I'd commit suicide."[19]

A nurse came toward them, pushing Lionel in a kind of bed on wheels. Sartre extinguished his pipe. Simone held Hélène's arm as she tried to remain calm. The two sisters told the nurse: "You can leave us, we'll take care of him." To their great surprise, Lionel smiled and seemed pleased: "I'm so happy you've come to visit!" he explained. Nobody in his family had come to see him. His mother, more interested in the needs of her third husband than in those of her son, could hardly find the time to write to him. Lionel was appraising the price of faithful love and friendship. In a joking tone, Sartre ordered him: "Well, my disciple, you will now get better!" Lionel burst out laughing. Finally they were all together again, and that surely was the most important thing. Hélène moved behind the cart and they took Lionel to a café in town that was especially set up to receive "the bedridden."

Lionel calmly told them that he was going to have surgery. An abscess

had developed on his spine. Contamination had to be avoided. The operation was risky and success was not very likely. As they left him, Sartre, Simone, and Hélène had trouble hiding their feelings. "I'll be back soon!"
Hélène promised him. In the train, she began to sob.

■   ■   ■

"My dear Castor, some day you will be published!"

In the Café de Flore everyone was engaged in conversation. Sitting on
a red imitation-leather bench, Sartre crushed a cigarette in an ashtray. His
collection of short stories, *Le Mur (The Wall)*, would soon come out. After *Nausea*, he was hoping for another success. Gallimard had rejected Simone's
manuscript, *Primauté du spirituel*. All she could do was start again and not give
in to despair. Hélène didn't doubt her sister's talent for a second and supported her with conviction. She turned out to be a most diligent reader; Simone and Sartre had asked her to type their manuscripts in return for
some financial help. After standing for hours in front of her canvases,
Hélène had typed *Le Mur*, *Nausea*, and then *Primauté du spirituel*. She had
trouble deciphering Simone's handwriting, but Sartre brought her impec-
cable sheets of paper, neatly covered in his small, fine, round handwriting. Copying the final draft was a moment of pure bliss for him, during which
the constraint of creation weighed less heavily.

Hélène had executed this thankless task very rapidly, and she worked
well. Sartre had a special affection for her. One day Hélène told me that he
had always dreamed of having a little sister and that for him she occupied
that place. That is why, without any doubt, she was the only woman whom
Sartre never courted.

Simone had gone to the library every day for several weeks. This time, she
seemed to be reaching her goal. She felt strong. Building chapters, inventing
characters, all of it suddenly seemed easier to her—this novel embodied her
future. One or two years from now, it would really and solidly exist and she
was heading there jubilantly. She dressed especially well that winter. She had
black and yellow shirts made with matching ties.

Clad in one of these new outfits, Simone went to visit Hélène in her studio. She loved the pungent smell of the canvases, was amused by the mice that scattered when she came up the stairs. When Hélène opened the door, she exclaimed:

"What a beautiful shirt!"

"It's new . . ."

"It looks wonderful on you. I've got to do your portrait . . . "

"I can't stay very long. Sartre is waiting for me."

"Just hold still for a few minutes. . . . There you go, don't move!"

Hélène grabbed her sketchpad and quickly drew the outlines of the figure. Soon the face appeared. She put down her pencil. The sketch would be enough for her to start working. Then Simone opened her purse and pulled a few bank notes from her wallet.

"Here, for your canvas and your paints . . ."

"But you're already paying the rent on this studio."

"Be quiet. And don't forget our pledge. One day we'll be famous, you as a painter and I as a writer!"

Hélène kissed her sister exuberantly. Once Simone had left, she took a medium-sized canvas and readied her brushes. On that day and the following days she painted a radiant Simone. Her black hair framed her magnificently blue and spirited eyes, lit by a smile. Dressed in her yellow shirt and a black tie, Simone was holding a book in her hand that she appeared to be skimming. Perhaps it was a manuscript notebook. With a self-assured hand, Hélène signed the painting in the lower right-hand corner.[20]

■   ■   ■

"Come now, don't waste your energy."

Sitting at Lionel's bedside in Berck, Simone and Hélène on either side of him, Sartre was grumbling. The gravely ill young man was interested in politics and felt an affinity for the Front Populaire.[21] Far from the turmoil of Paris, he now had hours of solitude that provided him with time for reflection.

Sartre, Simone, and Hélène had little time to think about such questions;

not one of them seemed concerned with the Civil War in Spain, even if it had roused them from their indolence. With the Munich Accord, thinking they had avoided the worst, the Beauvoir sisters felt visible relief. Only Sartre reacted: "One can't give in to Hitler indefinitely!"[22] He understood that war was becoming inescapable. Simone and Hélène worried. They had grown up surrounded by friends whose fathers, brothers, and uncles had died in combat. Filled with the stories of Georges de Beauvoir, they were haunted by visions of the gassed, the mutilated, and the amputees. Wouldn't it be better to negotiate peace? No, Sartre answered, "I don't want to be forced to eat my manuscripts."[23]

Hélène thought of Lionel and how weak he was. She now saw his illness from a different perspective: thanks to his tuberculosis Lionel would not be mobilized. But what would his life be like when totally restricted? Simone, on the other hand, grew afraid. Sartre would be mobilized and separated from her. The news only added to their feeling of distress. On August 23, 1939, to everyone's astonishment, the two Ministers of Foreign Affairs of Germany and the Soviet Union signed a nonaggression pact in Moscow. In France, Communists were arrested. A few days later, the Second World War broke out. In the cold dark of night, Sartre joined the 70th Division in the East. He was now caught up in a world of hierarchies—the army. Hélène sought refuge in the country in one of the family homes. Simone was alone. History had swept down on them with unheard-of abruptness and changed their direction. Their journeys to freedom would now move through politics.

▮   ▮   ▮

In September 1939, Lionel finally returned to Berck. To everyone's surprise the operation seemed to have been successful, but it looked as though convalescence would be long and difficult. To her dismay, Hélène found him much thinner and very pale. In the wheelchair, a blanket over his knees, Lionel told her he was leaving for Portugal to recover at the house of his mother, who finally seemed to have understood the gravity of the situation. She would put him up in the nicest room of the house, which was quiet and sunny, and promised to prepare the food that was good for him.

After invading Czechoslovakia, Hitler demanded the restitution of Dantzig from Poland. Hélène and Simone were both nervous. The world around them was in a dangerous state of flux. On September 3, France and the United Kingdom declared war on Germany. Simone reacted immediately: "I'll give you what you need to go and see Lionel for a few weeks." This way her younger sibling would be safe. Hélène thanked her, hugging her closely.

In the morning fog, on the platform of the Austerlitz Station, Simone watched Poupette's train leave to go south. "See you soon!" her sister said, eager to be with the man she loved. Simone didn't have the strength to respond but kissed her fiercely to hide her anguish. Her mind went back to Zaza's death. If only nothing would happen to Hélène!

The people she loved left one by one. Simone was alone in Paris, forced to deal with her parents; her father was growing weak and no longer had any income other than a wretched pension, so that she had to see to their needs. All she had left to console her were a few female friends, young girls with whom she had an ambiguous relationship, mixing friendship and desire. Neither Hélène nor her family could know anything about these loves; they were her secret and she fully intended to keep it that way. She didn't even dare imagine the scandal it would create and the distress it would have caused in her circle of friends and family.

■　■　■

Sitting next to Lionel in a Faro café, Hélène savored a cool drink. The trip had been long and exhausting, but she had finally arrived. Soon she would send postcards to Simone and her mother. As he was about to settle the check, the waiter leaned over to Hélène and asked: "Are you French, mademoiselle?"

"Yes, I am."

"Well, then I am very sorry for you. The Germans have just invaded France."

Hélène started to shake. What would become of her family? The French borders were closed. "You'll have to stay with me," Lionel told her. The future looked dark on May 10, 1940. After the Netherlands and Belgium, France too had been attacked; in three weeks the Germans had the

Maginot Line. The French army conquered, Paris was soon occupied. A few weeks later, the Parliament voted to give Marshall Pétain full power.

Hélène had no idea where Simone and her parents were and received no news. She didn't know that her sister was suffering from loneliness in Paris and that Sartre was a prisoner of the Germans. When the defeat was announced, Simone decided to leave the city, as did so many other French people. She had only one thing in mind, not to be cut off from Sartre and not to be trapped inside occupied Paris. However, a few days later she returned to the capital. The armistice had been signed, and perhaps Sartre would return. Letters reached her at last from the stalag. He was fine, he was working, and he didn't expect to be liberated for quite a while. At the Bibliothèque Nationale Simone was immersed in reading Hegel again. Sartre, meanwhile, entertained himself with the writing of a play, *Bariona*, which dealt with Palestine under the occupation of the Romans. He staged it and cast his fellow prisoners in the various roles. This is how he discovered the power of words on a theatrical stage. His career as a playwright had begun.

■　■　■

In the middle of March 1941, Sartre managed to get himself liberated by passing for a civilian with a serious vision problem. At the end of the month he found Simone in Paris. He seemed thoughtful and mature. Freedom implied responsibility and involvement in the life of the city. He intended to struggle against the German Occupation but didn't know how to go about it. Together with Jean Pouillon, Jacques-Laurent Bost, and Jean and Dominique Desanti, he tried to establish a Resistance group, symbolically called Socialism and Liberty. Unfortunately, these intellectuals did not trouble themselves to take any precautions: One of them lost a bag containing group members' names and addresses, and their discussions could be heard from the street because they made their plans with the windows wide open. They frequently met at the Hotel Mistral, near the Gare Montparnasse, where their comings and goings were anything but discreet. They were soon noticed because of their carelessness. Sartre and

Simone became aware of the futility of their actions and moved away from a battle for which they were not prepared. He went back to writing the second volume of *Les Chemins de la liberté*,[24] while Simone worked on the rewrite of *L'Invitée* (*She Came to Stay*), a novel she hoped would be published this time. She also thought of Hélène, who had now been in Portugal for more than a year. They were in contact again thanks to preprinted postcards, the only mail allowed, by which they could send each other short bits of news. Life in Lisbon seemed less hard than in Paris, where several hours each day had to be devoted to finding something to eat. Out of a sense of duty Simone spent a great deal of time with her parents. Her father's attitude toward the occupying enemy had brought them closer. After being in open conflict with him for years, she could now sit down with him and have calm discussions. As a patriot, Georges de Beauvoir couldn't bear the German presence on the sidewalks of Paris. The fact that a majority had rallied around Pétain and the Vichy government devastated him, and the support Pétain enjoyed among the aristocracy and most of Beauvoir's friends was a cruel disillusionment to Georges. Simone watched her parents and their gradual decline. Françoise de Beauvoir experienced attacks of arthritis, and Georges, who forbade his wife and daughter to resort to the black market but had always been a great eater, suffered from hunger. Simone spent hours sitting next to her father's bed. She couldn't talk to him about her book in which two women and one man were having an extramarital relationship. She preferred instead to hear him recite the lines in verse of his favorite plays and dream aloud of the actor's career he had not fulfilled.

On July 1, 1941, Georges de Beauvoir died of prostate cancer. Simone didn't shed a tear. In spite of her attempts at reconciliation, the gulf that had separated her from her father had not been bridged. As he lay dying, he had told her: "You, you earned your living early on. Your sister cost me dearly."[25] The older sister was speechless in the face of such flagrant injustice.

Françoise de Beauvoir was now under the authority of her daughter. She had been familiar with her husband's impiety but she didn't suspect that soon scandal would become a steady companion.

■ ■ ■

In the south of Portugal, it fell to Lionel to establish a French Institute in Faro, where, under the cover of culture, the objective was the promotion of Free France, a precarious goal in a dictatorship that was allied with Germany. Lionel welcomed musicians, writers, and artists who had fled France. They were all inflamed with the same wish—to bring back to life the spirit of the country so humiliated by the occupying enemy. During this period, Hélène taught French at both the *lycée* and the institute. Between courses and with Lionel's encouragement, she sketched Portuguese farmers, villagers, and fishermen on her canvas.

Sometimes, English people stopped at their house, spent the night and left again with the first light of day. Hélène asked no questions and Lionel was cryptic about the reasons for their presence. When they returned to Lisbon he was even more guarded. Having become the director of the French Gaullist Institute in Lisbon,[26] he received an emissary of General de Gaulle who brought them detailed information about the war and its developments.

In reality, Lionel was working for Free France: many German submarines actually stocked up in Portuguese ports, and information on the movements of the fleet of the Third Reich was invaluable. French agents and those of the Intelligence Service, coming from or on their way to London, also passed through Lisbon. Organizing their passage turned out to be a perilous task to which Lionel dedicated himself body and soul, without breathing a word to Hélène. His sad and solitary youth had brought him a taste for secrecy. A discreet man, he also knew how to be brave.

The news from the front was worrisome. Stretched out in the sun on a beach, Lionel exclaimed: "The situation is quite serious, Hélène—nothing is to prevent the Nazis from invading Portugal anymore. They're talking about it a great deal at the Institute. They told me they'd send me to Algeria if the threat becomes more definite. I don't want to leave you behind. . . Let's get married!" Hélène answered that she didn't want to get married; she refused to start mending socks. Lionel swore that he would never require her to do such chores. He kept his word: "When I think that I married a woman who has the perfect nimble fingers for sewing!" he would later say, half-joking and half-disappointed. In December 1942, Hélène became Madame de Roulet.

At the same time, after two years of correspondence with France on preprinted Red Cross postcards, Hélène finally received a real letter from Simone, in which she recounted in detail the deprivations, her separation from Sartre, the illness and death of their father, and their mother's bravery. The letter had taken six months to reach Hélène. She burst into tears, although she found some solace in the fact that she could finally exchange real letters with her sister.

█   █   █

A year later, as she walked along an elegant Lisbon street, Hélène saw her sister's name on a copy of *L'Invitée* in the window of a French bookstore. Her heart pounding, she bought Simone's first book. Their dreams had come true: the older sister was a writer, the younger one preparing a new exhibit in Lisbon.

She quickened her pace going home and began to read as soon as she arrived. Across the pages, she felt Simone's presence, recognized her strength, and admired her style. The novel was constructed like a detective story. Sartre, Olga (whom she had met on several occasions), and Simone were clearly recognizable beneath the features of the fictional characters. Imagination mingled with memories. The atmosphere of Paris had been rendered to perfection. One sentence attracted her attention. Alongside the descriptions of war, there was the presence of politics. When Xavière explains to Pierre that she cannot see joining a political movement, the hero responds: "Well, then you'll be a sheep. You can only fight society in a social way."[27] Hélène read that excerpt to Lionel who reacted with an ironic little smile. Not long before his bout with tuberculosis, he had wanted to establish a small socialist group. Sartre and Simone had made fun of him. Of what possible interest could it be to intellectuals to get entangled in politics? But now Simone's writing seemed to resonate a growing awareness.

The publication in 1943 of *L'Invitée* (*She Came to Stay*) was an immediate success. In Paris, the book was even mentioned as a candidate for the Prix

Goncourt.[28] Sartre made inquiries. In spite of the Occupation, the National Committee of Writers, which brought together authors who resisted, told her to accept it. However, the prize was not awarded to her. During this time, Simone reread Sartre's manuscripts. Her lover had been incredibly prolific during this wretched period: between *Les Mouches* (*The Flies*) and *L'Être et le néant* (*Being and Nothingness*) he wrote the play *Huis clos* (*No Exit*) in two weeks, with the intention that the roles be played by his mistresses. Simone might have taken offense, but she had other things on her mind: following the complaint lodged by a student's parent, she had been expelled from the university. Her closeness with the young girls in her senior class had shocked conservative dispositions. Her bisexuality was confirmed during the Occupation. She had relationships with women who were also enamored of Sartre, one of whom was Olga. She presented her dismissal as a reaction of the occupier and a sanction by the Vichy regime, and her family believed her. Freed from the constraints of teaching and urged on by Sartre, she devoted herself fully to literature. In the evening, they would meet up with Albert Camus, who was involved in the adventure of *Combat*, a newspaper dedicated to the Resistance. The first performance of *Huis clos* took place in May 1944 at the Vieux-Colombier Theatre. Despite the bombs and air raid sirens, the play was a triumph. Every word pronounced on the stage rang out like an act of liberty. "Hell is other people" pointed to the enemy, and the public was hugely enthusiastic.

On August 25, 1944, amid the crowd, Sartre and Simone applauded the parade led by De Gaulle on the Champs-Elysées. The dark years that were coming to an end had allowed them to gain fame, although they still didn't know where it would take them. For now, their greatest wish was to leave France, travel, and discover the world.

■   ■   ■

In March 1945, Simone, very thin and badly dressed, emerged from the train at the Lisbon station. Sartre had been invited to the United States as a special envoy of two opposing newspapers, the *Figaro* and *Combat*. As Simone was alone, Lionel had invited her to give a series of lectures in Portugal. For the two sisters it was the dreamed-of opportunity to renew contact, as they had not seen each other for almost five years. Simone looked at Poupette tenderly—she was blooming with health. On her left hand she now wore a wedding ring. Simone's predictions had come true: the younger one had actually ended up becoming middle-class. She teased her about it, then threw herself on the food: fish, vegetables, fruit, white bread, and chocolate. It was a dream for someone who had been subjected to the deprivations of wartime, ration coupons, and rutabaga. They spent the night chatting and laughing.

Shortly thereafter Simone was invited to the embassy for a gala dinner, where she made a bit of a blunder. When a magnificent fish, served with vegetables, was brought to the dinner table, she quite naturally cried out: "Oh, what a beautiful fish!"[29] Everyone looked down their noses, not hiding their disdain, for in the controlled world of Portugal it was inappropriate to comment on the food that was served. Appalled by the disdain shown to her sister, Hélène almost expressed her anger, but Lionel managed to keep her from doing so. It was pointless to cause a scene, especially because the couple was about to turn over a new leaf. Nothing kept them in Lisbon any longer, and peace brought the opportunity to return to Paris.

Financially the future was less than secure. The sale of a few of Hélène's paintings didn't even cover the cost of canvas and paints. Without any diploma other than a bachelor's degree, hard won after his stay in the sanatorium, what profession awaited Lionel? With the Liberation came the obstacle of looking for work. Perhaps his Gaullist activities would help him. In any case, that is what he hoped.

Hélène, on the other hand, was filled with expectations. In Portugal she had worked very hard on her technique. By this time her body of work consisted of almost a hundred paintings. She hoped that the Parisians would esteem her art as they had esteemed Simone's first novel.

■   ■   ■

"Come on now, hurry up!"

Lionel was impatient, they were going to miss their train for Paris. Hélène was counting the hams, pineapples, and other fruits hidden in their luggage. Presents like these would delight her family, for her mother and Simone, who had returned to Paris after a three-week stay with them, were still not getting enough to eat. Rations, never-ending lines, and indigestible food were still the Parisians' daily lot.

Lionel and Hélène finally clambered onto the train. The tracks had not been replaced in Irún, and between Spain and France they had to cross the border on foot, pushing a cart with their luggage. Finally, another train took them to Paris, from which they had departed five years earlier. At the station they discovered the grayness and misery the German Occupation had left behind. Overcome with emotion, Françoise de Beauvoir wept when she saw them and held her younger child to her breast for a long time. Simone was shouting with joy. They ate ham and drank Portuguese wine. In silence, Lionel watched the three women, reunited at last.

CHAPTER THREE

Achievement

With a cry of surprise Simone opened the door of her apartment. Her sister was in uniform. About to leave France once again, Hélène came over to kiss her.

"You joined the army?"

"Yes, so I can be with Lionel."

Hubert Beuve-Méry, a former resistance worker and director of *Le Monde* was familiar with Lionel's activities on behalf of Free France. Thanks to his intervention, Lionel had just been named Director of Information at the French Diplomatic Representation in Vienna, with the rank of colonel. Austria, completely destroyed, was occupied at the time by the Allies and by France.

"What exactly will he be doing there?" Simone asked dryly.

"He will be in charge of the press," Hélène answered gently.

"But why wear a uniform?"

Hélène explained that only officers were allowed in Vienna, which was officially liberated but in reality was under Soviet control. The mission was a delicate one.

"Still," Simone went on, "wearing a uniform! Leaving with the rank of colonel, sent out by the Ministry of Foreign Affairs! You've really joined the system, you'll end up like true bourgeois, that's all."

Stunned, Hélène remained silent. Discussing it was pointless—for Simone and Sartre, to be part of "society" meant exclusion from their world, where freedom was all that mattered, even if it implied misery.

■   ■   ■

Lionel met Hélène and Simone at La Coupole. While Hélène looked radiant beneath the pinkish light of the chandeliers, her older sister looked pale and thin and seemed tense. Invited with other journalists to the United States by the State Department, Sartre was producing reports for daily French newspapers. In and of itself this was nothing out of the ordinary, but during his previous trip to America he had found a new love, and Simone was well aware of it. All Sartre could think of was Dolores, a young French woman, divorced from her American husband, who had introduced him to intellectual and political circles. From then on, he would spend two months a year with her on the other side of the Atlantic. The waiter, in his large white apron, approached to clear the table but changed his mind—Simone usually had a good appetite but had hardly picked at her food. It was 1945 and she certainly deserved everyone's attention because of the success of her latest novel, *Le Sang des autres* (*The Blood of Others*). Hélène was not in the least jealous and showed great pride in her sister. The book's female protagonist was named after the younger sister. After *She Came to Stay*, in which the main character was named Françoise, after their mother, Simone continued to give her heroines names from within the family. It wasn't clear if this was a willed or an unconscious gesture, and Hélène didn't dare ask. She tried to cheer her up instead. Exhausted and frequently dissolving in tears, Simone greatly needed some support. Was Sartre going to leave her? Did the new affair mean that the end of her relationship with the philosopher was near? She watched Hélène and Lionel laughing and exchanging knowing looks. Their stay in Portugal and their marriage had made them into a stable and trusting couple. Why shouldn't she find the same kind of happiness? As if to reassure herself, the thought came to her that Hélène and her husband had turned into solid bourgeois citizens, precisely what she abhorred. To top it all off, Lionel would be wearing a colonel's uniform. The previous evening she had said some very harsh things to Hélène who had become indignant and fiercely stood up for herself. Lionel's studies had had to be abandoned because of illness—what else could he hope for? To be free but live in poverty? That was a rather odd notion of liberty, Hélène had added, ready to defend her husband tooth and nail.

Simone dismissed the incident from her mind and tried to get hold of herself so as not to spoil the evening. Even if her literary success brought her scarcely any solace, she would still return to the first draft of her novel, *Tous les Hommes sont mortels* (*All Men Are Mortal*), in which she described the sad condition of an immortal being condemned to go through the centuries alone. She would take up the pen once again, and always.

▮ ▮ ▮

After sunny Portugal, Lionel braced himself for Vienna, a city in ruins where everything functioned via the black market. Since Hélène had been married in Lisbon, she was still listed as Hélène de Beauvoir in the citizens' register of Paris. Under her maiden name, with a lieutenant's rank, she was assigned to the post of decorator of the French Information Center in Vienna.

"You know," Hélène added, "if it's any consolation to you, in Vienna we'll have nothing. It will be poverty rather than a bourgeois lifestyle. The Russians are occupying the city and the Americans and English haven't left much for the French."

With a heavy heart Simone took Hélène to the station. Sartre was extending his stay in America to spend more time with Dolores, and Poupette was joining her husband. In spite of her friends' support, her writing, and the launching of the journal *Les Temps modernes*, loneliness weighed heavily on her . She hugged Poupette, regretting her accusations.

"You'll write, won't you?"

"But of course."

Standing on the steps of the train, Hélène turned around. In the early morning fog her sister seemed so small on the platform. After her five years in exile, they were separating again, but for how long? It was impossible to tell. She wiped away a tear on her powdered cheek and blew a final kiss to Simone.

▮   ▮   ▮

In the reception hall of the Soviet general, the foreign diplomats waited to be welcomed. The minutes crawled by. Lionel paced the room with his superiors. They were bored stiff.

"If we only had a deck of cards," the French general whispered.

A few moments later, a Russian soldier came in and presented the general with a magnificent deck of fifty-two cards on a silver tray. He looked around triumphantly. Clearly the microphones were working well!

"Be careful what you say!" Lionel had exclaimed as soon as Hélène arrived. "Everyone here is a spy and will inform on everyone else."

Hélène had other things to worry about. She was discovering the rationing problems Simone had known during the war. Out of solidarity with his co-workers Lionel refused to eat in the officers' mess, and he and Hélène were having trouble finding food. In the chaos of the city, only the black market flourished. Six months after her arrival, Hélène had still not retrieved her crates of canvases and books, which were stuck at customs. The reason they gave her was that they had come from Portugal, a country suspected of being sympathetic to the Third Reich. When customs finally figured out what the real contents were, the crates were at last delivered—opened—to the addressee.

"How can I paint in an atmosphere like this? I love life and I love beautiful things; there's nothing here but ruins, misery, and grief. . . ."

Lionel encouraged her, although he was exhausted from his long days at work.

"Try anyway, it's too important to you. We won't be here forever... And while you wait you can paint the walls of the French library, perhaps with a mural? They certainly need it badly."

Hélène got to work and rediscovered her joie de vivre. In her long letters to Simone she described the Allied occupation and the attitude of the Soviets, of which she disapproved. It was said that the soldiers of the victorious Red Army had raped all the women when they arrived in Vienna.

As for the Americans, their behavior seemed more under control, sometimes verging on prudery. She went into detail in one of her letters to Simone. During a gala evening of expatriates, she had been seated next to a very American "boy." Among the attractions of the evening was a contortionist who could move her legs over her head, twisting her limbs in an extraordinary way, and this shocked the American:

"It's disgusting to watch!"

"But she's an excellent acrobat!" Hélène answered.

"Madame," the offended American came back, "would you like to see your sister doing things like this?"

The image of Simone with her legs above her chignon came to Hélène's mind and she burst out laughing.

"Yes, I would find that terribly amusing!"[1]

In reality, Hélène had very few opportunities for entertainment. Two years had passed since her arrival in Vienna, and she had only seen Simone and her mother twice during quick visits to Paris. She missed her sister in spite of the many letters they exchanged.

Throughout this period, Simone spent long days in Paris at the Bibliothèque Nationale, not far from the windows on the Palais-Royal gardens where Colette was writing her last words.

Bent over her table, Simone filled page after page as she wrote about the condition of the world's women without casting so much as a glance at anyone else studying there. Sometimes she would put down her pen and shiver. What she was discovering went beyond anything she had imagined when she began her research. In her historical and philosophical reading, she was dumbfounded as she measured the extent of the oppression of women through the ages and on every continent. She didn't know how the public would react. Her first novels had been received favorably, as had her play, *Les Bouches inutiles* (*Who Shall Die*) at the time of the Liberation. This time, though, her goal was different. Perhaps this book, for which she hadn't yet chosen a title, would interest no one.

As she left Rue de Richelieu and the gardens of the Palais-Royal, she walked past the Comédie Française, took the Pont-Neuf across the Seine, and returned to Saint-Germain-des-Prés. She thought of Vienna, where Hélène and Lionel were packing their bags. She wondered what Hélène would think of her book. Having become a faithful model wife who followed her husband everywhere, she had chosen the very path Simone condemned. She never rebelled. Still, Hélène could have judged her harshly as well, if she had known about some aspects of her life. In fact, Simone had found consolation with regard to Sartre, who was still spending long months in the United States with Dolores. She had an "American friend" herself, Nelson Algren, whom she had met in 1947 in Chicago. Poupette would never have been able to comprehend free love. Besides, she didn't understand anything about politics or the tension between the Soviet Union and the United States. What was worse, socialism and communism meant nothing to her. The shining future of the proletariat seemed to leave her indifferent. Over the years, a gulf had opened between the two sisters. Simone had created a new family of friends and comrades for herself. Still, she wrote to Poupette regularly to maintain the connection.

Simone quickened her step as she approached the Café de Flore to meet Sartre, who had just returned from America. In spite of her pleasure at the prospect of seeing him again, the only true urgency she felt was to cross the Atlantic to see her beloved in Chicago. She missed her lover. His caresses seemed so far away that her flesh ached. That was an emotion Poupette wouldn't understand.

However, she thought, as she noticed Sartre at a table at the Flore, Lionel was a handsome man, certainly much more attractive than the philosopher of her life. Poupette was obviously not unhappy, and at least she didn't have to share her husband with a swarm of scheming young women. Simone sat down, ordered a whiskey, and told Sartre about her sister's most recent letter describing ruined and occupied Vienna. Despite Poupette's lack of political awareness, her epistles supplied both of them with a current perspective on what was at stake in the Cold War in Central Europe. It was obvious that Lionel didn't much appreciate the Soviets and the paranoia of the Russian officials. It was aggravating. The "brother-in-law" didn't understand what was really at stake in France at the time. His political opinions were poles apart from theirs.

A group of gorgeous, made-up, and elegant young women passed their table, and smiled widely at Sartre without even glancing at Simone. The separation continued.

■   ■   ■

In a swirl of glacial wind, fog, and snow, Hélène descended the icy steps of the train with Lionel's help. They walked along the platform looking for the exit, which was easy to spot since the Belgrade station had been destroyed. Hélène sighed—ruins everywhere! In 1948, the scars of the unrelenting battles of World War II were far from healed. Everything in this wretched landscape had to be reconstructed. The Yugoslavian people had distinguished themselves with their strength and courage in resisting the Nazi invader. In contrast to the Austrians, the Yugoslavs were on the side of the conquerors, but they had paid a steep price: a city razed by the Germans, deadly hand-to-hand fights, and the Danube's water running red with blood. The economic situation was hardly any better than in Vienna. Even so, Hélène and Lionel were shocked—they had expected a city, but Belgrade was no more than a large rural town. People in assorted and ill-matching clothes rushed toward the trunks and suitcases standing in the middle of a herd of squealing pigs. Despite the destruction, Vienna had continued to be an intellectual center, while here everything reeked of desolation.

"Come, let's go. Let's not waste any time here," Lionel said when he saw his wife's nervous face.

Lionel was worried. He knew how much Hélène needed to paint. It was imperative for her own stability and that of their relationship.

"I will get materials so you can work comfortably, I promise you that."

They were taken to the only hotel, where the diplomats stayed. As they entered the room that would function as their apartment, Lionel examined the walls, the ceiling, the mirrors.

"After the bugs in Vienna, now the bugs of Belgrade! We won't feel homesick."

In her mind Hélène compared their situation to that of Simone and Sartre. She lived in a small studio on Rue de la Bûcherie near the banks of the Seine, and Sartre could see the Place Saint-Germain-des-Prés from the windows of his mother's apartment and go down to the Deux Magots or the Flore to write for readers who were eager for freedom and adventure. Parisian life seemed heavenly compared to the life the couple was going to have to put up with in Belgrade, an existence marked by rations, lack of heat, lack of privacy, and espionage.

In addition, as the attaché of culture and information, Lionel was answerable to the embassy. Keeping his post would be up to the goodwill of the ambassador and his wife. When paying her courtesy visit, Hélène thought of her older sister. Simone would hardly believe how Hélène had to flatter these people to help her husband's career along. Sartre and Simone were autonomous and didn't owe anything to anyone. As for herself, her painting certainly didn't allow her to attain economic independence and she would have to endure these ridiculous diplomatic incidents inherent in the life of a cultural attaché's wife. There were times, though, when she simply couldn't bear this microcosm any longer.

The French owned an enormous edifice that looked like a fortress, built on the banks of the Danube. Spared from bombardments, the building overlooked the modest homes around it. The ambassador's wife intended to keep a tight rein on the small French community and remind everyone of her rank.

Hélène entered the private apartments of the building. Shortages were still rife in Yugoslavia, and despite diplomatic packages everything was lacking. Madame de Roulet—now thirty-eight years old—was suffering from hunger and braced herself for the long hours of boredom ahead. She greeted the ambassador's wife, a beautiful, slender woman with piercing blue eyes, and shored up her courage when she saw the *petits fours* meant for tea. The ambassador's wife followed her gaze and said to her servant:

"Ah! You brought out the foie gras? But surely we need not bother serving Madame de Roulet any foie gras, do we, my dear?"

Politely, Hélène smiled ironically.

"Certainly not, Madame, there wouldn't be any point."

"Well now, since it's here," the ambassador's wife continued, "help yourself, Madame, eat, eat. . . ."

Discreetly, she took one hors d'oeuvre, finished it quickly and took another. The ambassador's wife chatted about galas, goodwill, and diplomatic receptions. Hélène nodded her head as she savored the foie gras. Simone would never believe her! She was in a rush to tell her sister these anecdotes of another era. Soon after, Hélène got up, put her white gloves back on—gloves that in this setting every woman had to wear—and returned to her apartment.

The whims of the ambassador's wife didn't end there. Every time she returned to Belgrade she insisted that the whole embassy greet her at the station. No one could escape it—neither diplomats, secretaries, or bailiffs. The offices were closed while the assembled courtiers awaited the train's arrival from Paris. The women dressed warmly, and the men pushed their felt hats down over their ears. Still in ruins, the Belgrade station was drafty, only the damaged platforms remained, exposed to the glacial wind. Trains might be six hours late. No matter! Stamping their feet and rubbing their hands, the French diplomatic community paced back and forth, waiting minutes and then hours. Passersby sniggered and Tito's policemen watched it all with a glint in their eye. The ambassador himself didn't say a word. Was he afraid of his wife's wrath? Telegrams and dispatches could wait. The return trips of the ambassador's wife were becoming affairs of state. Woe to those who missed these command performances! They would be forever marked and out of favor, even if they were out of town. Hélène and Lionel committed this egregious mistake just once. The ambassador's wife didn't want to accept their apologies. Later on, however, she agreed to forgive them, a leniency that was extraordinary, and for which Hélène never did discover the reason.

■   ■   ■

Lionel found a house on the heights of Belgrade. It was an unexpected bit of luck and a privilege that didn't trouble Hélène. Nor did she question the latitude enjoyed by Lionel, who could move freely through the country, unlike his colleagues. Without special authorization, the other diplomats were not allowed to stray more than thirty kilometers beyond the capital city limits. It was a procedure that would continue in all the countries behind the Iron Curtain until the Berlin Wall came down. Despite his defiance toward the Soviets, Tito applied one method that was dear to Stalin: he confined foreigners to the villages, while the countryside was forbidden to urban dwellers.

Lionel and Hélène explored many of the sites in the region, harbors and industrial areas that were often close to military sectors. For a few hours, Hélène set up her easel at the edge of a field or a road; Lionel would go walking by himself with a camera around his neck as if he were suddenly excited about the sad landscapes around him.

Some of the visits they received at home didn't surprise Hélène. There was a Frenchman who came to see Lionel regularly. It was rumored that he worked for the secret service. They would disappear together behind locked doors and ask not to be disturbed. But with every visit, the man asked to see Hélène's last painting and would admire her sketches. Hélène always thought he truly loved her work.

Many years later, during a conversation when I was alone with Lionel while visiting the Roulets in Alsace, he explained this strange situation to me.

"During the war, " I asked him, "did being the director of a Gaullist cultural institute in Lisbon mean that you were in the Resistance?"

"Are you asking whether I worked for the Gaullists? Yes, but Hélène doesn't know that."

The door of the room was open, so I lowered my voice and asked:
"Are you sure?"

"Oh, perhaps she suspects it. . . . De Gaulle needed people to bring the Resistance workers who passed through Lisbon to the English submarines."

"Why didn't you tell Hélène?"

"Too risky."

I caught my breath and waited a moment. Moving closer to him, I whispered:

"If you didn't tell Hélène it's because you continued defending Free France after the war, isn't it?"

Lionel closed his eyes. Without raising his voice, he told me about his work for Free France after the Liberation, in occupied Vienna and then in Yugoslavia. The war between Stalin and the Allies was raging. He was on the side of France.

Stunned, I gauged the rift that must have widened between him, Sartre, and Simone during those Cold War years when the two writers defended the Soviet Union and reviled the Americans. The question flew out by itself:

"Lionel, were Sartre and Simone told about your work for General de Gaulle's France?"

He remained silent for a few moments, then added cryptically:

"If they were informed it wasn't Hélène who told them, since she doesn't know about it."

Actually, Communist agents and the Communist Party in France—powerful and influential as they were at the time—must have been aware of Lionel's activities at the time and would have told Sartre and Simone about them. This likely was the cause of their disagreements, which were never openly tackled.

Simone's sister and brother-in-law were a popular couple in the country under reconstruction, their allegiance coveted by both the Soviets and the West. In fact, their association with Sartre and Simone represented an ideal cover that undoubtedly suited the secret service very well. In Paris, the two writers openly defended the cause of the Russians against the Americans. Lionel and Hélène were navigating a world split in two, in which Lionel had chosen to work for the West.

At receptions, he watched Tito from afar. The Yugoslav leader didn't come near Western diplomats and conversed only with Russians and Bulgarians. In such a climate of mistrust, Lionel sometimes went to Paris to meet with the head of the government. Would such a person normally have received a minor information attaché in a private audience? Hélène seemed to think it was normal.

Attempts were made to back them into a corner, unmask them. Agents

provocateurs appeared at their door. Lionel immediately escorted them back
to the front steps, always pretending not to understand a thing.

Without knowing everything about their brother-in-law's activities,
the two lovers of Saint-Germain-des-Prés condemned his anti-Soviet attitude. Certainly, the letters Hélène sent to Simone and her mother recounted every detail of the life in a country where the political police
were on a par with the Soviet Union's, but no matter.

The existentialists and their followers vilified the Americans and their
support of fascist regimes:

"We did love them, those big soldiers in khaki who looked so peace-
loving. They represented our liberation. Now they are defending leaders
who are imposing dictatorships and corruption from one end of the earth
to the other: Chiang Kai-shek, Franco, Salazar, Batista. Their uniforms are
a threat to our independence,"[2] Simone would write later.

■   ■   ■

Early in 1948, Simone finished two books simultaneously: one on women
that was more than a thousand pages long and the other an account of
her first travels to America. She continued her research at the Bibliothèque Nationale. It was a strange predicament—she devoted her days to
describing American cities and this people whose "boys" had liberated
France four years earlier. Now she no longer liked the country, even
though she had a lover there. Even as she wrote her critical and inflam-
matory texts on America, the process immersed her once again in the atmosphere of a distant paradise. Every word was actually directed at
Nelson Algren. She was ready to take another plane to meet up with
him as soon as she could.

In her letters to her lover she sometimes mentioned Poupette. Her
sister's anecdotes about diplomatic escapades left her thinking. Simone
watched the young women who spent time with Sartre. The "family" the
two writers had created now clung to them, thirsting for recognition.
Their bohemian life and their interminable discussions in cafés about
Sartre's plays made them feel they were rejecting bourgeois patterns. Yet,

they all lived off the philosopher's money, just like many traditional couples. Only Simone preserved her liberty.

It was the end of the day. One by one, researchers left the Bibliothèque Nationale. Her writing day had gone by too quickly. Crossing the Palais-Royal gardens, Simone delightedly breathed in the cool evening air. In front of the fountain, passing onlookers sitting in iron chairs, she smiled inwardly. Each page she added to her work reinvigorated her. She was like Poupette, she thought as she hurried on, who survived only thanks to her painting. It had been a long time since she had last sent some words of encouragement to Belgrade. She knew by heart the words that would renew her sister's strength to create. Tomorrow, she would sit down and write to her.

Try as she might to free herself from her blood ties, she found it was not easy. Besides, since her father's death, she had become the head of the family. She sighed at the thought as she entered the Flore, where Sartre and Camus awaited her. The world of ideas took over. She wanted to tell them about the last chapters of the two books that were taking shape in her thoughts. She gulped down a whiskey and began to talk.

If her work on America was emotionally important to her, she was far more attached to the one on women. Every day she discovered new forms of injustice. It would be a work of both philosophy and sociology. It would become her "J'Accuse."[3] Reading ancient authors such as Seneca, Plato, and Aristophanes, she could feel the anger rise inside her. The misogynist phrases followed each other from one century to the next and nobody had thought of protesting. Nobody but she. The public would no doubt be shocked, but that wouldn't stop her. The project would have to be gigantic, as the subject demanded. In France, General de Gaulle had granted women the right to vote, and in 1945 they had used it for the first time in municipal elections. Intellectuals were preoccupied with politics, commitment, and socialism, but no one was interested in the condition of women. In the United States, technology was supposed to lighten women's household chores. Nothing hinted at the feminist consciousness-raising that was to come.

■   ■   ■

In November 1949, after leaving Belgrade, Lionel had accepted a position in Casablanca. In the filtered ochre light of her Moroccan house, Hélène placed her brush on the easel. She moved back a few steps to contemplate her latest painting—a tea vendor kneeling in the narrow alley of a *souk*, the local market. Here, in comparison to the villages of Portugal and Yugoslavia, a more vivid light brightened the scenes of everyday life. She was happy. Her canvases were becoming more diverse, as each country she visited provided her with new subjects.

Hélène wanted to avoid doing abstract and post-surrealist work, the styles of the period. During a visit to Paris, she had organized an exhibit and sold some of her paintings. She decided to take a break in the heavy shade of a cypress tree. Sitting in an easy chair, she poured herself a glass of mint tea and opened the package the mailman had just delivered. She cried out with pleasure—it was *Le Deuxième Sexe (The Second Sex)*. She forgot about her paints and brushes and immersed herself in the book on which Simone, who had not revealed its contents to her, had worked so hard.

The indictment represented a gigantic effort. Moved and proud, Hélène skimmed through the chapters that criticized the alienation in which half of humanity had been submerged for centuries without managing to attain freedom. The book systematically examined the private lives of men and women and did so with a fine-tooth comb, comparing the smallest details. The blatant differences were brought to light, prominently exposed by Simone's critical pen. "One is not born a woman," she concluded, "one becomes one." The book surpassed Hélène's expectations; it offered the reader a perspective unimaginable at the time. Fascinated and awed, she knew this book would change society's values.

She couldn't simply return to her studio and pick up her brushes. Every page taught her something about herself. One subject in particular concerned her, the one that addressed her own situation and that of other women artists. She had often discussed it with her sister and looked for the chapter on the topic. Simone knew how much attention and allegiance men had won and to what a great extent women were refused these same rewards. Surely she had written about it. Hélène came to the last chapter with the promising title "The Independent Woman." Perhaps here she would find an echo of their earlier debates. When reading the final pages, she gave a start. What she read about women painters was not what she had hoped.

> But the very circumstances that turn woman to creative work are also obstacles she will very often be incapable of surmounting. When she decides to paint or write merely to fill her empty days, painting and essays will be treated as "ladies' pastimes"; she will devote no more time or care to them, and they will have about the same value. . . . Even if she begins fairly early, she seldom envisions her art as serious work. . . . She masquerades as a Beaux-Arts student, she arms herself with a battery of brushes; as she sits before her easel, her eye wanders from the white cloth to her mirror; but the bunch of flowers or the bowl of apples is not going to appear on the canvas of its own accord. . . . Instead of giving herself generously to a work she undertakes, woman too often considers it simply an adornment of her life; the book and the picture are merely her inessential means for exhibiting in public that essential reality: her own self.[4]

Hélène stopped reading and painfully caught her breath. How could Simone be so harsh with her artist colleagues? What she found out about Elisabeth Vigée-Lebrun bothered her. She adored the eighteenth century, the purity of the colors this artist used. And here was her older sibling disparaging the work by declaring that the painter "never wearied of putting her smiling maternity on her canvases."[5]

These lines broke her heart. Simone certainly knew of her sister's admiration for Elisabeth Vigée-Lebrun, whom she saw as one of the most talented painters of her era. How many times had she sat in front of one of her paintings in the Louvre? The grace, the play of light, the atmosphere of that pre-Revolutionary eighteenth-century era filled her with wonder. She felt close to this aristocrat who, despite her privileged status, had devoted her life to her work and had indefatigably produced an oeuvre of eight hundred paintings. Born in 1755, the daughter of a portrait painter, she had enjoyed

the support of her father in a period when high-society ladies only performed acts of charity and did not think of having a profession. She was so
precocious that, when she was noticed as a twenty-year-old student at the Louvre, she was asked to do portraits of well-known personalities. In 1783,
when she was twenty-eight, she was one of the rare women in history to be
elected to the royal French Academy. Most important, however, Queen
Marie-Antoinette had invited her to Versailles. Her wish had a political
purpose: the portrait was to serve as a means by which to try to rehabilitate
the queen, whom the public at large had accused of neglecting her duties and,
supreme offense, being a bad mother. Elisabeth Vigée-Lebrun produced
other paintings of the hated Austrian princess. Completed just months before
the Revolution, some could not be shown. It was feared they would be mutilated because of the rage brewing among the starving people.

Moved in her contemplations, Hélène thought of the painter's flight
across Europe: after traveling to Italy and Vienna she had found refuge at
the Russian court in Saint Petersburg. Her reputation had preceded her, and
the grand dukes all scurried to her with commissions, which made it possible for her to survive. Back in France in 1792, she lived off her art and died
at the age of eighty-seven, leaving an enormous oeuvre behind. By the
power of her work and her extraordinary influence, she was a true ex-
emplar and inspiration for Hélène. Brushing this artist's work aside with a
stroke of the pen as Simone had done was cruel, unfair, and abhorrent—
especially if one claimed to be defending the cause of women. Hélène
closed the book and got up quietly. In her Moroccan garden with the
birds beginning their evening song, she was pervaded by sadness.

Of course, she knew Simone's aversion to motherhood, pregnancy, and
the disfigured body, all of them symbols of the imprisonment men impose upon women with procreation as the only objective. Without a doubt,
this was the reason for her angry words about one of the rare female
artists across the centuries who had been recognized. Hélène was also
aware that her sister had never felt any particular affinity for painting, no
matter what the genre. But neither had Simone taken any offense at the fact
that museum walls were filled with paintings done by men, paintings that
also depicted family scenes or the court, commissioned by middle-class

and aristocratic patrons who granted the artists their means of survival. Women had far greater trouble finding benefactors, and when it did occur, it often resulted in all sorts of crude insinuations. Simone's point of view reminded her of the critics' condescension.

She grabbed her brushes and tried to concentrate. The next time they met, she would bring up the terribly unpleasant passage. She would find the courage to confront her sister. Art for her was not a mere distraction, a time filler for a lady of leisure; for her it was the true purpose in life.

■　■　■

Simone crossed the Place Saint-Germain-des-Prés. It was November 1949 and criticism of *The Second Sex* came flying from all sides. In viciousness and vulgarity, it surpassed anything she could have imagined. Incensed letters, death threats, and insults poured in, including comments from the otherwise very pious novelist François Mauriac, who usually chose his words with such care but who this time had written to one of his friends who worked at *Les Temps modernes*: "Now I know everything about your boss's vagina."

She had dared to claim that women were kept within a system of oppression that prevented them from attaining the existence of their choice. Worse yet, she had the audacity to express herself on sexuality and discuss abortion, a subject so taboo in France that the word was never uttered, either in public or in the press. At most, women might mention among themselves their anxiety about being late with their period and the prospect of an unwanted pregnancy.

Broaching the subject of the condition of women throughout the ages and civilizations right in the middle of the Cold War seemed untenable. While the tension between Truman's United States and Stalin's USSR was at its peak, she had the audacity to bring up a problem of a totally different nature—a war within society. Albert Camus's sarcastic remarks were flung in her face—"You are making the French male look ridiculous"—as were many more of this sort. It was fortunate that many women sent her letters of support and gratitude: "Reading your book has changed my life!" Even Hélène wrote her, and she needed to be comforted this way.

Simone entered the café Les Deux Magots, which was filled with people, noise, and smoke. Out of breath, she sat down in the back behind the two Chinese mandarin statues. She had been obliged to run so she would be on time for her appointment with Raymond Queneau. A cold rain beat against the windows. Ever since they had started yelling at her in public places she felt ill at ease. She was in a hurry to get this over with. Queneau had talked to her about a documentary on life in Saint-Germain-des-Prés and arranged for her to be filmed in an interview with the director. At the time she had no idea what to expect. When the spotlights came on, every eye turned toward her, the disgraceful one. Students from the Beaux-Arts recognized her: "As soon as they had plugged in the spotlights and began to film me, hundreds of guys standing on the tables shouted at me: 'Off! Off!' Then they screamed: 'She writes too fast, she doesn't think' and other niceties like that. Well, what could I do, other than pretend not to hear or see anything and continue to write until they had finished shooting? That's what I did, but it was quite a nasty fifteen minutes I went through."[6]

Exhausted, Simone left the café and hurried off to describe the incident in letters to Nelson Algren and to her sister. What increased her anger were the sarcastic comments Hélène had to endure on her behalf. Simone would fight for this book and for its distribution both in France and abroad. She wanted her work to breathe strength into those who would read it. She arrived at Sartre's apartment on Rue Bonaparte across from the Saint-Germain-des-Prés church. Her determination was greater than ever. Even if she were to be the only one, she would go on condemning injustice. If that was the price for creation, she felt ready to pay it.

■   ■   ■

The Roulets did not stay in Morocco for long. The Ministry for Foreign Affairs had suggested a promotion for Lionel in Italy.

"Lionel was named cultural attaché to Milan? How lucky you are to settle in Italy!" Simone exclaimed. "Do call Elio Vittorini and mention my name."

As soon as they arrived, Lionel and his wife were caught up in a whirlwind—meetings with Dino Buzzati, Franco Fortuni, the inauguration of the Piccolo Teatro with Strubler and Grassi, and the reopening of La Scala. More so than Rome, which in the early fifties was still a rather provincial city, Milan was the intellectual capital of Italy. Hélène wrote long letters to Simone about the cultural life of the country they loved with such a passion.

"Where have you been?" Lionel asked his wife one evening. "You have a sunburn and you look exhausted."

"I went to paint the *mondines*, the peasant women who pick rice all day long, day after day. They work bare-legged, feet in the water, and go through life hunched over. In spite of the arduous work, they are singing continuously. They're seasonal workers, they're poor, and just glad not to be unemployed."

"Did you do any portraits?"

"Yes, and I plan on doing more. I'm really interested in the relationship between these women, the water, the sky, and the earth. Their motions remind me of those of the Portuguese women I sketched in the salt marshes. I'd like to pay tribute to these professions, which in France we hardly ever see anymore."

"I'm thrilled. I can tell the light and colors here are an inspiration to you."

Hélène smiled. Her husband's support was as important to her as Simone's. Like every artist, and perhaps more than most, she needed to be encouraged. Sartre and Simone's fame had crossed the border a long time ago. Her warm welcome in Milan was due in part to the prestige of her family, and although she was aware of that, she had every intention of proving that she had a life of her own. She worked eight hours a day in her studio and kept her evenings for important social affairs.

When she discovered how little Italian women were paid and how they were exploited, Hélène often thought about *The Second Sex*. With every passing day her sister's judgment on the condition of women was proving to be right. Misogyny, too, was increasingly apparent to her.

At the lunch she organized in honor of Fernand Léger, Hélène placed two Italian women next to him, one on either side. One was in charge of the largest bookstore in Milan and the other of La Bura Museum. The conversation was brilliant and very animated. By way of thanking his hostess when he was about to leave, Fernand Léger said: "Women who talk this much are terrible for a man."[7] Hélène did her best to ignore the comment.

Simone and Sartre went to Milan for Poupette's exhibit, where she finally showed the public her paintings of the *mondines*. They congratulated her.

"I hope to have an exhibition in Paris next year," Hélène said as she handed her sister a glass of champagne. Her Moroccan paintings had been very well received. Sartre stopped in front of every canvas.

"Keep it up," Simone told her. "Your paintings are very good, indeed!"

As she tasted some petits fours, she gazed lovingly at her sister. Hélène looked gorgeous in her dress by Jacques Fath, a famous Parisian couturier. It was hard to picture her standing in front of an easel with her hands covered in paint. The opening had attracted a great many people, and there was no doubt that the presence of Sartre and Simone had something to do with that.

■   ■   ■

Hélène feverishly opened the art publications. A year had gone by since the success of her show in Milan. She had left Italy for several days to inaugurate her new exhibit in Paris at the Greuze Gallery, and a few journalists had hovered around her there. Trembling, she read the articles.

"The sum total breathes a syncopated musicality and is bathed in a dazzling light," the *Arts* review stated. *Le Monde* was even more laudatory: "Through her constructions in air and light, Hélène de Beauvoir has produced her own talent, confirmed her intentions, which are to bring together landscape and the image of the human being."[8]

For Simone the period now coming to an end had been rough. Nelson Algren had decided to break it off with her. He couldn't spend his life waiting for a woman who was so closely attached to another man. It was a brutal and cruel shock to her. Of course, they continued their correspondence, but the news left a large hole in Simone's life. She reacted by throwing herself into the writing of *Les Mandarins (The Mandarins)*—eight hundred pages, two rough drafts, and four years of work. She wanted to describe the history of the postwar French intellectual world and the tensions of the Cold

War. Her love affair with Nelson Algren would be incorporated into the novel. As with *She Came to Stay*, she chose to include herself in the story, taking Sartre's advice:

"Really, you need put more of yourself in your written work. You are far more interesting. . . . Put yourself in there!"[9]

She was preoccupied with another matter. During a journey to Moscow, Sartre had been sick; it turns out he was suffering from high blood pressure. Communication with the USSR was very difficult at the time but Simone had still managed to reach Sartre at the hospital. She was astonished to hear his voice through the receiver.

"How are you?" she asked anxiously.

"Very well," he answered sociably.

"If you're calling from a hospital you're not well. . . ."

Sartre had not wanted to worry her unduly. Simone hung up but couldn't calm down. She realized that "like everyone else, he bore his death within."[10]

Fortunately, a handsome young man came into Simone's life. Her meeting with Claude Lanzmann eased her trials, and the love affair galvanized her. When *The Mandarins* finally arrived in the bookstores, it was an instant success. The book described the hopes and disillusionments of the postwar intellectuals. After the scandal of *The Second Sex*, its contents were less disturbing to the public, and in November 1954 the novel was awarded the Prix Goncourt. Simone quickly left her room and sought refuge first at Sartre's, then at her mother's. In her apartment on Rue Blomet, Françoise de Beauvoir served Simone coffee. She didn't know how to express how proud she was of her daughter. The work received nothing but praise and, even if it fictionally told of Simone's affair with her American lover, she couldn't wait to talk about it with her friends. The Prix Goncourt for her daughter! Few women had ever known such glory.

Hélène had devoured the book. She wrote her sister a letter to congratulate her and announce a surprise, too: she and Lionel had bought a house in a Medieval village, perched on a hill above the Boca di Magre not far from the port of La Spezia. You had to park the car in front of the ramparts and walk to the house on foot.

"You now have a studio in Italy, Hélène," Lionel had told her as he handed her the keys. "We can spend a lot of time here."

Simone absolutely had to come there the next time she was in Italy. Hélène scribbled the address on the envelope, then set up a trestle and opened the window. She saw the valley and the hills, and in the distance she could make out the sea.

■   ■   ■

Lionel and Hélène spent eight years in Milan. In 1956, Hélène received troubling news from her sister. The war in Algeria had broken out on November 1, 1954 and, because of their support of Algerian independence, Simone and Sartre's lives were in danger. They received death threats, and a bomb exploded in front of Sartre's apartment on the Place Saint-Germain-des-Prés. Being so far away increased her anxiety.

"Look, Hélène," Lionel said with his customary common sense, "there is nothing you can do about it. Would you like to come with me to Rome to the meeting the ambassador is organizing? It will be a change of scene for you."

She agreed. Not long thereafter, she and her husband entered the dining room of the French ambassador in the Farnese palace. Michelangelo's frescoes decorated the room, and they dazzled her. The guests had found a small mirror to the left of each dinner plate, allowing them to look at the ceiling without having to crane their necks.

Servants brought in the main course while the ambassador's wife chatted with a general. Hélène exchanged a few words with her neighbor, a foreign diplomat who loved French literature. The wine was poured—an excellent Saint-Émilion. Nevertheless, Hélène's attention wandered—anguished, she was thinking of her sister, side by side with Sartre in their struggle for the independence of the Algerian people. The militants of the OAS[11] wanted to get rid of them. Still, Hélène managed to react and, gracious and smiling, she pretended to pay attention to her neighbor, nodding her head when it was called for and answering with a few platitudes.

As Lionel cast tender looks in her direction, she relaxed over dessert. Dinner was coming to an end. Soon she would be thanking the ambassador and his wife for the delightful evening. Teas, coffee, liqueur, and cigarettes were served in the drawing room. Lionel had joined a group of men who were listening to their host's most recent feelings about Italian politics.

At that moment, the companion of a French writer who was passing through town launched a new topic of conversation: society life in Paris. She mentioned two people in particular who had been banished from French society, Simone de Beauvoir and Jean-Paul Sartre. She knew them very well, she added, had in fact dined recently at the house of the author of *The Mandarins*. At receptions of this sort, Hélène was introduced as Madame de Roulet and her maiden name was never mentioned. Only the embassy staff knew the truth. Hélène grew pale with anger. How could they suggest such ridiculous lies? Simone never invited anyone to dinner—she couldn't cook. At this very moment, she and Sartre were trying to escape the terrorists and would hardly be wasting on frivolous dinner parties!

Hélène soon lost count of the times she had been confronted with such situations. Every time Lionel was transferred, she had to put up with false statements about her sister, invented friendships, unfounded gossip: Simone was secretly married to Sartre; she had had an abortion; she had a child by him that they kept hidden; she was incapable of writing and Sartre revised all her books. . . .

At the Farnese palace no one dared react and let the lady know who Hélène de Roulet was. Furthermore, in a country like Italy it was considered improper to mention, in her presence, Hélène's family relationship to a woman who in 1950 had been excommunicated by the Church. The woman continued to hold forth, oblivious to the embarrassed looks of others. Hélène rose, left the swarm of wives seated near the ambassador's wife, crossed the drawing room and said: "Lionel, let's go home." Nothing surprised her anymore, but she continued to be baffled by some people's twisted imagination and audacity.

■   ■   ■

Nevertheless, Milan provided her with fantastic opportunities. She organized several exhibits and mingled with many artists, but most important she met the great Maria Callas and attended many of her performances at La Scala. It was an encounter that had a profound effect on her, and until the day she died the diva's voice would be with her when she painted. Other exhibitions followed; the one at the Greuze Gallery gave her the chance to be back with Simone in Paris again. Hélène sold several paintings and was excited when she received the money for her work—she was proud to show Lionel that to some extent she, too, was earning her living now. Over lunch, Simone spoke to her about *La Longue Marche* (*The Long March*), a book on China she was about to finish. The struggles for decolonization were taking up much of her time. The young People's Republic of China was then only about six years old and had not yet had its falling out with its Soviet big brother. Stalin had died two years earlier, Beria was quickly eliminated, and Nikita Khrushchev, who was now Secretary General, had read a report admitting to the abuses of power committed by his predecessor. A hesitant opening up of the political spectrum began to show in the East, and French intellectuals were watching the evolution with great interest.

"And then, Simone, what will you write about in your next book?"

"I don't know yet, but it may well be a more personal work."

Hélène listened attentively. More personal? Simone had already put so much of herself in her novels *She Came to Stay* and *The Mandarins*, and even in *The Second Sex*. She mentioned this, and Simone agreed that in her previous work she had drawn extensively upon her personal life. But there were still the notebooks of her youth and a journal she faithfully kept up, which should provide plenty of material. Changing the subject, she suddenly exclaimed:

"Come and see my new apartment! Thanks to the money of the Prix Goncourt I finally own my own place!"

The sisters passed the building on Boulevard Raspail in which they had grown up, then the Café La Rotonde where as adolescents they had admired the girls with their urchin haircuts in the Roaring Twenties. Now, the customers on the terrace muttered Simone's name as they walked by. They went as far as Denfert-Rochereau and then turned onto Rue Schoelcher. Simone's new apartment was on the ground floor with a view of the Montparnasse Cemetery and the Paris sky.

"What a marvelous painter's studio this would make! Such wonderful light! It's the perfect place to work."

Simone burst out laughing.

"Yes, and from the ground floor the sunsets are truly magnificent! You already have Trebiano and it's all yours. Just wait, you'll see, one day you, too, will have your own house in France."

Hélène didn't stay long, she was too eager to tell Lionel the news. For years on end Simone had lived in hotel rooms and here she was—at the age of forty-eight, she who had so often teased Hélène about her bourgeois lifestyle had settled down in a level of comfort that many might have envied.

■   ■   ■

"Just pass that car! Can't you see he's not letting you by on purpose?"

Sartre was squirming in the passenger seat next to Simone in a little Aronde beneath the Italian sun. In spite of his small size and his bad vision, Sartre was checking the road. Like the knight of Pardaillan in the comic strips of his childhood, he was ready to do battle with the jerks at the wheel who were harassing Simone. Castor's driving exasperated Sartre. He had never obtained a license but that didn't prevent him from giving her endless advice and reprimands at every turn. Simone's patience was beginning to wear thin.

"Be quiet or I'm dropping you by the side of the road!"

"But that guy is keeping you from moving along, my dear!"

"I'm warning you, I'm going to tell Poupette everything!"

Sartre grumbled a few incomprehensible words and then said no more. He knew he had gone too far. Her hands gripping the steering wheel, Simone tried to avoid the Italian drivers who were passing on hilltops and sometimes in the wrong direction. She sighed deeply and clenched her teeth. If she were to listen to the little man beside her, it would lead to their certain deaths, and not for the sake of freedom but just to gain a few seconds on their trip.

They finally made it to the highway where Simone picked up speed.

Sartre relaxed and left her in peace. She had heard the story of Hélène's debut at the wheel in postwar Yugoslavia. When her sister had mentioned that she wanted to learn to drive, Lionel, who was usually so calm, had blown up.

"You don't need to! I'm your chauffeur, isn't that enough?"

For once her sister had held her ground.

"No, Lionel, that isn't enough! It's imperative that I know how to drive. What if something happened to you? Besides, I may need to go places."

"That's ridiculous, we can't afford to buy a car and we may never have one! You'll be wasting money."

"Fine then, I'll pay for my lessons with the sale of my next paintings!"

Lionel had to admit defeat. When Poupette wanted to, she could be just as stubborn as Castor. To top it all off, her older sister had decreed that driving was necessary for everyone to be free. Women needed to get around just as much as men. Hélène had looked at Lionel with a triumphant little smile.

Simone helped the couple purchase their first car at a time when she herself didn't own one. Of course, it was a bourgeois object, a symbol of capitalism, but it was also a tool that brought the liberty she held so dear. Today, the journeys with Sartre gratified her. She had always loved discovering new horizons. She consumed the world and unexplored regions, decided on her own which road to take, and allowed herself to be surprised by the beauty of the landscapes.

At last they arrived in the noisy and hot city of Rome, went around the Forum and found their hotel. Simone went to wash up and ordered an ice-cold whiskey. The next day she would phone Poupette in her summerhouse.

▮   ▮   ▮

Sitting in the living room in Trebiano, sipping a Bellini[12], Simone leaned over to Hélène.

"Show me your new paintings."

They jumped up and went to the studio. Hélène placed two self-portraits on an easel; one, very realistic, was a full-face image showing her in her living room in Milan; the other, more abstract, was a profile. In her studio, the paintings were piling up. Thrilled with the light and colors of Venice, she had brought back from a stay there her *Variations sur Venise*. Rather than mixing hues, she had juxtaposed them, playing with the perspective. She did her best to explain her approach. Space held a primordial place in her painting. She was still groping to find her own style. Looking to differentiate herself from what was fashionable, she had given up on studying perspective in accordance with Renaissance ideas. She had thus spontaneously turned to the abstract. The paintings paraded by as Simone expressed compliments and encouragement. Slowly but surely, Hélène was won over by her enthusiasm. She had never been an early riser, but in Venice she got up at five in the morning every day. She went through the apartment on tiptoe so as not to awaken Lionel; then, in the cold of winter, she took a *vaporetto* and, armed with her box of watercolors and folding stool, settled down on one of the bridges.

"At the end of December, there weren't many tourists in Venice and its colors belonged to me."

Simone asked for another apéritif. Planting herself in front of her sister's last canvas, she declared:

"You remember that I told you I wanted to start a more personal book. . . ."

"Yes, and what do you mean by that?"

"Well, I realized it while I was writing *The Second Sex*. As women, we didn't have the same childhood as the boys our age."

"That's very true. . . ."

"So I began to write my memoirs, starting with our youth."

Hélène froze.

"Are you planning to mention our relationship with our parents?"

"Yes. . . ."

"But Mother is still alive. Aren't you afraid you'll hurt her?"

"Some passages might bother her. But I'll try as much as I can not to hurt her. Who knows?—maybe she'll understand me better."

Another question was burning on the younger sister's lips.

"Will you describe the relationship we had as little girls?"

Simone smiled.

"Of course, it meant a lot to me, you know. You needn't worry."

"I trust you. Having said that, I must admit I wasn't expecting this news. . . . Have you made some progress on this project already?"

"A bit. . . . I'm wondering if it's of any interest. It's so hard to predict the success of a book."

The sisters rejoined Sartre, Lionel, and the others at the table filled with Italian appetizers. Hélène was stunned. Simone had already given her first name to one of the heroines in *The Blood of Others*. This time around she would become a character in her memoirs. The prospect filled her with fear and curiosity.

❚   ❚   ❚

"Come on, Hélène, we have to leave. . . . Paris is waiting for us."

Since the cultural attaché position was not a permanent one, after eight years of good and loyal service, the Roulets had to leave effusive Italy and their comfortable life in Milan to return to Paris. Hélène and Lionel drove all the way to Paris in the fog and the cold. In the back of the car on top of their luggage lay the bouquet of flowers their landlord had given them, as thanks for having paid the rent so regularly.[13] In her mind, Hélène replayed the disconsolate farewell of her Italian housekeeper, Giuseppina. The woman had become very attached to them and especially to Lionel. Her affection was so great that one evening when she saw a guest take too generous a portion of dessert, she decided to intervene:

"Don't take so much, there won't be enough left for Monsieur!"[14]

Eight years of Italy, eight years of happiness. Paris seemed dreary by comparison. The drama of the Algerian War weighed heavily. Passersby disappeared hurriedly into the gaping mouths of the metro to go to work. On the threshold of the door to her apartment, Françoise de Beauvoir welcomed them effusively. Hélène and Lionel were going to live with her; she wouldn't be alone anymore.

A few months after their arrival, Lionel heard on the radio that the Information Center of the president of the French Republic, where he had held the position of secretary general, had been dissolved. What was to become of him now? The fear of unemployment haunted him. They rehired him at the Ministry of Information, where he refused any file remotely dealing with political life. It wasn't easy to be the brother-in-law of the two intellectuals most hostile to the French government. At the office Lionel became doubly careful. Sartre and Simone were calling for civil disobedience and support for the FLN[15] "terrorists." They had to change addresses frequently, while Hélène and her mother lived in trepidation. She feared for her sister's safety. Simone and Sartre could be assassinated. In addition, Lionel seemed at the end of his rope. In this explosive family context he was having trouble assuming his new post and performing his duties for the French government. And in spite of the success of some of Hélène's exhibits, the painting sales barely covered the expense of materials.

Nevertheless, Hélène did not despair. The Synthèse Gallery was organizing a new show for her. She received her guests with her usual charm. Despite the heavy climate caused by the war in Algeria and the risks involved, Simone was fearless enough to attend. She stopped by briefly, her presence assuring that the exhibit received the recognition of the intellectual crowd.

In spite of the political tension, 1957 was a fine period for Hélène, who in that one year had six exhibitions outside of France: in Berlin, Mayence, Pistoia, Milan, Florence, and Venice. She and Lionel kept their bonds with Italy alive and often went to their house in Trebiano.

■ ■ ■

In May 1958, as the Algerian conflict deteriorated, part of the army threatened to secede, as did the French in North Africa who were opposed to Algerian independence. When confronted with the crisis, to avoid a civil war the last government of the Fourth Republic turned to General de Gaulle.

The General accepted the position of Council President, decided to dissolve the National Assembly, and was elected President of the Republic. René Coty, his predecessor, declared:

"The permier Frenchman is now the permier of France." The Fifth Republic would soon be born. In spite of several trips to Algeria and his famous statement "I have heard you!" General de Gaulle couldn't help but notice the complexity of the situation. The Evian Agreement[16] would not be signed until 1962.

In Paris with Sartre, Simone criticized the torture of Algerians. She was accused of "demoralizing the French army." She felt cut off from her country and from public opinion and was no longer in the mood to work. She had submitted the manuscript of *Memoirs of a Dutiful Daughter* to the publisher Gallimard in the spring of 1958. Hélène had not seen it; only Olga—the heroine of *She Came to Stay*—her husband Bost, and Sartre had read it. Simone's family and the public would all discover the book at the same time. In a taxi taking her to a demonstration against the French army's presence in Algeria, she queried herself. Writing a novel in a climate such as this seemed out of the question. While waiting for better days to come to France all she could do was focus on writing in her journal. The din of marching feet was already heard on the sidewalks. Many intellectuals recognized her: Pontalis, Chapsal, the Adamovs, Anne Philipe, Gégé Pardo, a friend of her youth, and . . . Poupette! It was a shock. Her sister was marching next to her, yelling "Fascism won't work!" What would Lionel think? He was taking a risk by letting her demonstrate. This political reunion made her smile. She knew that her sister was worried about her safety. Did she want to show that she, too, was a woman of the left?

■ ■ ■

A few months later, a florist rang the doorbell of Françoise de Beauvoir's apartment. He handed her a bouquet and a package. Inside an envelope she found a note from Simone asking for her forgiveness. *Memoirs of a Dutiful Daughter* would be in the bookstores a few days later. Hélène ran over to her mother:

"Show me!"

Together they leafed through the book. That night, as she discovered herself as the heroine of her own story, Hélène didn't sleep.

And what a story! While in *Who Shall Die* Simone had presented the character of Hélène as a superficial artist, here she displayed an immense affection for her sister. Certainly, she had sometimes been a brusque and authoritarian sister, but in her *Memoirs* the author brought the years of complicity with Poupette back to life.

"I was thrilled to have a little sister. As soon as you were old enough to follow, for instance, I loved giving you lessons. I remember that it was I who taught you how to read,"[17] she was to say sometime later.

While Lionel slept next to her, Hélène kept reading. She was filled with emotion and joy. The love she had for her older sister really was reciprocal. In the room next to theirs, Françoise de Beauvoir couldn't sleep. How would her husband be depicted? She relived the arguments between father and daughter, the screaming, the silences. Their private life would be revealed to the entire world. To reassure herself, she remembered how Simone had tried to protect her ever since her husband's death in 1943. Besides, Hélène had seemed delighted as she skimmed the pages.

As Sartre's mother, who proclaimed her son had understood nothing about his childhood, would later do with his book *Les Mots* (*The Words*), Françoise de Beauvoir rediscovered her life through the sharpened eyes of her daughter, a look that was quite critical of the education she had given them. Journalists liked the book, and it sold well. Hélène, too, felt acknowledged. She told her older sibling with childlike joy that the Museum of Modern Art in Paris had bought one of her paintings and that she had an order for a Gobelin tapestry!

Simone congratulated her. The future looked brighter. Thanks to all these commissions she felt sure that her paintings would continue to sell. That same evening, Lionel told his wife they had offered him a very lucrative post at the European Council. From now on he would enjoy a stable position. They packed their bags for Strasbourg. Françoise de Beauvoir watched her younger daughter depart once again. Simone, however, wasn't too upset, because Strasbourg was not far.

∎   ∎   ∎

Simone took a notepad and packed it in her suitcase. The summer vacation of 1963 was coming to an end. She would leave Rome the following day to return to Paris. The phone rang:

"Your mother has had an accident. She fell in the bathroom and broke her hip."[18] Sitting on the bed, Simone listened wordlessly to Jacques Bost, who lived in the same building as her mother. "We had to knock down the door of her apartment."

That same day, Hélène and Lionel moved into their new house in Goxwiller. Without water, electricity, or heat, the old farmhouse lacked everything. For a year they would have to camp out and face the cold of the Alsatian winter. While the movers were stacking all their furniture in what was once a stable, the mailman delivered a telegram with the sad news. Hélène left for Paris right away, promising her husband she wouldn't be gone for long. As it turned out she was away for more than a month.

"Mother has cancer, you know," Simone said.

"But I thought she had broken her hip?"

"Yes, but she also has cancer."[19]

For thirty days, the two sisters took turns staying with Françoise de Beauvoir, so she would not be lonely. Faced with her mother's withered body deformed by a tumor, Simone let her thoughts wander; memories of joyful moments but of conflict, too, came back to haunt her. Since her father's death she had executed her role as the head of the family with devotion.

Still, the writing of *Memoirs of a Dutiful Daughter* had not resolved the old quarrels. In the hospital, Simone recalled her earliest years when she was surrounded by admiring, loving parents. Then, after the First World War came the rupture as her father sank into a life of alcohol, gambling, and women. The financial troubles. Her embittered mother who dared not learn a profession and took revenge upon her daughters. How Poupette had suffered!

Simone relived the rejection by her biological family and her earliest conversations with Sartre on the importance of choosing one's own "family." They had both managed to do just that and yet, sitting by her dying mother's bedside, she felt bewildered. Once so authoritarian, she now seemed so frail. She needed her children and begged them not to abandon her. After their father's death, Simone had seen to her needs and given her trips to the Netherlands and to Italy. Françoise had carefully accepted the first novels of her oldest daughter and made no comment when she discovered that the main character in *She Came to Stay* had her name. The publication of *The Second Sex* and the scandal that followed baffled her completely. Her daughter had achieved fame, but at what cost! "A cousin had broken her heart stating: 'Simone is the shame of the family!'"[20] On the other hand, the 1954 Prix Goncourt for *The Mandarins* had overjoyed her. She was equally mystified by Hélène's work—painting for days on end and organizing exhibitions. Protected by her daughters, she sometimes had the feeling that their success had eclipsed her, but she was impressed by their energy.

Still, her pride was tinged with disappointment. Neither Hélène nor Simone had given her any grandchildren. Familiar with her daughters' opinions on motherhood, she didn't dare bring up the subject, knowing it would be too painful. She also appreciated the visits of Lionel's sister, Chantal. Sweet, intelligent, and a beautiful blonde, Chantal sometimes came to lunch with her three sons. Françoise loved her times at Meyrignac as well, where her cousin Jeanne de Beauvoir, who was the mother of nine children, invited her to stay.

"The first few days," Catherine, one of Jeanne's daughters, recalls, "we were happy to see her. But very quickly she would try to run the household. After two weeks, we were glad to see her leave again."[21]

And now this same woman was bedridden. Simone and Hélène couldn't bear to watch her suffer. She was attached to all kinds of tubes but was given no morphine, the doctors claiming that it might block her intestines. However, Françoise's days were numbered. The sisters rebelled against one arrogant and insensitive doctor, and insisted that their mother's pain be alleviated. Every now and then they managed to have someone give her an injection. The patient began to plead:

"Don't leave me alone, I'm still too weak. Don't let those beasts get at me!"[22] Her ordeal became more critical. She asked for additional shots of morphine. The doctor looked at Simone with hostility:

"There are two points where the self-respecting physician draws the line: drugs and abortion."[23]

The allusion was obvious. In *The Second Sex*, Simone had criticized the law that made abortion a crime. Now, fourteen years after the book had been published, they were making Françoise de Beauvoir pay on her deathbed for her older daughter's stance. The doctor openly showed his animosity. Simone and Hélène had to resign themselves—there was nothing left to do but hope that the end would not be long in coming.

Back in her apartment, Simone collapsed in Sartre's arms. Gnawed by remorse, she was sorry she had lied to her mother in the past, that she hadn't grasped the seriousness of her condition, that she had frightened her at times. She had not wept over her father's death, horrified as she had been by his words concerning Poupette. She thought she would have the same reaction when her mother's time came. Sadness, a little nostalgia, maybe. It was very different, however, and soon her world disintegrated. She couldn't deal with her despair. Compassion was ripping her apart. The old woman had given life to her; theories denying blood ties went out the window. Her mother's flesh was her flesh, her mother's story her own childhood story. Simone felt lost. The tears, grief, anguish all took her by surprise.

In the depressing atmosphere of the hospital, Simone and Hélène now had only one goal—to help their mother suffer as little as possible. At a time when Catholicism still had a strong grip on society, a patient's pain was seen as an inevitable and natural passage, and even as a road to redemption. Since Hélène was exhausted, Simone decided to spend a few nights at the hospital. Another shock awaited her. When they were washing her mother, she glimpsed the nude, deformed body. This unveiled privacy embarrassed her. In spite of her adventures, her relationships, and her love affairs, Simone still had the modesty of a young girl of the early twentieth century. She mentioned this to Poupette, who was less embarrassed by nudity. In her art classes she had had many occasions to see the naked body, young and not so young, beautiful, ugly, worn out, or grotesque.

Lying down in her mother's room, Simone revisited the stages of her own life. She was over fifty-five. Her affair with Nelson Algren was in the distant past and the one with Claude Lanzmann had come to an end. These two bygone love stories gave her the bitter impression of having moved into old age. No man would take her into his arms anymore, she thought sadly. Sought-after, surrounded, and pampered by very young women, Sartre didn't have the same experience; his fame guaranteed him easy conquests.

A few days before her mother died, Simone felt a strange peace come over her: "While we were talking in the half-dark, I assuaged an old regret: I picked up the dialogue that had been disrupted during my adolescence . . . and the old affection that I thought was gone completely was resuscitated."[24] The surge of tenderness extended to her sister. She once again found the intimacy that geographical distance and divergent viewpoints had diminished. During the years of separation, letters and intermittent meetings had maintained their affection, but now Hélène's daily presence and the torment they were enduring together revived their mutual devotion. Poupette lavished love upon their mother and showed no rancor whatsoever. Simone was surprised to find herself living behind closed doors, day in and day out, in this family room, as if it had always been the center of her world. Was it the effect of aging, of the problems she had encountered with Sartre? Once so exacting, she suddenly felt indulgent toward her loved ones.

The last few nights, Simone and Hélène took turns by the old woman's bedside. From time to time, the doctor would stop in, observe the patient in her final hours, and make some acerbic remark. Too overcome with grief, the sisters no longer reacted. The last night, Simone went home to sleep for a few hours.

"Simone undoubtedly didn't want to believe the end had come,"[25] Hélène confided to me later. Perhaps she wasn't able to bear the idea of this death. Alone with her younger daughter, Françoise de Beauvoir murmured: "I don't want to die. . . ."[26]

Hélène saw her hiccup and then fall asleep. She closed her eyes, kissed her, and ran to alert her sister. At two o'clock in the morning they stood together by the body. They slid her golden wedding ring onto her emaciated finger.

The burial took place in private. Sartre and Lionel walked silently beside Simone and Hélène, who were both hunched over with grief.

■   ■   ■

In December, Hélène returned to Goxwiller. It was icy cold in Alsace and the house was unheated. Everything in the studio was frozen. She sat close to a makeshift stove and made engravings. Not one of them represented her mother, but all of them evoked separation.

As night fell over her studio apartment, Simone flipped through an album of family photos she had brought from her mother's place. Turning the pages one by one, she felt an overwhelming need to write the story of this suffering. She had to. Tell every moment of this dying process, bring the woman back to life, let her speak, as she had done for all the other women whose condition she had described.

She allowed her sadness to burst forth. For several months she did not lift her pen off the paper. She composed line after line of what would become *Une Mort très douce (A Very Easy Death)*. She called Françoise de Beauvoir "Mother" and not "my mother." The writing became a cry. Amid tears and smiles she relived her childhood and dreamed of the unique moments she had shared with her younger sister. She had never felt this close to Hélène. When she wrote the last word, the dedication seemed to write itself: "To my sister."

"The book you wrote about Mother is magnificent," Hélène said on the phone.

"Thank you. I wonder how the public will react."

The book came out in 1964. In the conservative and modest France of the sixties many were offended by it: she had dared to describe the intimacy of the final moments of a dying woman. Others reacted violently to the description of the medical world. Her criticism of prolonging life by medical means scandalized some people. She deplored the fact that physicians were not sufficiently preoccupied with pain. What was she getting mixed up in? Had she been taking notes while her mother lay dying?

"I don't regret a single word I've written."

"I should hope not," Poupette answered.

Simone remembered the attacks against her when *The Second Sex* was published. This time, because the subject was more personal, it was more painful.

Many of her readers understood that her need to write this book was part of a grieving process. Many of them congratulated her on her candor and the way in which she criticized the social circumstances of old people and of the sick. Pierre-Henri Simon of the French Academy paid homage to her:

"Perhaps in these 160 pages, Simone de Beauvoir has given if not the best then at least the most secret part of herself."

▪   ▪   ▪

The Algerian War era was behind her and the future looked dark. Without the prospect of love, only her writing could restore her taste for life. Like Hélène, Simone was bruised and wounded from the ordeal. Old age was catching up with them. Still, Hélène seemed serene. With the companionship of Lionel, who had become an international government official at the European Council, she seemed to accept both aging and their mother's death more serenely. Her husband had a stable position that guaranteed him a pension and a reasonable financial situation. For Simone, things looked shakier and more unsettled. Gradually, a topic came to her, an extension of her last book. It would require a great deal of research and reflection, as much as she had done for *The Second Sex*. After criticizing the condition of women, she would do the same for the aged across the centuries and civilizations. Break another taboo. The prospect of a new scandal did not frighten her.

"I've gone back to the Bibliothèque Nationale," Simone told her sister one Sunday.

When Hélène understood why, she smiled.

"Go ahead, it will be great. For Mother and for us, too." She hung up and went back to work. Her paintings would be more sorrowful that year.

CHAPTER FOUR

The Women's Cause

It was November 1964, and it was raining in Paris. Simone watched Sartre. Bent over his worktable, his eyes glued to the accumulating pages, his fingers yellowed from nicotine, the little man seemed at the end of his rope. She wondered anxiously how long they could go on like this. Sartre had just refused the Nobel Prize for Literature.

To escape from the journalists he had sought refuge on Rue Schoelcher. Simone let out a sigh, her heart tight with sadness. In the eyes of the world they still personified one of the great literary couples. However, their love was foundering. Once again Sartre was enamored of a very young girl.

The phone rang. Three rings, silence, and another set of rings. Simone recognized the code meant only for those very close to her. Hélène was on the line. Far away, isolated in the Alsatian countryside, she had been following the Nobel affair through the press. She knew what Simone was going through. Covering up her concern, she announced lightly:

"We've finally moved into our new house in Goxwiller! Why don't you come for a change of scenery? You can go out and walk in the street without people bothering you, you can climb Mount Sainte-Odile or go to the Charbonnière Pass, and you can write in peace and quiet!"

Simone quivered with emotion—leaving Paris for a few days seemed like a dream! No rival would get in her way there. Being with her sister and brother-in-law would be a comfort even if Lionel irritated her. Goxwiller appeared to her now a sanctuary, a haven of serenity. She asked Sartre with a glance—for once, the author of *Nausea* was not repelled by the thought of going to the country and they left a few weeks later.

On Rue de l'Eglise, where the vegetable gardens began, Sartre and Simone passed some farmers going to the fields on their tractors. A few dogs barked as they came by. They stopped the car in front of the last house. Facing them, behind a pale wooden gate, two farms connected by a barn comprised Hélène and Lionel's new domain. The courtyard, which had been neglected by the previous owners, was covered with weeds, and the bottoms of the pools were green with thick layers of moss.

Climbing the stone steps, the Parisians inhaled the welcoming scent of a simmering veal stew. Poupette had prepared the dishes she knew her sister loved. Before dinner they opened a bottle of champagne. Simone sat down on a bench in the kitchen of the old Alsatian home. The younger sister was busy cooking, and a gentle heat emanated from the stove. The older one was talking non-stop as if drunk on freedom—a physical sensation she had long since forgotten, the feeling of being loved and protected. Goxwiller reminded her of their childhood in Meyrignac, of the smell of toast and hot chocolate.

Why wouldn't they ever leave them alone? She knew the answer all too well—because that is how Sartre wanted it. She was a woman in love and suffering wordlessly; she preferred enduring all of that to losing him. After lunch, Sartre and Lionel retired to the small library. He lit his pipe and sank happily into the red velvet easy chair, a Beauvoir family heirloom. Behind him were bound copies of rare eighteenth-century books; Voltaire and Rousseau stood side by side with his own and Castor's writing. The volumes covered the shelves of the attic room with their sweet scent of wood and wax, and time seemed to stand miraculously still.

Workers were busy in the courtyard that had been transformed into a temporary construction site (goldfish ponds were in the making). Lionel picked up a pickax and decided to give them a hand. In admiration, Sartre watched his former student dig with all his strength. He, too, grabbed an ax, rolled up his sleeves, and sank the tool into the grass. Suddenly water spurted straight into the air. Alerted immediately, the village mayor came running and saw a badly dressed, plumpish little man, bolting into the street crying:

"Mr. Mayor, Mr. Mayor, I discovered a spring!"

Goxwiller's foremost magistrate came closer to observe the gaping hole that continued to gush water; he finally shook his head. What had really happened was that Sartre had perforated a water pipe. Having to announce this bit of news to Lionel, who had a hard time covering up his mad laughter, and to the silent but amused sisters, the philosopher turned pale. His first attempt at garden work had pathetically come to nothing. Sartre went back up the steps into the house and collapsed exhausted into a chair. Clearly his hatred of chlorophyll was well founded. He could hear Poupette and Simone downstairs, giggling like girls.

A few days later, as the finishing touches were put on the goldfish ponds, it was time for them to leave. Simone effusively hugged her sister goodbye. She had no idea what the future had in store for her. A new book would not be enough to alleviate her melancholy. She braced herself to face Paris again, with Sartre's companions, both young and old, all eager for his time and love.

■　■　■

Simone opened her mail. There were more letters from women in distress. Cheated on or deserted by their husbands, these women told a timeless tale of loneliness. Often without any professional skills, they sank into despair or madness. What Simone had described in *The Second Sex* had not been remedied. Seated at her small worktable, she reread the pages of her most recent manuscript: three dark short stories, all too close to her readers' life stories. Three disillusioned lives of solitude. She understood their situation all the better since she herself felt betrayed. Arlette El Kaïm, a young woman of Algerian origin and Sartre's intimate friend, occupied a dominant place in the life of the philosopher who had legally adopted her. Among Sartre's "women," she was the only one who bore his name, and it was she who scheduled his time. Simone had intelligence and character, but Arlette had one major asset: her glow of youth.

A fortuitous new encounter brightened Simone's life. A philosophy student at the Ecole Normale Supérieure for women wanted to interview her about her work. Sylvie Le Bon enchanted Simone with her lively spirit. They became fast friends, and this brought her the solace she so badly needed.

Not long thereafter, in 1966, Simone had some good news. Together with Sartre she was invited to Japan by some of the writers there. The journey was a triumph. They were welcomed like movie stars, their words quoted repeatedly in the press.

Before a jam-packed hall, with photographers' bulbs flashing away, Simone broached a subject she hadn't mentioned since *The Second Sex* had been published: women and creativity. She had prepared her speech with Hélène in mind. This time she defended women painters and did not treat them disdainfully. In a strong voice, she spoke of how difficult it was for a woman artist to finance a studio and sell her paintings: "It is expensive to have a studio. Yet to make money you need the support of an art dealer and you need collectors. Now, I am close enough to the art circles to know that an art dealer will not put his money on a young woman."[1]

She described in detail the obstacles a painter had to confront and reminded the public how rare it was for a woman to find assistance within her own family, as Van Gogh had found in his brother. She herself had played that role by giving Hélène both moral and financial support so that she could exhibit both in France and abroad.

Having come to the end of her analysis, she descended the podium steps to thundering applause. The trip to Japan had gone beautifully, and her only regret was that her sister had not heard her speak.

■ ■ ■

In the silence of her apartment, Simone put the finishing touches on her short story collection, which would bear the title *La Femme rompue* (*The*

Woman Destroyed). Suddenly she had an idea, leapt up, and phoned Goxwiller. She suggested that Poupette create engravings to illustrate the issues, and the distress of the women she had described. Mad with joy and impatient to start working, Hélène could hardly wait to tell Lionel the good news that night. That year, the sisters would come together on a single work, with pen and brush complementing each other for the first time.

In her house in Alsace Hélène created a series of engravings in a matter of weeks.

"They're absolutely superb!" Simone exclaimed on seeing them when her sister came to Paris. An art gallery on Rue Saint-André-des-Arts was willing to exhibit them. *Elle* Magazine published excerpts of the book with photographs of a few of the engravings. Poupette and Simone anxiously awaited the public's verdict. It was merciless: the press did not criticize Hélène's work, but the commentary on the stories, on the other hand, turned out to be excruciating. In *Le Figaro littéraire*, Bernard Pivot[2] declared it a "novel for shop girls." Others couldn't understand why Simone would want to describe women's bondage when in *The Mandarins* she had expressed the values of involvement and existentialism so well.

The fiasco hit the sisters hard. Simone went back to the Bibliothèque Nationale to continue writing the essay she had started after her mother's death, a condemnation of the dismal condition of older people. This would become *La Vieillesse* (*Coming of Age*). Hélène fervently defended Simone's book, but Christmas 1967 was still a bleak time.

▨   ▨   ▨

Sartre and Simone were walking along Boulevard Saint-Michel and couldn't believe their eyes. Young people were tearing up the streets and ripping out the protective wire around the trees in the Latin Quarter—May 1968 promised to be stormy.

Simone moved along in silence. Too many painful events had transpired lately. She had not yet digested the mordant reception of *The Woman Destroyed*. Sartre's love for Arlette El Kaïm was even more upsetting to her. Happiness lay behind her, she thought, as she watched the adolescents running in every direction. Their nonchalance and energy seemed to have no limits. Their heads were covered with makeshift helmets and on the barricades in the Latin Quarter they kissed each other wildly. Simone looked at them and felt her weariness increase. No more happiness, she repeated to herself. Of course, Sylvie's affection helped, but she could not keep herself from envisioning the inescapable decline of aging, both her own and that of the man she loved.

Simone reflected on the fact that she had turned sixty on January 9, 1968. Poupette had called her from Alsace, expressing once again her unconditional love. For years this had irked her, and in her letters to Sartre and Nelson Algren she had written some terribly condescending words about her sister. Now she understood it better. Since Arlette had come into her world, she realized that the condition of ordinary women, which she criticized in *The Second Sex* and which she thought she had escaped, had become her fate as well. Now she was like a wife who had fallen from first place. For forty years her books had allowed her to have a special spot in Sartre's heart; today, the reviews were tossing them in the trash. Cost what it may, she simply had to concentrate on her writing, her ultimate reason for living.

Sartre pulled Simone out of her reveries, making her jump back. The CRS—the state security police—was charging, unleashing a fog of tear gas on the crowd. An oppressive cloud choked them and Sartre was coughing furiously. Amid the screaming and shouting of the demonstrators they found shelter in a carriage entrance. They were getting too old for such stampedes.

The young, of whom she was particularly fond, were not interested in Simone. They would meet Sartre, have discussions with him on the radio. In France, paralyzed by strikes and riots, you could hear Sartre and Cohn-Bendit, Sartre and Geismar, Sartre and Sauvageot[3]: at this revolution's every stage their words were an inspiration. Not once did anyone think of interviewing Simone. Words spoken by women didn't count. Her thousands of published and translated pages, the hundreds of thousands of books that had been sold across the world brought her no recognition whatsoever in a country so much in need of new perspectives. May 1968 was a revolution led by men; once again, women's place was parenthetical. They remained invisible, like the knick-knacks on a shelf you no longer see because they've become such a part of the overall décor. Never having hesitated to speak out and criticize injustice of any kind, Simone realized she had been confined to silence.

And yet, how she would have loved to participate in the exaltation of those crazy days!—with Sylvie, of course, but with Poupette as well. They called each other daily. Excitedly, Hélène described the initiatives of the students in Strasbourg. They were invading the European Council, debating with technocrats and politicians. Brazenly, they would lay into the arrogance of civil servants in gray suits. Hélène felt she was back in the atmosphere of her art student days; at fifty-eight she was rediscovering her youth.

She told her sister she had attended a feminist meeting on the subject of battered women. In her elegant pearl-gray suit, galvanized by the fiery words of the speaker, she had clapped wildly along with the rest of the audience. Sitting beside her, Lionel had turned pale. Poupette, usually so discreet and well bred, was allowing herself unexpected excesses. Controlling his annoyance, he had whispered in her ear:

"Don't clap so loudly, my colleagues are looking at you."

Hélène laughed, not leaving out a single detail; on the other end of the line, Simone rolled her eyes. Since they couldn't be together, the telephone bills of the Beauvoir sisters grew larger. Sitting next to the window from which she could make out the church's bell tower, Hélène listened to her older sibling describe the turmoil in Paris.

"How I miss our old neighborhood!" she exclaimed. The artist had left her studio. With the radio permanently on, she felt completely in tune with the youth that rejected the arrogance of the affluent and their stuffy speeches.

After the Grenelle agreements,[4] the workers returned to the factories and the student demonstrations disintegrated. Simone did not hide her pessimism from Hélène—the forces of order would again take the upper hand. The highly placed civil servants who had fled their ministerial offices reappeared. Daniel Cohn-Bendit, a German who had been a key student leader, was ousted from France. Everything seemed to have come to an end. That summer, more than ever before, the sisters continued to have lengthy exchanges both by phone and mail.

■ ■ ▌

In the fall, Hélène returned to her canvas and brushes. She rose early and as soon as Lionel had left for the European Council she would have a small cup of espresso, cross the courtyard, and retreat to her studio. The vast and luminous space with its high ceiling put her at ease. In a corner stood a couch covered with an old Moroccan blanket where she could sit and contemplate her day's work. From the bay window she had a view of the flower garden and the trees Lionel had planted. Paintings from several periods were piled up behind a huge, heavy drape: the Venice series from the fifties, rural scenes of wartime Portugal, the warm colors of Morocco.

In the stillness of the countryside, Hélène felt a new emotion pulsating within her. Aimlessly, she put some lines on the canvas, then stopped. Colors followed. In her memory she heard the sounds of the turmoil, the shouting, and the demands of the previous May. The slogans of the young, their insolent gaiety, their rejection of the established order had marked her in the depths of her being. She stepped back. On the canvas helmets appeared, iron bars, the CRS smudged with dirt and blood, their eyes owlish in metal goggles. These were the shapes in the center of the composition; in a corner demonstrators emerged from the cobblestones, white as shrouds in front of a wall red with blood.

Exhausted after many hours on her feet, Hélène went back to the painting and wrote the title that came to her: "Fascism will not prevail." She went back to the quiet house. Other ideas for paintings sprang up within her as in a dream. The events had awakened a thirst for liberty and justice. *"Aimez-vous sans entraves,"* one of the 1968 slogans had stated—"Love without shackles." That evening when he returned from the European Council, Lionel found his wife in the kitchen. She had made a delicious dinner while thinking about the next day's painting. It would be even more violent, more intense than the one of the CRS.

As winter approached, the temperature in the studio came close to freezing. With icy hands, Hélène continued to work relentlessly. Her sister and Sartre talked about involvement—she was following in their footsteps. When the Alsatian cold made the studio unlivable, she set herself up in the living room, put down her metal frames, and made some engravings. Women passed beneath her window, all bundled up, their heads wrapped in scarves. The water lily pond was frozen and the goldfish were moved inside the house. At teatime Hélène went downstairs to feed them while the cats stayed in the living room near the heater and the pieces of fruitcake they were hoping to steal. Deep inside, however, she was growing impatient. She wanted to get back to her work on May 1968. She was in a hurry to get it down on canvas, feeling an immense need to create. With a steaming cup of Lapsang Souchong warming her hands, she thought how lucky she was—she had been able to build her life around the miracle of painting.

Finally spring arrived in Goxwiller. Since her studio was still freezing, Hélène wrapped herself in woolen sweaters and tried to protect her chapped hands. She dipped her brushes in the sensually dense paints. Hurriedly, she placed violent hues on the canvas, full of the fury and hope of the youth that had stormed France. Flags, truncheons, visages in face paint were emerging from the fog. Within a few months she finished a major collection, more than thirty paintings in all. Lined up side by side, they provided a rare testimony of a turbulent page in France's history. In comparison, her earlier work seemed insipid to her now. This time, reality matched the image. As had Simone and Sartre, she had just remade the world her way, by painting it. She really wanted to know what her sister's reaction would be.

First she had to find a gallery, and she knew it would not be easy. She had two handicaps to overcome: her isolation in the country and the nature of her work, which was less abstract than that of the painters then in vogue. Furthermore, there was a risk that her choice of such a recent and painful subject would provoke the public. A gallery on the right bank of the Seine was willing to host a show on the basis of the title of the series: *Le Joli Mois de mai* (*The Lovely Month of May*) had entranced the gallery owner, who undoubtedly imagined a more classical theme of springtime, but she abandoned the project when she saw the paintings. Another attempt failed as well. Hélène was disturbing to a traumatized France that had grown fearful again.

At home, Simone was getting upset:

"Don't let it discourage you!"

Hélène raised her head, exclaiming:

"Of course not! I'm going to keep fighting."

She met Franck Thomas, the cultural organizer of a youth center, a young man with the face of an angel who very quickly became a friend. With enthusiasm and determination he pounded the pavement and found a space for Hélène that was not only available, but legendary as well. Eighty years earlier, Toulouse-Lautrec had created his sketches of French cancan dancers there: the Moulin Rouge! The opening was extraordinary. In the mixed crowd, duchesses rubbed elbows with writers like Simone, Sartre, and Prévert,[5] as well as prostitutes: as someone took a photograph of Hélène with Jacques Prévert, the Duchess de La Rochefoucauld entered the gallery in a magnificent red coat. A prostitute called out:

"Hey there, the lady in the red coat, you're getting into the picture, move over!"[6]

As usual, Hélène couldn't avoid a few rude people who, seeing her sister there, insisted they be introduced. It happened at every opening. Still, this particular evening she forgot the hurt of the past. One by one, her paintings were snatched up by buyers. She had managed to re-create the spirit of May 1968. Under Simone and Sartre's eyes, she was coming to be recognized for her own work.

Would there be any reviews? The next morning, Hélène skimmed the art page of *Le Monde*. Low down in a column, next to a boxed piece about Chagall and the Bible, she found a brief article about herself. The comments were full of praise:

"Luminous, gentle colors come alive in a prismatic breakdown, newspaper pages are splattered with abstract signs, ghostly figures (the wounded or fighters) respond to the compact crowds of helmeted troops. Precise sketches of sites and actions seemingly caught in mid-gesture, are integrated into the whole. . . ."[7]

For a moment Hélène raised an eyebrow: the article opened with a quote from Simone, the eternal reference. In spite of the unexpected sale of all of her paintings, her older sister's glory again cast its shadow over her accomplishments. But she decided to forget this minor note and serenely took the train back to Goxwiller. She was bringing Lionel tangible proof of the attention her work had received in the form of a tidy little sum of money. Announcing the total figure of her earnings, she saw a pride in his eyes that overwhelmed her.

In Paris, Simone and Sartre met with the Maoist students. One of their leaders, Benny Lévy, a student educator better known by his revolutionary pseudonym Pierre Victor, fascinated Sartre. Brilliant, authoritative, he comfortably addressed the author of *Being and Nothingness* by the informal form of "you" (*tu*). Together they burned with excitement over their idea to launch a revolutionary daily paper to be named *Libération*. Simone observed that very few women would be sitting on the editorial board and wondered if they were going to keep quiet. A few days later, Anne Zelensky asked to meet with her. In May 1968, this young feminist had established a women's center at the Sorbonne, which had been received with indifference.

▮   ▮   ▮

In the spring of 1969, sitting on her yellow sofa at home with a glass of whiskey in her hand, Simone listened intently to Hélène. Her sister was spending a few days in Paris with Lionel and had hurried over to visit her. Poupette always surprised her. This time, though, Simone couldn't believe her ears and had trouble keeping a straight face.

"You're actually spending your days with workers and hooligans?"

Hélène burst out laughing. At last she had made an impression on her sister. Sartre and Simone no longer had a monopoly on relationships with the working class, and not every factory was in Billancourt. The success of her exhibit at the Moulin Rouge and the record sales of her paintings showed that revolutionary actions could be taken, even far from Paris. She had captured the spirit of May 1968.

Simone looked worriedly at the small clock. Her appointment with Sartre was fast approaching. But Poupette couldn't stop. In a high, excited voice she was recounting every detail of her stay at Montbéliard. They had asked her to take charge of setting up an Altuglas studio for the Peugeot factory workers. Altuglas was a "very resistant synthetic material, translucent or tinted, that could serve artistic purposes or industrial applications." In the morning she taught courses to students at the *lycée* and in the evening to young, hardened, and sometimes aggressive workers.

"My dear Hélène," she had been told, "you'll be teaching a group of very difficult young people, future delinquents, terrible types. Be careful. The other day, they told the pastor's wife to go f– herself."[8]

Simone's eyes opened wide.

"I started by being polite, greeting them with a 'Good morning, gentlemen,' and using *vous* [the formal "you"] with them. Since they were so used to being treated rudely, contemptuously, and disrespectfully, they were totally adorable with me."[9]

The leader, a tall redheaded youth covered with tattoos and jewelry, became her protector. Hélène described the months she had worked with them and how they had put together an exhibit, which everyone in the region had come to see. At fifty-nine, she had found a bohemian atmosphere again, a joyous chaos she no longer wanted to leave. Still, she had to. When the former dutiful daughter said goodbye to her "students," they picked her up in their powerful arms and planted noisy kisses on her cheeks. In their own way they thanked her for everything she had taught them.

Openly showing her amusement, Simone asked:

"And what about Lionel?"

"Well. . . One evening when he thought I was taking a long time, he came to get me!"

Sartre's brother-in-law had been very surprised to find guys in blue overalls kissing his wife to say farewell. It was time to go back to Strasbourg and a quieter life. Simone suddenly jumped up. These stories had made her forget the time. She had her appointment to keep with Sartre!

▌   ▌   ▌

General de Gaulle had resigned a few months earlier. In January 1970, Georges Pompidou, backed up by Minister of the Interior Raymond Marcellin, put leftist groups and the intellectuals who supported them under surveillance. Simone and Sartre's lunches at La Coupole had begun to make them look as if they were plotting. The owner, a dignified older gentleman, highly respectful of the two writers' privacy, kept the neighboring table reserved so troublesome people would not come and bother them. Nobody dared sit there. They felt sheltered, sitting in the back of the restaurant without being disturbed and situated in such a way that they could see who came and went. They hadn't counted on the new government that was now in place. As soon as Simone and Sartre had begun their appetizers, policemen in civilian clothes sat down at the next table. The owner insisted they move to another table. Impassively, they took out their identity cards displaying the French flag and ordered their meal. What followed was a game of hide-and-seek in which the two accomplices slipped away to a different table to finish their meal, to the delight or concern of the other patrons.

Simone poured another glass of wine. Her new book *La Vieillesse* (*Coming of Age*) had been in the bookstores for several days. The memory of the failure of her two previous books, *The Woman Destroyed* and *Les Belles Images*, still lingered painfully. The subject matter was very dear to her heart, but she wondered if her own aging process might not have diminished her analytical gifts, and she was drowning her anxiety in alcohol. It was true that an American publisher had paid a considerable advance to obtain the publication rights in the United States and the other English-speaking countries. Other countries had tried to acquire exclusive rights as well. Nevertheless, her confidence both in herself and in her readers was disintegrating. She had sent a copy to Poupette and awaited her reaction.

In Goxwiller, Hélène devoured the book in just a few nights.

"It's a masterpiece. Your work is of the same quality as in *The Second Sex*. This will be a triumph! And, you'll see, the topic is less sensitive than that of the women's issue. There will be fewer attacks."

Simone hung up, deeply touched. Dear Poupette! She was always so loyal and enthusiastic.

■   ■   ■

Taking the plane back from New York in June 1970, I was apprehensive about returning to Paris. I had gone back and forth between the United

States and Europe since childhood. Robert Oppenheimer, the inventor of the American atom bomb, had invited my father, a mathematician, to the Institute for Advanced Study in Princeton, where Albert Einstein was working. Having also been in close contact with Russian scientists at odds with the powers that be, I had become interested very early on in what was happening on the other side of the Iron Curtain. As a *lycée* student I went to Leningrad, Kiev, and Moscow every summer to learn Russian and visit my father's colleagues. In the fall, I would return to Princeton and American civilization again. My best friend at school was African American, and at the time I was the only one who would speak to her. Apartheid was still so much a part of the mentality that I was openly rebuked for sharing my meals in the cafeteria with her. The intolerance of both systems impelled me very early on to struggle for a little more justice in the world. Strengthened by this ideal, I threw myself into the Movement of March 22 in 1968 in Nanterre, which was led by a young red-haired student. Daniel Cohn-Bendit was a talented storyteller and a ladies' man—with a good sense of humor, lively and intelligent, he captivated the crowds, especially young women. However, I refused to add myself to his list of conquests. He didn't hold it against me; on the contrary, we established a sort of complicity.

It was hot and humid in the great amphitheater of the Sorbonne on May 14, 1968. Sartre sat down at the small table on the podium. The students, myself among them, piled in, occupying benches, steps, and aisles. A huge cloud of cigarette smoke blossomed above our heads; the hero of existentialism found a note on the desk that was to become famous: *Sartre, keep it short.* In a warm, spellbinding voice, he expressed his approval of our movement in a few dynamic sentences. We applauded him wildly and with deafening noise.

Looking modest, Sartre left the building. Thanks to support such as this, we were going to have a successful Revolution. I, for one, felt slightly disappointed, however. I had expected to see Simone de Beauvoir, but instead a young girl with fine features and dark hair, barely any older than we, had accompanied the philosopher. It was Arlette El Kaïm. Why, I wondered, didn't the author of *The Second Sex* have anything to say? I was not yet aware of the fact that May 1968 was a male matter.

The collapse of the student movement bewildered me, as it did so many others. The revolution I had naively believed in had vanished the same way it had come. For a change of scenery, my parents sent me to an American university for a year. A few months after my arrival in the United States, the demonstrations against the Vietnam War intensified. My university friends were distraught when they received their draft cards. They refused to participate in this distant war where a population was being burned with napalm. They destroyed their cards in the university chapel and then fled to Canada. Their lives were ruined. I left America in a fit of intense passion.

What kind of a country would I find upon my return to France? In 1970, order reigned again. Georges Pompidou was president. Traumatized by the country's paralysis, strikes, and riots, the authorities were trying to dismantle any groups that had emerged from the 1968 movements. In addition to pursuing my studies in literature, I wanted to rejoin the political movement in which I believed. I joined *Les Amis de la Cause du peuple* (Friends of the People's Cause), a group of intellectuals, led by Sartre and Simone, who supported the Maoists and published a banned newspaper. There I found some of the former leaders of May 1968. Among them was Sartre's secretary, Pierre Victor. He responded to every political comment uttered by a female activist with the same scathing answer: "Be quiet!" Other comrades in the struggle went a step further: "You wouldn't understand." We were only women.

Older, less obtuse intellectuals, among them Michelle Vian, the first wife of Boris Vian[10] and the mother of his children, joked around with us. An intelligent, lively blonde, she had beguiled Sartre and he saw her frequently; she belonged to the "family. " Michelle introduced us. His utterly mesmerizing voice amply compensated for his ugliness, which was more unsettling than in the photographs—grainy skin, waxy complexion, wall-eyed gaze, tobacco-stained fingers—but when you listened to him the rest of the world no longer existed. His melodious conversation gave you the illusion of exchange and complicity.

How could he stand the arrogance of the revolutionaries around him? I wondered. No doubt they gave him the impression they were participants in changing the course of history. Aged and sick, he livened up in their presence, and the endless discussions delighted him, so much so that he often left exhausted.

My status as a woman brought me a few privileges in the student movement, such as typing pamphlets and, at six A.M. in the cold and fog—while the comrade leaders, nice and warm in their beds at that hour, pondered the future of the Revolution—going off to factory gates to distribute them to the workers. It was an experience that taught me a great deal.

My most vivid memories are of the moments spent with the women workers. I had become close to some of them and learned about the conditions of their lives. Young and pretty, they were often subjected to being fondled by the foremen. In spite of the harassment, some of them refused the advances and were then laid off on some trumped-up pretext. Alone with each other in the bathroom, they would discuss their main concern: were they pregnant by their husband, their companion, or lover? With their meager salaries they could not afford more pregnancies. In whispers they exchanged their confidences and the addresses of backstreet abortionists. Where and how could they get a clandestine abortion? Their whole world revolved around this vital question. One of them had to be hospitalized after she had hemorrhaged; the secret abortion, performed on a kitchen table, had ended bloodily, leaving her mutilated. Curettage sessions without any anesthesia in sealed rooms and the fear of being found out haunted their memories. Every one of them had a story to tell: humiliation, fear, and pain were their daily lot. And society wanted nothing to do with this sad reality. Simone de Beauvoir had described it in *Tout Compte fait* (*All Said and Done*): in 1970, eight hundred thousand secret abortions had been performed in France.

When I mentioned this disgraceful situation to other activists they chided me with a lighthearted look and said:

"That will take care of itself when the Revolution comes."

I was skeptical. The Revolution of 1917 and the Communist regime hadn't improved the lot of Soviet women. Contraception was practically nonexistent there (they believed the pill to be carcinogenic). Only married women could get an abortion, and these were performed under deplorable sanitary conditions. Every time I brought up an important topic they referred me to some hypothetical future. I had had enough, as had several others. I didn't feel like waiting for some radiant tomorrow. The slogan of May 1968 was mine, too: "Change life and now!" Moved by this desire, I joined the Women's Liberation Movement—the MLF—and finally met Simone. That day would change my life.

■ ■ ■

Anne Zelensky had asked me to be punctual. Since I was early I was pacing back and forth in front of the white building at 11bis, Rue Schoelcher, near Montparnasse, overcome with emotion. I had just turned twenty. My parents had given me Simone de Beauvoir's books , and I was dying to lead a life as impassioned as hers.

It was October 1970 and Simone was sixty-two years old. To me she appeared a respectable old lady, ensconced on the pedestal of her fame. For us feminists Simone surpassed Mao, Kennedy, or Indira Gandhi because of her charisma. Her writings had changed our view of the world and our way of living in it. Our mothers' generation had been bowled over by it. What could I possibly say to a person who had had such influence over the turn the world was taking?

It was raining. My hands shaking, I pushed the glass-paneled door and entered the building. I found Simone's door on the ground floor. Ready to faint from nerves, I rang the bell.

In less than a second she was there, her eyes the color of a smile. I was bewildered. My idol was a slender woman, barely five feet two. We were the same height. Used to seeing her beside Sartre, who was very short, I had expected her to be quite tall.

Her beauty was arresting. Large blue eyes stared out at me. Her headband framed an oval face with clear and satiny skin beneath black hair. In her painter's studio, the light poured in through huge, towering windows. Two yellow sofas and two armchairs rested on mauve carpeting. Above one of the sofas was an Egyptian mask, its gaze motionless and mysterious: "Nasser gave me that," she told me one day in passing.

Against the windows facing the sofas sat a whole army of dolls from all

over the world in the traditional costumes of their countries. An old refrigerator hummed behind a Mexican blanket.

During the meetings Simone always sat in the same place on one of the
yellow sofas, a vantage point that allowed her to survey the whole room and
keep an eye on the hideous little alarm clock that was always seven minutes
fast. She couldn't do without it. Nothing made her more nervous than
the passing of time. Writing, the priority in her life and Sartre's, required
time, solitude, and concentration. Their numerous activities, literary, philosophical, and political work; their amorous and, above all, activist adventures, each required iron discipline and precise timing.

Thus they had both established very strict rules. Simone did not answer
the phone in the morning. Her line was connected to an answering service,
and an operator took messages. Even Sartre couldn't reach her. Fortunately, he spent two nights a week with her, and every now and then Simone
slept at his place. The hours reserved for friends were closely timed, and the
MLF meetings obeyed the same rules.

I sat down across from the Egyptian mask in the one free chair. Simone
was to my right, sitting in the corner formed by the two sofas, dressed in a
tunic of yellow silk over black pants. Among the ten "girls" of the MLF were
lawyer Gisèle Halimi, actress Delphine Seyrig, writer Monique Wittig,
and philosopher Christine Delphy. All eyes were on Simone. She would listen, agree, and encourage others. Because of who she was, and her enthusiasm for our initiatives and youthful exuberance, and because she felt
our love for her, we were prepared to go to the ends of the earth. Sunday
after Sunday, we were going to change it a little.

The dialogue about the abortion campaign was hot and heavy. Simone and her energy exhausted us, but after a moment's silence, the
conversation would begin anew. We all shared that extraordinary feeling then that we were remaking the world, or at the very least remaking
French society. After two hours of heated discussion, Simone tensed up. It
was time for her to go meet Sartre. We rose as one. Night was falling
over Montparnasse, and we often went to have a bowl of onion soup at La
Coupole or La Closerie des Lilas.

The Manifesto of the 343 appeared in April 1971—not without

difficulty. Several weeklies had refused to publish it, fearing the papers would be seized and prohibited from going on sale. We had to negotiate vigorously with *Le Nouvel Observateur*. As it turned out, the magazine had one of its largest press runs and was not sued.

The scandal was enormous. The word "abortion" was taboo, but after only one day, thanks to the news flashes on the radio and the newspaper headlines, it was the most frequently spoken word in France. In my academic and intellectual family I had only heard the word mumbled twice. By declaring that we had had abortions, that is to say that we had committed a crime as far as the law was concerned, each of us risked years of imprisonment. During the Occupation, one woman had even been put to death by guillotine for that reason. Our families reacted violently or had a falling-out. My parents were frightened and feared I would be arrested. Attacked and maligned, we had nevertheless achieved our goal: to break the law of silence.

Simone smiled and joked. This victory was hers above all. Twenty years earlier, she had been the first to dare broach the question. At that time she had faced the abuse alone; now she felt supported. Her words in *The Second Sex* had found concrete success. Yet, we had never mentioned the book in her presence. Simone had a rule of not referring to her own writing. If someone were to mention one of her books, she would blush, answer quickly, and turn the discussion back to what actions should be taken. We were about to embark on several battles. A few months later, we decided to organize a demonstration to condemn the ban on abortion. We would not let up the pressure.

We marched through the streets of Paris with activists who had come from every region in France. Armed with balloons and banners, we demanded women's right to choose their form of contraception and their sexuality. At the front of the procession we carried a coffin that read "To the victims of clandestine abortion in France." Simone marched in the crowd next to Sylvie. How far we'd come in just a few months! What a payback for the insults and aggravation experienced in 1949! A new generation was following her and surrounding her with love. Simone's Sunday meetings became a regular event, joyful and studious occasions. We overflowed with vitality and dragged her with us from one struggle to the next. We really were her "girls"[11] as she called us when she was with Sartre.

■ ■ ■

One day, Simone took advantage of a moment when we were alone:

"How did you get into the MLF?"

I then told her my mother's story. She knew her name, because at the time my mother was director of the Ecole Normale Supérieure for young women where Sylvie Le Bon had been a student.

"In 1949, my mother married a mathematician. Since he was looking forward to a fine future, one of his friends suggested that she abandon her research and devote herself to her husband's career. My mother refused. A few months later, while she was pregnant with me, she read *The Second Sex*, which had just come out. It's thanks to your book that she found the strength to become a chemist and a scholar."

I caught my breath and added lightly:

"In a way, Simone, I read your book before I was born. . . . I am the child of *The Second Sex*."

"If that is so," she answered smiling ironically, "then you are actually its *enfant terrible!*"

■ ■ ■

After the manifesto of the 343 "bitches" and the demonstration of 1971 that demanded that abortion be legalized, much remained to be done. We wanted to condemn the condition of unwed mothers in France. At the time, you did not reach majority until the age of twenty-one. Young and pregnant adolescents, often raped by their father, an uncle, or a so-called family friend, were not able to get a secret abortion under decent conditions due to lack of money. Moreover, when the faculty discovered a girl was pregnant she was expelled from secondary school, and once the child was born she could not return. Before she even reached adulthood, her life was wrecked. Her parents, fearful of the criticism of their neighbors, would put her away in a kind of reformatory, a bleak home far off in the dreary suburb of Plessis-Robinson.

One exception was a fifteen-year-old who was expecting her boyfriend's baby. She loved him, but as she was a minor she was not allowed to have him visit her in the home or meet him elsewhere, even for a few hours. The girls arranged for him to come and see his girlfriend in the dormitory. The principal discovered them and told the parents that their daughter had been expelled. The following day her father arrived, grabbed his daughter—eight months pregnant—by the hair, threw her to the floor, and beat her up. The social worker, Claude, tried to intervene. The principal yanked her violently by the arm and cried out:

"Don't you ever come between a father and his daughter!"

The father continued beating his child and left her, inert, on the ground.

For the first time in their lives, the other pregnant girls rebelled. They begged their social worker to call the MLF for help. They were determined to break the law of silence. In protest, they went on a hunger strike, not letting their pregnancy deter them.

The strike spread panic. The following day, the Minister of National Education decided to close this site of subversion. The principal sent word to the parents, requiring them to come and get their daughters before the week was out. The girls were terrified, afraid they would undergo the same punishment as the one who had been battered.

"Please come quickly!" they begged us.

The following Sunday, I went to pick up Simone early in the morning, and with other young women from the MLF and a few journalists we gathered at the bottom of the hill below the house. A guard tried to prevent us from forcing the gate but with a few good kicks it gave way. Pulling Simone by the hand, I scrambled up the hill at a run and a few minutes later we were inside the home.

To our surprise, an inspector from the school board was waiting for us. Simone immediately declared that until she had obtained an appointment with the Minister of Education she was not leaving the building. Then she sat down across from the pregnant girls, took the microphone and the tape recorder a journalist handed her, and began to ask them questions that were broadcast live on national radio. The girls did not appear to be intimidated. They seemed comforted, instead, now that they were able to tell their stories and talk about what they had suffered.

One by one, over the airwaves in a France that was still asleep that Sunday morning, they recounted how their lives had been wrecked by their pregnancies, for the most part unwanted ones. At the end of each testimony Simone stated her political and feminist viewpoint on this injustice, which French society kept hidden.

It became a scandal. The air waves stopped their regular programming to do special broadcasts every half-hour. The French stayed glued to their radios. Simone got an appointment for the following day with a high-level official from the Ministry of Education.

"That's fine," she said, "but the girls of the MLF will occupy this home until a decision has been made in favor of these minors." We stayed. We sang and danced part of the night in a cheerful atmosphere—these young girls' lives were finally going to change.

We had reason to be hopeful. In her meeting, Simone expressed her indignation about the hypocrisy of French society that offered no education about birth control whatsoever, that tolerated rape of women and minors, and that treated these young girls both as minors and as guilty parties. Very quickly, Simone managed to have the laws changed and made it possible for girls to return to school after the birth of a child.

The action brought us unexpected success and recognition. The media and the politicians had accused the MLF of being nothing but a group of middle-class women, which, of course, was false. Suddenly, however, the press, the radio, and the French realized that we were actually helping women from every background. The attention we received was positive in every way.

A few days later, I ran into the concierge of my building. Until then she had felt nothing but mistrust for our movement and saw us as a bunch of eccentrics. That morning, as she was sweeping and I passed by her, she didn't raise her head, but I heard her whisper in my direction:

"What you did on Sunday is really good. I once knew a girl like that myself. It's really very good."

It was one of the finest compliments I received, and for the MLF it was the moment that our actions began to be recognized. Messages of support and testimonies streamed in. The women's cause was finally becoming the business of a whole nation.

■   ■   ■

In order to acquire a larger platform for our cause, we decided to organize two days of indictment of crimes against women. Unknown women would come forward and publicly attest to rape, incest, sexual harassment, and unequal treatment in the workplace. In spite of the risks they ran, others would talk about the trauma of the clandestine abortions they had undergone. They were in danger of being arrested on the spot.

"We'll be there," Delphine Seyrig and Simone exclaimed in chorus. "We'll be arrested with them. And Gisèle Halimi will defend us."

The notoriety of those who had signed the manifesto of the 343 made us hope that the authorities would hesitate to intervene. Describing in front of thousands of witnesses such a private act, one that, furthermore, was considered a crime, required extraordinary courage. The memory of it was so painful that we were afraid they might lose control, break down, or find themselves unable to speak before a crowd. But the obstacle course was just beginning. One by one, doors were closed in our faces. Everyone quailed at the thought of renting us a hall. At last, the manager of the Mutualité, a meeting hall in the Latin Quarter, accepted our request, albeit reluctantly. The staff who received us were antagonistic. Other meetings had taken place there during the Algerian and Vietnam wars. The site was well known and in a good location. The hall could hold five thousand people. We had provided for childcare to be handled by the men. Nevertheless, the place cost us a great deal of money.

"Don't worry, I'll pay a good portion of that!" Simone retorted the following Sunday.

"And I'll pay the rest!" Delphine Seyrig added.

As we were about to express our gratitude, Simone spoke a phrase that was becoming customary with her:

"Above all, no thank you's. If I do this, it's only because I can afford to do so."

She spoke with firmness and frankness. These two qualities characterized her more than any other, but I was also beginning to discover her already legendary generosity, which I would witness many times in the years to come. As we were very much in demand since the Plessis-Robinson affair and often called upon for help by unwed mothers and female workers in distress, I told Simone about a few particularly desperate cases. Her answer always came instantly:

"How much does she need?"

I would give her an approximate figure.

"Fine, you'll give her that amount in a few days, but on one condition: you'll tell her that it came from the MLF without mentioning my name."

Unbeknownst to them, many women were aided by Simone—her discretion and lack of pretension impressed me deeply. A few years later, when Hélène confided to me that Simone had always been generous with her, it hardly surprised me.

I strongly doubt that we could have organized the tribunal at the Mutualité without her help. It was a large amount of money and most of us were living on very tight budgets. On May 13 and 14, 1972, the crowd invaded the hall. Radio stations broadcast each presentation. One by one, in voices tense with emotion, women told of the agony of their abortions in front of five thousand people crammed into a sweltering space. In support of them and to give the unprecedented moment a political tone, Simone spoke after each one, offering a critique of the case and, in a few caustic phrases, summarizing her positions in *The Second Sex*. The audience, composed of as many men as women, held its breath. That evening, before an awestruck public, Simone concluded by demanding that the inhumane and obsolete laws on abortion be changed. The hall burst into deafening applause. Simone came backstage where we were waiting and declared triumphantly:

"We have won the first round. We'll keep going."

∎ ∎ ∎

Hélène followed the events closely from Alsace.

"How I wish I were in Paris!" she told her sister on the other end of the line. Yet she had become used to her village near Mount Sainte-Odile and the Vosges Mountains. In one year she and Lionel had renovated the former farm in Goxwiller. Every weekend they explored the forest together.

In Paris, Sartre's health was declining. The survival of *Libération* seemed to be in jeopardy. The crushing responsibility of the project—creating a daily paper constantly targeted by those in power—was weakening him. Legal suits came in from all directions and Sartre, the publication's director, was paying one fine after another. His royalties were swallowed up, and soon he needed Simone's financial support. She didn't hesitate and helped him as much as she could. In spite of the difficulties, the Sartre-Beauvoir couple withstood the storm.

Simone went to Alsace. Inside the book-lined library–living room, the sisters discussed the rumors from Paris and the wild adventures of the young women who charmed Simone every Sunday. Who would have guessed that a new start like this would be awaiting them after May 1968? Simone loved the house with its thick walls, but Poupette felt far removed from everything. Simone studied her most recent paintings and then said enthusiastically:

"We're getting ready for a huge lawsuit in Paris, the one about secret abortions."

"Tell me!"

Simone told her about the young girl who would soon be in the media limelight.

"When are you returning to Paris?"

"Next week, for the demonstration. I'll be testifying in court. And I'm going to tell the judges a thing or two!"

Simone kissed her sister on both cheeks. She was in a hurry to get back to Paris. She felt energized and strong in the face of this new battle. As she took her to the airport, Hélène felt a yearning. How she missed Paris! She was envious of Simone.

"Don't forget to tell me what happens next," she said to her before she left.

■ ■ ■

In Paris, Simone brought us together to fine-tune our strategy. In fact, the trial at Bobigny promised to be rough. Marie-Claire, an eighteen-year-old girl, had discovered she was pregnant by her boyfriend. Her mother, who as an employee of the Paris public transportation system had raised three children by herself on a very small salary, had suggested she keep the baby. The girl didn't want to and resorted to a secret abortion. At the same time she decided to break off her relationship with the young man. In revenge, he had gone to the police station and informed on her. The police went to Marie-Claire's family and arrested her, her mother, and the woman who had performed the abortion. All three were threatened with a heavy prison sentence. The mother, an energetic and brave woman, came up with the idea of writing to Gisèle Halimi and asking for her help. Her reputation as a defense lawyer for women in distress had been established in the Algerian War and by the Djamila Boupacha affair.[12] The following Sunday, Simone and her "girls" heard about the story.

"It's disgraceful!" Simone cried out. "We're going to fight to save them. This trial will be all about the oppression of women!"

We all shared her feelings but were unsure how to attract attention to the case. We decided unanimously to organize a demonstration on the Place de l'Opéra at six P.M., rush hour, just before the trial was to begin. We were prepared for a scandal to break out.

"Let's hope people will show up."

Simone gave her last bits of advice. We were counting on crowds of pedestrians and cars at an hour when offices were emptying out. We would have to get the banners up before the security police could arrive and disperse us.

"This demonstration has to be a success!" Simone decreed. "The trial must become a historic one."

We arrived at the Opera building, some of us with children, others with banners and balloons. Dumbfounded drivers, some of them furious, watched us from their cars. Traffic was very quickly blocked. But not for long. A few moments later, motorcycles emerged onto the square in front of the Opera. Clubs in hand, the police officers struck at the women and children. Panic ensued. The wounded put their hands to their bloodied faces. Children were screaming and crying, but the motorcycle cops charged again, spreading terror. The police thought they had achieved their goal—which was to disperse us. In reality, they had just rendered an invaluable service to the women's cause. The next day, *Le Monde* devoted its last page to the beatings of the evening before, condemning the shameful reaction of the police force. The journalist who had written the article told the story of Marie-Claire and her mother, easy prey for the justice system because of their social class. On the radio, protests flooded in. In just a few days, Marie-Claire's trial became a national affair.

On the day of the hearing a crowd gathered around the courthouse. I arrived early with Simone and a few of the MLF women. As a witness, Simone had been authorized to enter the courtroom. In front of the cameras of the world, we came up against the police, who prevented us from entering. We made our dissatisfaction known loud and clear.

Suddenly, one of the cops, a young man who was holding us back, whispered to me:

"Fine, go on in. But fast. Just because we're confronting you here doesn't mean that we're against you. We also have women in our lives."

A dozen of us crossed through the police chain and into the courtroom.

A surprise awaited us there: the room was already filled with policemen in civilian clothes, dressed in trenchcoats worthy of a Humphrey Bogart film. We offered quite a contrast in our brightly colored clothes and blue jeans. Once seated in the remaining chairs, we looked around the room and were impressed. What was about to happen would change the future of the women of France. In front of us to our left sat Gisèle Halimi, the lawyer, with Marie-Claire, her mother, and the woman who had performed the abortion. The latter looked terrified.

The judges entered and everyone rose in silence. I trembled. These men standing above us, their faces like steel, draped in their black robes, were going to pass judgment on three poor women. It was the world of men, makers of laws, against that of women, who weren't entitled to have their say. Society's injustices were glaringly evident and revolted me all over again.

After a deeply moving plea, Gisèle Halimi had witnesses testify, eminent physicians such as Jérôme Monod—winner of the Nobel Prize for Medicine—as well as Delphine Seyrig. Then, under an impressive silence, the person we were all waiting for emerged.

Walking fast and apparently in a bad mood, Simone came forward. I looked at my watch. It was close to her lunchtime with Sartre. The courtroom was located in a suburb, about an hour from Boulevard Montparnasse and La Coupole. Simone was going to be late for her meeting with him. She faced the judges and stated her name. Discreetly a bailiff brought her a chair and placed it behind her.

"You may sit down if you wish," the judge said to Simone.

"Of course I may," said Simone, and proceeded to do so.

Simone seemed small in the chair. I was afraid that this might weaken the impact of her testimony, but I had forgotten how determined she was. In a loud, sharp voice, she was going to give these judges a memorable course in the daily lives of women.

"Your Honors," she exclaimed as she pointed a threatening finger at them, "do you know what society is telling little girls? Instead of saying 'When you're grown-up you'll have to clean floors, do housework, cook, take care of children, dust furniture, vacuum, in short, be a servant,' do you know what society tells little girls instead, your Honors?"

The judges blushed and lowered their eyes. They looked like little boys who had misbehaved and were waiting for their mother to stop scolding them.

"Well, your Honors, what they very excitedly tell little girls is this: 'You're going to get married!'" The sermon went on for half an hour, in total silence. The prosecuting attorney, a bald man who was blushing to the top of his skull, did not dare ask Simone any questions.

Full of hope, I left the courtroom. Two weeks later, when the sentence came down, the president of the court declared that the abortion law was no longer in force. The accused, both the young girl and her mother, were given symbolic sentences. It was a crushing victory for French women. For the first time in the history of our country, abortion was no longer considered a crime. Simone was exultant but had no intention of leaving it at that.

Shortly thereafter, the country's new president, Valéry Giscard d'Estaing, had the law decriminalized despite the virulent objections of the nation's deputies.

■   ■   ■

My frequent trips to the United States led us to compare the evolution of the situation on both sides of the Atlantic. For the sake of effectiveness, our battle had to become international. The American feminists were well ahead of the French in many ways. In the United States, abortion had become legal following a decision by the Supreme Court on January 20, 1973. Nevertheless, women still struggled to find a place where they could have them done safely. The opening of the Feminist Women's Health Centers was enormously successful. Women from all walks of life, from Mexican-American women in Los Angeles to actresses in Beverly Hills, wanted to go there. Whereas the typical American doctor gave no more than a few minutes of his time to his patients and had a nurse do most of the questioning, these clinics offered women a place where they were patiently and attentively heard, and where general physicals were combined with gynecological examinations. The fees were five times lower than elsewhere. These initiatives, although a great success, were the object of growing hostility from the medical profession. Centers for women's health, the importance of which was unquestionable, posed a danger to the income of the medical establishment.

The clinics put a lot of work into finding the most natural, least invasive, and least dangerous means of treating women, especially for minor infections. "Our bodies are our own," they were saying on both sides of the Atlantic. One of the objectives therefore was for women to better understand their own anatomy and health. One of the founders of the Los Angeles Feminist Women's Health Center was Carol Downer, a young Californian, who one day decided to try an old method for curing yeast infections, which consisted of inserting yogurt into the vagina. It was a prescription that had been handed down from mother to daughter both in Western rural regions and among Native Americans. Carol wanted to check the efficiency of this procedure and served as her own guinea pig. The attempt reached the ears of the medical world, which had her arrested for practicing medicine illegally. By blocking her initiative, the medical community wanted to force the clinics to close, anticipating that she would surely not have the means to pay any lawyer's fees.

They had not taken into account the women's movement's quick reaction to her arrest. Nor had they considered the support of women across the United States who had been visited by Carol and Lorraine Rothman.[13] They also had not counted on Carol's monumental energy. Born into a poor but proud family, her parents had migrated to California in the 1930s in search of new opportunities when she was still a toddler. The eldest of four children, she was given a great deal of responsibility at a very young age. At eighteen, she married a sailor. Four children were born from their union. The family lived in precarious circumstances while her husband attended college and worked full-time as a taxi driver. He then fell ill with a serious case of tuberculosis and was treated at the Veteran's Hospital for a year. Carol had to care for four young children with very little income or assistance. Within a year of his release from the hospital her husband died of pneumonia. With only a pittance from the government and some help from her family, Carol was left widowed with four mouths to feed. She had been working temporary jobs since her husband's return from the hospital and she was able to provide her family with a simple but decent life. While working at a state agency, she befriended a man, and their relationship ripened into romance and then marriage. Together they had two more children.

Their future looked calm when, following the Vietnam War and the birth of the feminist movement, she began to feel the spirit of rebellion rise within her. American women of every social background should enjoy access to a decent health system and medical care without becoming destitute. Her experiences with giving birth had traumatized her forever.

These women of modest means, who worked tirelessly in the clinics for very small salaries, prepared the trial together. Two feminist attorneys agreed to defend Carol for reduced fees. She wasn't afraid to confront the city prosecutor or the truculent medical world. She would tell the story of her life and that of her sisters in misfortune whose trials and tribulations she knew all too well. The press and media came running. In the courtroom, photographers' flashbulbs and television cameras converged on Carol. She didn't blink an eye. In a calm voice she laid bare the reasons for her action and kept her cool when confronted with the prosecutor's aggressive words. The society where money is king did not impress her, and she maintained her dignity throughout the proceedings.

The verdict shook America: Carol was acquitted. The determination, clarity, and common sense of this unknown woman had impressed the jury. In a few days' time, in the fall of 1972, she was thrust from the shadows into the glare of publicity. *Time* and *Newsweek* both devoted articles to her. She continued her battle. The group decided that Carol should come to Europe and share her experiences, and Simone asked me to organize her visit in November 1974.

Women had been prevented from knowing their own bodies for too long. Studies on female diseases, gynecological questions, hormonal functioning, and finally menopause, a taboo subject, were still very rare. On the other hand, men's health, sexuality, and hormonal functioning were the object of numerous studies. Women had to act, first and foremost, by participating in meetings where they could exchange what they had learned and observed. They were very dissatisfied with their gynecologists. In the meantime, their bodies went through changes and cycles. They needed to be able to discuss these issues, to understand their own reactions, and to know how to detect signs of illness such as an abnormal lump with a breast self-examination. If caught in time, breast cancer could be treated early.

With this in mind, Carol Downer and a few other American women came to Paris and attended a feminist meeting one evening, each of them armed with an oblong box, an electric light, and a mirror. To the bewilderment of everyone there, Carol took off her pants, took a plastic speculum from the box, inserted it into her vagina and with the help of flashlight and mirror shined the light on it. To the dumbfounded, entranced women Carol explained:

"Women are born, grow up, have children, and die without ever knowing their bodies. While men are used to seeing their sexual organs, since they are located on the outside, women go through life ignorant of one of the most important parts of their body. They do not know what a cervix looks like or what its color or physical features are. It is as if they carry a dark cavity inside. Only the gynecologist knows the secret of their body."

One by one, the women took speculums and examined themselves.

The following Sunday, I told Simone about the experience. I thought it was a true step forward. Simone listened to me intently. Yet she stiffened when I told her that the Americans had brought a film with them.

"You should really see it. It's an extraordinary document!"

Simone didn't dare thwart my enthusiasm and acquiesced.

"Fine, arrange a screening for me."

We went to a movie theater in Saint-Germain-des-Prés, next to the Deux Magots. There were about twenty of us in a room that could hold two hundred. Seated next to another woman writer, Simone was discussing literature when the lights went down and the first frames of the film *A New Image of Myself* appeared. For ten minutes during the film, women inserted speculums into their vagina and discovering their private parts. The images weren't shocking, and yet they showed people in the most graphic state of nudity.

I watched Simone in the dimness. Each time a speculum was inserted, the author of *The Second Sex* closed her eyes. At times she put her right hand over her eyes as if to protect herself further. I felt confused. Had I gone too far? Her speeches for women's liberation, her support of our actions, her youthful spirit had made me forget that she was born early in the twentieth century, in 1908. I began to dread her reaction. The lights came back on. Simone turned to me and said:

"That was very good! It's an excellent film, in fact! These women are doing remarkable work! Please congratulate them on my behalf!"

"Do you really think so, Simone?"

"Of course. Look here, you know perfectly well that I always say what I mean!"

She questioned me about the American women, whose methods were so different from those of the French, who were more theoretically inclined.

She planned to read the books of Kate Millett and Shulamith Firestone. I made it clear to her that "these women from the clinics are immersed in the realities of everyday life. Because of that, they are existentialists and authentic feminists." Simone listened attentively when I added:

"They all claim to follow *The Second Sex*. Several of them told me that your book changed their lives."

I was flustered when I left the movie theater. I'd been afraid there would be a burst of anger, a refusal to go this far. To my great surprise the screening strengthened my bond with Simone. She told her entourage that I was a "serious" activist. Coming from her, the word sounded like the greatest possible vote of confidence.

■   ■   ■

In May 1973, Georges Pompidou, president of France, was completing the final year of his presidency. Traditionally, Mother's Day was the occasion for awarding the Medal of Merit to the mother of a large family, often escorted by her twelve or fourteen children. It seemed unbearable to us that our role should implicitly be limited to one of motherhood.

"Simone, next Sunday is Mother's Day. Come with us!" I proclaimed at our regular Sunday meeting.

"Oh, that holiday Pétain invented! But you seem awfully enthusiastic! Do you have something specific in mind?"

"Yes," I said with a wink of complicity at Anne Zelensky, Christine Delphy, and Delphine Seyrig. "We plan to get ourselves invited to the Elysée Palace."[14]

Simone suddenly sat up. The Right Bank of the Seine would witness something unexpected. At the end of our briefing, she burst out laughing and said:

"Well, I won't be able to come because I'm having lunch with Sartre and Sylvie at La Coupole, but you know where to find me. And I'll be thinking of you!"

Just before noon on Mother's Day, a colorful crowd formed at the upper end of the Champs-Elysées. Passersby saw a lady of a certain age, all dressed in black, in lace and crinolines. About thirty little girls, although they were adult in size, accompanied her. We had actually disguised ourselves as kids, with braids, balloons, and lollipops. Having reached the Normandie Cinema and Avenue Georges-V, we unfurled banners that read "Celebrated for a day, exploited all year long!" and "Mother, free yourself, you are before anything else a woman." Stunned, the onlookers turned around. Police cars began to drive up and down the avenue. We sang slogans condemning women's exploitation and raised our banners high . We were determined to march to the Elysée peacefully.

Unfortunately, at the Champs-Elysées traffic circle, the CRS, special police units used for maintaining order, awaited us. The Avenue Marigny was barricaded, as were the gardens next to the Elysée. Crossing the barricade was impossible. We sat on the ground, still brandishing our signs. The Parisians in their Sunday clothes stared at us, glancing quickly at our slogans. Tourists, who were more tolerant, took photographs of us. Our shouting was heard up and down the world's most beautiful avenue.

Several patrol cars approached and in seconds we were surrounded. The police leapt on us immediately, insulting us and dragging us to the ground. Ten minutes later, the famous paddy wagons screeched off and sirens howled. They were circulating around the area—Boulevard Haussmann, Place de l'Etoile, and then the Champs-Elysées again. Finally the procession stopped in front of the Grand Palais. Below the museum was a police station. Unceremoniously, they made us get out two by two. The CRS were prodding us, calling us hysterics and dykes. It only reinforced our resolve. If they thought we were scared they were wrong. If they found our behavior shocking, they hadn't seen anything yet. Locked behind steel bars, we were held in a room for questioning. The least little sound resonated—and so we improvised two-line verses about Georges Pompidou, Mother's Day, and exploited women. We sang at the top of our voices, thirty women together, united by the same sense of contempt. The racket quickly became unbearable. To add to the scandal and to agitate the cops, we held each other close, like couples, uttering endearments to each other at a time when female homosexuality was still a matter of horror and disgrace.

The officers bustled about, making phone calls and putting their fingers in their ears. One of them begged us to be quiet and stop behaving this way, or else "the whole station was going to end up being gay!" It was enough to get us started on a new refrain, with ever more ironic lyrics.

The cacophony went on for more than an hour. Finally, they opened the door:

"You will be called two at a time."

Another mistake: we came out as pairs with arms tenderly around each other. To state our name, we had to scream because the shrieking of our sisters filled the police station. Then they pushed us to the exit, "Get out!"

I immediately went to our meeting point. The party continued. On the Avenue des Champs-Elysées, the café-brasserie Le Colisée was a choice establishment. In this family restaurant, all the patrons were elegantly dressed for the Sunday ritual. Sons brought their wives, children, and in-laws to this classic and refined place. The menu was excellent and served by maître d's in tuxedo. The place was a bastion of serenity and good taste. Our descent upon Le Colisée was like a tornado. Every five minutes two more girls dressed like little kids would come in and join us. From our table, we loudly applauded their arrival, making jubilant noise, and laughing uproariously. In the corner of the restaurant, men in coat and tie and their families threw us dirty looks. Half an hour after we arrived, a waiter came over to me and whispered:

"You wouldn't be part of the MLF, would you?"

"Yes, why?"

"There is a phone call for you. . . ."

I thought it was a joke or a journalist and went to the phone booth.

"Hello, is this the MLF? This is Simone de Beauvoir."

I let out a cry of surprise and told her every detail of our arrest. She burst out laughing.

"Well, that's very good! I'm calling you from La Coupole. If any one of you has not yet been set free within an hour from now, let me know! I'll make a statement to the press."

Then she went on:

"I'm going to tell Sartre about this, it will amuse him terribly!"

And she hung up. I joined the other girls whose laughter grew louder with every new arrival. A maître d' came to lecture us:

"Could you please make a little less noise? You're bothering our customers who would like to be able to have lunch quietly."

"Excuse our noise, sir, but we just came from jail. . . ."

"Mademoiselle," he said to me sarcastically, "when people get of jail they do not come to this establishment!"

That very day, the radio broadcast the event. The following Sunday, Hélène was treated by telephone to a detailed description of our mischief. She then told her sister that she, too, wanted to meet the girls of the MLF.

■ ■ ■

Simone was dumbfounded. What would her younger sister want to do with feminists? She knew to what extent Hélène tended to model her life after her own. At age sixty-four, Poupette, a good wife, surely wasn't going to join her "girls" of the Movement. Simone forgot that there is no age limit for liberation.

In the train that brought me to Strasbourg, I reflected on the past. Eight years earlier, on my seventeenth birthday I had dreamed of meeting the Beauvoir sisters. I had just read Simone's memoirs. I was burning to lead as impassioned a life as hers and to fight injustice. In 1967, I read an article that had set my heart racing. Right in the Latin Quarter near the Odéon, in the Kieffer Gallery, there was a show of the sixteen original drawings Hélène had made as illustrations for *The Woman Destroyed*. The younger Beauvoir sister, a painter, who seemed so warm, human, and almost accessible, intrigued me. In front of the gallery on Rue Saint-André-des-Arts, I was terrified. Would I dare speak to the Beauvoirs? I went in, being careful not to wet the art books with my umbrella. Sadly, the two were not there. However, I had seen the exhibition. The engravings were beautiful, but gradually a huge sense of disappointment came over me. How could I possibly have imagined I would meet my two heroines? They would continue to be distant, mythical beings. Now my dreams had become a reality. I had been close to Simone for five years and now I was on my way to meet Hélène.

Simone had told me somewhat mysteriously:

"You'll see, my sister has heard a lot about you. I've told her about the MLF actions of the past few years. She's eager to work with you."

When the door opened, I was shocked. Hélène was a blonde replica of Simone, with the same high cheekbones. On the other hand, her elegant suit surprised me. I was used to seeing Simone in pants, outfits that more closely resembled the way we dressed in May 1968. Hélène wore a silver necklace in the shape of a snake, a family heirloom. While her older sister never took the Mexican ring Nelson Algren had given her off her left hand, Hélène wore her engagement ring, a pearl surrounded by diamonds, and her silver wedding ring.

She smiled at me warmly and approached me with less reserve than Simone would have. She had just established a home for battered women in Alsace. In one year's time, four women had died—one was thrown out of a window while the other three had succumbed to violent beatings. With the support of a feminist who in her childhood had witnessed ferocious battles between couples, they had found a house to shelter women who were seeking refuge with their children. But in 1975, French society still refused to recognize that this calamity existed. Sexist prejudices remained very much alive, and it was believed that the assaults on women were exaggerated, or even deserved. While they were the ones to endure men's brutality, it was the victims who became suspect or guilty. The lives of many turned into a nightmare. To help them both legally and practically, Hélène sought the support of the MLF. She took me to visit the home, greeted the residents, hugged them, and played with the little ones. She laughed, made tea, and offered cookies with charm and natural ease. More ingenuous and warmer than Simone, Hélène made easy contact where her sister was more likely to inspire a sometimes forced respect.

That evening, Hélène suggested I have dinner and spend the night in their home in Goxwiller. Lionel sat across from me at the dinner table, looking inscrutable. Tall and slender, he had an oval face with fine features and deep blue eyes. Sartre's former student intimidated me. In Simone's memoirs I had read of his exceptional courage when he had faced his bone tuberculosis and learned to walk again. He moved lithely and elegantly and showed no vestiges of his earlier disease. Hélène told me right away that her sister couldn't boil an egg, even though her grandmother and mother were both superb cooks.

Indeed, she herself served us a sumptuous meal whose aroma permeated the house while Simone's favorite dessert, a cherry clafoutis, awaited us. Lionel silently ate the dishes his wife had prepared. He later confessed to me that he had been reluctant to have me visit. He'd wondered what a feminist could possibly be like—probably a woman who despised men and wouldn't be interested in food. He was already concerned enough about his wife's frequent trips to Strasbourg. Hélène had been elected president of SOS Battered Women.[15] He dreaded that his colleagues at the European Council might think he himself was violent with her. All those feminists about whom the two sisters spoke could only disturb his tranquility and privacy. He couldn't wait for me to leave.

Over dessert he began to relax. He asked me questions about my youth among mathematicians in France and in the United States, and about my studies in the USSR. The atmosphere lightened, although I hadn't managed to beguile him yet.

Hélène took me to the library, where she had made up the bed for me. On one of the shelves stood an Egyptian mask that closely resembled the one given to Simone by Nasser. Many twentieth-century books were lined up, particularly works by linguists Emile Benveniste and Georges Dumézil, and ethnologist Claude Lévi-Strauss. In one corner I found copies of Sartre's and Simone's books inscribed to them. "To my disciple," it said on the first page of *Nausea*. "To Poupette and Lionel with all my love," Simone had written in *Memoirs of a Dutiful Daughter*. Before retiring for the night, Hélène glanced at the small serving cart filled with bottles of whiskey, port, cognac, and other liqueurs. She hesitated, then asked me in a neutral voice:

"Would you like a nightcap?"

"No thank you, Hélène, I drink very little. And especially no liqueur." She smiled.

"When Simone is here, we try to put the serving cart in another room."

I was actually using the bed in which her older sister normally slept. As I lay down beneath the blankets, I reflected that I had realized my adolescent dreams. My feelings were so intense that I had trouble falling asleep.

■　■　■

The next morning I saw the rest of the house. The main rooms faced the garden and Rue de l'Eglise, across the street from other similarly structured and typically Alsatian buildings. I noticed the goldfish ponds down below. Hélène's room, the largest one, served as the living room. The Louis XIV chairs were scratched up by the cats. Near the window I saw a white table that held some of Hélène's tools, and she explained that she did her engraving there.

On the wall were pastels showing animals and women in natural settings.

"Would you like to see my studio?"

"Of course!"

After crossing the porch, we came to the second garden and an adjacent house that contained a studio measuring fifteen by twenty-one feet. Bathed in light, it looked out over rose bushes and flowers. On a pedestal next to a jar filled with brushes were some framed photographs of Sartre and Simone. Paintings were piled up everywhere.

"I'll show you this year's paintings."

Women and children, lions, tigers, and other animals paraded before my eyes; the style combined the abstract and the naïve. Other paintings reflected a darker mood. Human beings encased in blocks of snow or ice. It depicted an unsettling society with nuclear facilities, destroyed vegetation, and engineers cloaked in white coveralls.

"I worry more and more about the systematic destruction of nature that mankind is busy producing."

The suicide of Gabrielle Russier, a *lycée* teacher in love with one of her students, had inspired *Un Homme livre une femme aux bêtes* (*A Man Leaves a Woman to the Beasts*).

"That is my first feminist painting. Now that I have some experience with the traumas of battered women, I think I'll be doing more of those."

When she showed me that picture, Hélène explained why she had wanted to meet me and, through me, come into contact with the MLF.

"I've already painted women who've been raped, I've done scenes of hardworking peasant women, especially during my time in Portugal. What I want to do this time is show the oppression in its most insidious forms. I feel great solidarity with all these women."

She paused for a moment, then added in a strong voice:

"Besides, I was a feminist before Simone!"

Surprised, I showed no reaction. Simone's memoirs had not given me that impression. Then she explained:

"As a young girl, I was less 'dutiful' than my sister, who went to the Sorbonne with young people from good families. In the art courses I took, I met boys who came from more modest families and who used vocabulary that was not exactly refined. Then, too, it is easier in our society for a woman to be recognized as a writer than as a painter. How many of my women colleagues are accepted for every Michelangelo, Picasso, or Matisse? It's very hard. The men who would come to my studio were more interested in seducing me than in looking at my work."

"So you think that the artistic universe of painting is less accessible to women?"

"It is a macho world in which only men are taken seriously. The great painters have always had wives beside them who would handle the daily chores, thereby allowing their husbands' 'genius' to fully bloom. We, on the other hand, have no wives to support us. Worse yet, our painting is seen as a hobby. Women painters are treated much less well than women in Simone's profession. I've been talking to her about this for years, but nobody wants to hear it."

"Simone hasn't mentioned it to us."

"She should have."

I sensed more than exasperation in her; she was discouraged. If her own sister didn't bother to pass judgment on the condition of women painters, then who would? I felt embarrassed myself. Why this silence? I tried to think of painters who had been recognized: Elisabeth Vigée-Lebrun, Niki de Saint-Phalle, Berthe Morisot, and Sonia Delaunay. A few names came to mind. Hélène brought out more canvases of animal scenes.

"Do you know why Rosa Bonheur, one of the greatest French painters, used to paint horses and lived with a tigress she had tamed?"

"No. . . ."

"Because at the end of the nineteenth century, women who studied painting were not allowed to draw male nudes. They were told to paint cows! I like her work very much. She never married, but lived with two women who were painters as well. She must have had quite a personality and a fierce sense of independence—Rosa Bonheur had short hair and wore pants. Since women were forbidden to dress that way, she had to go to police headquarters every six months to request a written renewal of the permission she had obtained. I believe that in France this artist did a great deal to promote her women colleagues. Furthermore, she was the first woman to receive the Légion d'Honneur[16] in 1865. But there is an enormous amount of work still to be done. We as women artists are not recognized, and it is even worse for women sculptors and musicians. Alongside Bach, Mozart, Lully, Beethoven, can you mention a single woman's name to me besides that of Clara Schumann?"

Indeed, I couldn't. In 1975, there were no female prefects, no female ambassadors. The worlds of research and finance were closed to women as well. I then realized that in spite of the success Simone had gained between 1970 and 1975, we had a long way to go toward true equality between the sexes. Later on, I learned that an English university study had drawn up a list of three thousand female composers from various centuries! Not a single one had received any public attention. We returned to the living room where Hélène made us some tea. The scent of Lapsang Souchong wafted in as I got to know the two Abyssinian cats, Tëtka and Pimpernel, who wouldn't leave her side. Instead of sprawling all over manuscripts as Colette's cats did, they nestled near the brushes in the studio and, warmed by the sun, watched their mistress work, summer and winter. She would return to the main house only at sunset when Lionel came home from work.

The next day, Lionel took us to the to the Charbonnière Pass in the Vosges Mountains. We walked through the forest not far from Mount

Sainte-Odile at a nice pace, stopping occasionally. Lionel went ahead, cane in hand. I was definitely impressed by his stamina.

"When I watch him walking like this in the woods," Hélène confessed to me, "I have a lump in my throat. He is alive and he is walking. When I came to Portugal in May 1940, his doctor told me he thought he wouldn't be able to save him. They had no idea of his courage and his overwhelming will to live!"

Sartre and Simone's brother-in-law had become more talkative. Having answered his questions about my relationship with the two writers, I in turn wanted to know more about him. I knew the story of his meeting Simone and Hélène in a train, so I asked him about his connection to Sartre. Lionel happily recalled the teacher who used to love getting together with his students in cafés. On the other hand, he revealed a certain bitterness about the growth and change of their relationship.

"In *Nausea* and *Les Chemins de la liberté* (*Of Human Freedom*) he depicted a character inspired from my life, but he described him as a conservative and that hurt me. People thought that was my true self. "

I sensed some nostalgia for the years when the two writers, then still unknown, showed a more human and intimate side to their entourage. Then Lionel said with a sparkle in his eyes:

"So, tell us about May 1968! It seems that you were in Nanterre with Daniel Cohn-Bendit?"

I told them about the wild nights of May, the occupied university buildings, our hopes, our intoxication with liberty. I mentioned the sensational beginnings of the MLF, the scandals, and our Sundays with Simone. They were aware of all this, but wanted to hear it from me. I realized I was infusing them with the energy of my youth. We were actually forty years, almost two generations, apart. Hélène and Lionel did not have any children. On that day, as I told them about my adventures, I thought of my grandparents, whom I hadn't known and whose absence had been so painful in my childhood. That Sunday dinner in the Vosges felt like a family meal to me.

When they took me back to the train station in Strasbourg, Lionel kissed me goodbye and Hélène asked me shyly if I would come back.

■ ■ ■

"Will you please sit down!"

On that cold November day in 1975, I couldn't stay still. I was pacing back and forth in Simone's studio. The story of my visit to Goxwiller bewildered her. Hélène represented the ruined aristocratic family that Simone had rejected early on. And here was Hélène, at the age of sixty-five, claiming to be involved with feminism! The older sister was pensive. That, however, was not what most preoccupied me.

"You won't refuse it, will you?" I asked anxiously.

"Absolutely not!"

A few hours before, a rumor had started circulating through Paris that Simone had been nominated for the Nobel Prize in Literature. They had called her from Stockholm to confirm that she wouldn't act like Sartre, whose refusal eleven years earlier had left bitter memories. I was overjoyed. What a fine recognition that would be for the figure who had launched the women's movement in France! This would have an enormous international impact. I already imagined the celebration with the girls of the MLF. I left in a state of excitement. There was nothing to do but wait.

I phoned Hélène later that evening. She hadn't heard. The Nobel Prize for her sister? That would be a dream come true! But would they dare, after Sartre had snubbed them? The next day the news came down—the Nobel Prize for Literature had been awarded to an Italian, Eugenio Montale. Like the other girls, I shook with rage and sorrow. Simone tried to hide her disappointment.

"Since 1975 was declared the International Year of the Woman," she told me, "they were afraid it would be too much of a good thing. So don't be disappointed, maybe I'll get it some other year."

Simone would die eleven years later without a Nobel prize. In fact, between 1975 and 1986 not one woman received the honor. And in one century only about ten women won it, compared to ninety men. Neither Colette, Marguerite Duras, Nathalie Sarraute, nor Marguerite Yourcenar,[17] to name but a few of the deserving, was awarded a Nobel Prize. Every year, Hélène and the rest of us would wait with a pounding heart for the news from Stockholm. We preferred not to mention the Nobel in front of Simone anymore.

"Some men simply won't forgive her for having written *The Second Sex*," her younger sister said more than once. Long after that book had been published she was still a thorn in some people's sides, and she was paying the price.

As for Simone, she had other worries. Sartre's health was declining. Weak and plagued by deteriorating vision that prevented him from writing, he was furious at not being able to finish his last volume, *L'Idiot de la famille* (*The Family Idiot*).

"My life is a failure because I'll never be able to write my work on *Madame Bovary*," he often told those close to him. Simone had started to tape interviews with him about his youth, his writing, and his life. Except for describing his childhood in *The Words*, he had not written any memoirs, nor anything about Simone. She, on the other hand, had described their intellectual, political, and emotional relationship in more than a thousand pages. She intended to breathe a new taste for life into Sartre, who was now almost blind.

A year earlier, France had elected a new president who was committed to liberalizing the abortion law. Valéry Giscard d'Estaing kept his promise. In the face of booing and racial slurs from the nation's representatives, Simone Weil defended the plan alone throughout an entire night. From their seats in the semicircle of the National Assembly hall, the deputies—almost all men—yelled at her filthy words hardly befitting their position. From her experience in the Nazi concentration camps where she had watched her mother die, the Minister of Health had returned with sufficient courage and broad enough shoulders to brave the insults. In spite of some despicable allusions to the gas ovens, she held her own. At dawn, a new law was voted in, giving French women the right to choose and make decisions about their sexuality.

It was about time. With Simone and the girls, we had spent years fighting for this. We were exhausted, but the struggle wasn't over. We now had a monthly column in *Les Temps modernes* with the title "Ordinary sexism." There we condemned language abuse and other degrading attitudes toward our female peers. Together with Anne Zelensky, Simone established the League for Women's Rights. There were still far too many texts that treated us like minors and that didn't grant us the status of full citizens, and many professions remained inaccessible.

That was when I decided to do my doctorate on Simone's work and commitment to women's rights. Between Sunday meetings with the girls of the movement, I interviewed her about her writing and sometimes mentioned Hélène. On one particular point—motherhood—I did not agree with her. Simone had explained in *The Second Sex* the extent to which motherhood had made women subservient; it confined them to the home and prevented them from having a career. I understood her analysis but presented my case to her: My mother, an academic and a chemist, was a feminist. She had inspired me with the will to fight and lead my life the way I chose.

"Simone, the more feminist mothers there are, the more relationships between men and women will be based on respect. I actually consider myself to be lucky to have a feminist mother."

Simone's face hardened.

"Of course, I understand, but confining women to the education of their children and to motherhood has allowed men to exclude them from society. Let's be very careful on this subject. . . ."

I then grew bolder:

"Hélène tells me that she, too, didn't want any children, so she could devote her time to painting. So you both decided this at a very young age, then?"

Simone's gaze became distant. Her bright blue eyes avoided mine. Sitting in one of her mauve chairs, I felt flustered. Had I been indiscreet? She regained her composure and stared at me intently:

"You know very well that's not the real reason. . . ."

"No, I don't know. . . ."

Blushing, she added:

"Since his tuberculosis and his prewar surgery, Lionel can't have any children. It is out of respect for him that my sister tells that story. She might as well say it's a feminist idea. . . . But don't talk to her about this. It would hurt her."

A friend of both sisters confirmed this version to me. I now had a better understanding of the affection that Hélène and Lionel felt for children and young people. Besides, Lionel had adopted the son of a friend, Monique.[18] The child, Sandro, was devoted to the Roulets and thought of them as his grandparents. He often spent his vacations in Goxwiller. Without a doubt, Sandro fulfilled Lionel and Hélène's desire for a child. Still, even after Lionel's death and despite our very close friendship, Hélène never told me her secret.

■   ■   ■

The door to the courtroom in Strasbourg opened. Hélène strode forward between the rows in icy silence; her heart beat wildly. She was playing a role that until now only her sister had played. Approaching the bar, she told herself that at sixty-five her life was taking a completely new direction. The feminist movement was providing her with a second youth. It was her turn to feel she had a mission to accomplish. The presidency of SOS Battered Women took up more and more of her time. In the eastern part of France the word had spread: Simone de Beauvoir's sister was ready to help women in difficulty and, if need be, testify at their trials.

Seated behind the bench, the judges watched the elderly lady coming toward them. While Simone walked quickly, more often than not dressed in a silk jacket and slacks, Hélène wore a severe but feminine suit, a small hat, and fine leather gloves. The older sister spoke tersely and in a clipped voice. The younger one expressed herself affably, as if she were in someone's living room. Simone rushed on, overwhelming the judges; with a fine smile on her lips, Hélène assailed them with courtesy. Faced with this audience for whom every word mattered, her good manners allowed her to be crafty.

Battered women, girls raped by their fathers or uncles, family tragedies—Hélène knew that French society wasn't yet ready to recognize that certain breaches could lead to murder, madness, or suicide. The young woman she was defending that particular day had left her baby in a garbage can. They had found the dead child, and now the mother might be sentenced for homicide. While Simone had defended many cases of tortured and imprisoned women—notably during the Algerian War—it was the first time that Hélène had entered the cold universe of a women's prison. The pain that emanated from its walls had made her shiver.

In a calm tone, she testified on behalf of this woman to save her, at all costs, from a dire fate. She told the judges about the life of the accused who was, only yesterday, just an oppressed young girl in a hellish family situation. She explained that the girl had been misled so she wouldn't be able to abort on time. With clarity and composure, she recounted how undesired motherhood could shatter someone's life. Then she fell silent. When she caught her breath her hands trembled slightly. She straightened her hat, smoothed her leather gloves, and walked out of the courtroom, her posture erect.

As she roamed the halls of the Strasbourg law courts, she worried about whether she had handled it well. Being the president of SOS Battered Women had already opened her eyes to the taboo of domestic violence. She wanted her testimony to sound like a challenge. A few days later the accused was given a two-year suspended sentence. She was free to go. Hélène was enormously relieved. She placed a huge canvas on her easel, picked up her brushes and, as her cats looked on, painted one of her most famous pictures, *Les Femmes souffrent, les hommes jugent* (*Women Suffer, Men Judge*). Locked inside a glass cube, a naked woman stands trembling, her head lowered before four male judges in red robes and black hats, their fingers pointed at the accused. A few days later, she did another painting representing women burning in the distance. She called it *La chasse aux sorcières est toujours ouverte* (*The witch-hunt is still on*). These two paintings were later to be shown in many exhibits. Hélène told me:

"I became involved in the women's liberation movement much, much later than Simone, but now my commitment will not let go of me anymore."

She came out of this ordeal stronger and more confident and told me many times:

"I've had the luck to lead a happy life. It's up to fortunate women to help those who are less lucky."

CHAPTER FIVE

The Twilight of the Mandarins

"Watch your step!"

Hélène held Simone firmly by her right arm as she helped her up to the studio in Goxwiller. The morning light came in through the immense bay windows, and a slight breeze swayed the flowers in the garden. Dressed in brown slacks and a yellow silk shirt, Simone sat down on the sofa, facing the easel.

Hélène bustled about with a smile. Her sister had always expressed an interest in her work, and she was eager to show her the latest results—her feminist paintings! Her heart racing, she displayed the first canvas and waited. Simone remained silent. She was thunderstruck when she saw a naked woman with her head down and an arm covering herself, facing huge men dressed in judges' togas and mortars. Faceless and without eyes, the judges seemed terrifying.

"I call this painting *Women Suffer, Men Judge*. Do you like it?"

Simone looked as though she were suffocating. The image of the defenseless woman made the canvas scream out. Poupette had told her about the trial at which she had testified on behalf of a mother accused of infanticide. Out of this court case Hélène had created a masterpiece:

"It is magnificent!"

Hélène set her paintings down one after another. They all portrayed women's hardships and deplorable circumstances. Simone smiled and said:

"How lucky you are—you can still create new paintings! I have no books left in me because I have nothing more to say. In spite of your age, you can still continue to create!"

Hélène was deeply moved. At last her older sibling recognized there was an area in which she, too, excelled. Simone envied her artistic talent. Never before had she offered her a tribute like this. She leaned back against the pillows. On her right, some old Italian vases stood among a forest of brushes. A smell of paint engulfed the room. Her sister was lost in thought. Dear Poupette! She had been so irritated by her youthful mania for wanting to imitate her out of pure admiration. Certainly, four years earlier in *All Said and Done*, her last volume of memoirs, Simone had admitted that her sister's life had been harder than hers.

Today Simone was struck by the very real achievement confirmed through these paintings. Like herself, Hélène had been liberated from her blood ties. And yet something kept her here in this studio, something warm and comforting. Their mother's death had brought them closer. She could confide completely in Hélène about Sartre, about his predilection for young girls, his physical infirmity, how blind he was with regard to the youthful schemers consumed by pretension and ambition. Hélène could read her sister's mind, let her talk herself out, and console her when she broke down in tears. Poupette was infinitely dear to her, Simone had never doubted that, but this morning she realized it with particular force. She smiled at Hélène.

"Shall we go back to the living room?"

"Sure."

As she helped Simone up, Hélène tried to hide her impatience. Lionel would soon be home from work. She couldn't wait to tell him about Simone's reaction. These words would warm her heart as long as she lived.

■   ■   ▮

When I suggested to Hélène that she come and stay with me for a week, she blushed with pleasure but hesitated at first to accept the invitation. Finally, she asked me shyly:

"When may I come?"

A few days later, she rang the doorbell. When Simone heard about it, she was annoyed. Poupette's return to Paris didn't suit her. Between Sartre and his mistresses, her friendships with Sylvie, Lanzmann, and Bost, and her activities with the MLF, she was overburdened. When was she going to find time to write? She tried to reassure herself. Poupette had always respected her schedule, and she would surely not disregard it now.

Hélène opened my apartment windows wide. The constant stream of cars on Rue d'Alésia was a stark contrast to the quiet of Goxwiller. She leaned over the edge of the balcony.

"Finally, breathing the air of Paris again! I really miss it!"

I watched in amusement.

"You have to understand," she said, "the fourteenth *arrondissement* is the neighborhood of my youth. Your apartment is just five minutes from Simone's, ten minutes from the Boulevard Raspail where we used to live when we were little girls. I can wander around Montparnasse again, see the galleries, and, who knows, maybe someone will still be interested in my art."

I answered at once that she had enjoyed a very fine artistic season. Hadn't she been exhibited in New York? And how about the show of a hundred of her paintings at the Palace of Arts and Culture in Brest? The press had covered it, and Sartre and Simone had even written the catalogue text. I read aloud to her what Simone had written about her painting:

"She always refused both the constraint of imitation and the aridity of abstraction. She found an ever more expert balance between formal inventions and references to reality. I did not see her exhibits in The Hague and Tokyo, which were very successful, but I loved the work inspired by Venice that she showed in Paris in 1963 and even more the complete cycle she did of the festivities and tragedies of May 1968."[1]

Hélène admitted that 1975 had, indeed, been a good year and had brought her renewed recognition. Still, Paris, her beloved city, had forgotten her. The capital had not forgiven her for living in the provinces. She still thought nostalgically of the success of her show on May 1968. Since then, France had slipped back into a certain form of conservatism.

■ ■ ■

A few weeks later it was my turn to go to Goxwiller. A strong wind blew across the snow-topped pine trees of the Vosges. Ahead of Hélène and me, Lionel pushed his poles and glided along the country skiing course. We were alone in the forest, the sound of the wind in the trees our only company.

"I'm so sorry that Simone no longer skis," Hélène said to me when we stopped for a rest. She had taken some sandwiches and a thermos with hot tea out of her backpack. The bitter cold turned her cheeks bright red.

"Simone never did feel really comfortable on skis. But like us, she would go up the peaks in her sealskin from morning to night. Even Sartre tried it. Now, partly because of him, she rarely leaves the city and hardly ever comes to the country anymore. The alcohol she consumes has affected her walking. How she must miss nature!"

We continued on our way for another two hours. Nothing could stop Lionel and Hélène, who, at over sixty-five, intended to stay in shape and lead a healthy life.

In Montparnasse, Simone was battling Sartre's entourage. By phone she told Hélène about the painful compromises she was forced to make. Pierre Victor, Sartre's secretary, had clearly gained influence over him and was poisoning Simone's life with his contemptuous attitude toward her. She knew, moreover, that the days the little man had left were numbered. She was in a panic: how would she live without him? She reported everything—the slow deterioration of the philosopher, his blindness, and his despair at not being able to write anymore. Despite the bonds that united the sisters, Paris and Goxwiller seemed to be two different worlds.

At the height of the winter of 1975, Lionel and Hélène invited me to come and celebrate Christmas with them in their Italian home in Trebiano.

The large house was located a few miles from La Spezia and Genoa. An old medieval fortress towered above the valley. The house, consisting of several floors connected by a spiral staircase, overlooked the surrounding hills. In the entryway stood a wooden sculpture of an Italian *carabiniere*, complete with hat and mustache. The first room was Hélène's studio. Many paintings were stacked up—images of Italy full of light and shimmering color. It was a country that had always enthralled the artist in her. Her series on Venice, done when she lived there in 1955, bore witness to this. They also owned the two adjoining houses. The sculptor Tacchini and his family lived in one; the other remained empty.

I went to my quarters and unpacked my books and notes so I could continue working on my thesis on Simone. Then a scream, followed by another one, interrupted my thoughts.

"What's going on?"

"It's the neighbor beating his wife. He is poor, he drinks, and when he gets paid he gets drunk, breaks the furniture, and knocks his wife around."

I was horrified. The screams were making me ill.

"Can't anything be done? Call the police?"

"We've tried, but then the man threatened us with a rifle. He told us to mind our own business."

I was dumbfounded. Twenty yards from the house of Simone de Beauvoir's sister, a man repeatedly abused his wife, who sometimes had to be taken to the hospital covered with bruises. My room overlooked the accursed couple's home. I thought I was living a nightmare right there in the enchanting atmosphere of northern Italy. I moved my things to Hélène and Lionel's living room, far from the noise of the neighbors.[2] I immersed myself in Simone's work again. It was a critical study, for I was going through her sentences with the eye of a firebrand, not allowing for any opinion that went against the feminist spirit of the time. I checked the orthodoxy of her writing without any leniency.

Often Lionel was the amused witness to my conversations with Hélène. I criticized the novels of her older sister, whose female characters seemed too agonized to me.

Then Poupette would turn to her husband and say:

"It's true! In Simone's novels women don't come out as being positive enough! I'll talk to her about it next time I'm in Paris."

"Hélène," I ventured, "that's not entirely necessary."

"Oh yes, it is! She needs to be told."

Lionel had trouble keeping a straight face. At times he'd glance at me reproachfully. Without a doubt, he could already imagine the conversation between the sisters in which the older one found her younger sibling preaching to her, giving her a course in feminism. Nevertheless, I continued to discuss the work and life of the writer with Hélène.

On several occasions, she returned to her favorite novel, *All Men Are Mortal*, in which Simone condemned the boredom that immortality would offer. Watching her, I realized how much Hélène loved talking about her sister's work. Simone's energy impressed her and her ability to write even when she was going through hard times fascinated her. And yet, although she was endowed with the same fierce will, Simone continued to be her point of reference. One evening while we were chatting about her writing, Lionel whispered to me:

"Hélène always needs to admire someone. She cannot get close to people without putting them on a pedestal. Sometimes I try to reason with her but most of the time it's pointless."

A certain annoyance showed through in his words; perhaps he was afraid that one day his wife's enthusiasm would blind her.

Hélène wanted to know my opinion—in other words the opinion of a new generation—of *The Second Sex*. Some passages surprised me because they were so harsh. Simone's view of women and creativity was pitiless. According to her, they were too preoccupied with being seductive, thus incapable of working hard enough to forge a body of work. Only Colette and Virginia Woolf were spared. The pages on artistic creation, and especially on women painters, intrigued me. Simone had a living example right under her eyes; through her sister's experience she could have gauged the almost insurmountable obstacles of a world even more male-oriented than that of writing. Why, under conditions such as these, had she not devoted more space to them in *The Second Sex*? Why had she not attacked this state of affairs more directly, with her usual vehement candor? It baffled me.

Hélène reflected but found no answer either. She had to admit that Simone had not wasted many words on creative women. Just a few lines on women sculptors and musicians. As she rose from her chair, she turned to Lionel and said firmly:

"I'll talk to Simone about it."

Lionel closed his book with a snap:

"No, Hélène, you won't."

"Why not, Lionel?"

"Because you're going to irritate her and hurt her feelings. With her anxiety about Sartre she has enough on her mind."

He rolled his eyes and turned to me:

"And, Claudine, what do you think about all of this?"

"I agree with Hélène. It's a pity that Simone doesn't stand up more for women artists."

"Now I understand why Simone told us you sometimes intimidate her!"

I nearly jumped out of my chair. In the past, in my youthful enthusiasm I had occasionally acted audaciously and always faulted myself afterwards. The youngest in the MLF and still a university student, I had very quickly been privileged enough to meet with Simone during the week in order to discuss the logistical details of our plans. During these times, I found myself confronted with her rigid schedule. One morning I had to contact her so she could write a telegram intended to save some Portuguese women from prison. I phoned, but her answering service told me she wouldn't respond to any calls before two o'clock. As always, she wanted to preserve the peace and quiet of her mornings for writing. I ran to her apartment and pounded on the door. Shocked at my brazenness, she came to the post office with me, but on our way back she added:

"Now you have to let me work."

"Yes," I answered with all the gravity of my twenty years, "but these women need you."

She went back to her work and I promised not to disturb her anymore.

Thus I didn't see what Lionel meant. With a trace of reproach in his voice, he explained:

"Two years ago you wanted her to postpone her vacation."

"Yes, Lionel, we needed her to be there to demand that other women in prison abroad be set free."

I saw the scene again, still very clear in my mind. At the time, Simone had told me rather timidly:

"But I need to leave with Sartre to go on vacation. . . ."

Without any compassion for Sartre's state, I'd snapped back:

"I need a vacation, too, but I've postponed it."

Instead of reacting sharply as she was wont to do, Simone remained speechless, her cheeks crimson.

We left each other without resolving the misunderstanding. That very evening I received a phone call from Delphine Seyrig. She scolded me gently, almost affectionately:

"Simone is not as young as you are, she is over sixty, she has worked hard all her life and Sartre is tired. She has a right to go on vacation when she wants to. Believe me, she's earned it."

I ended up by admitting that on that occasion I had perhaps been a bit sharp and that Lionel's comments were not unfounded. It was my turn now to try and put the brakes on Hélène's heated criticism. It did no good.

"No, I don't see why. I have the right to know why her female characters aren't more positive and why she has so little to say about women artists. She's my sister, after all!"

I decided to retire for the night. Christmas was coming. The New Year's celebration was going to be happy. Nevertheless, I was determined to prevent any tension between the two sisters and I hoped that time would work in my favor.

❚   ❚   ❚

"What did you say to my sister?"

Sitting on her yellow sofa, Simone blushed as she asked me the question. Dressed in an elegant silk shirt that matched her headband, she seemed ill at ease. Now I felt embarrassed as well. Upon my return from Trebiano, Simone had not welcomed my New Year's wishes with her usual kindness. The thought of hurting her terrified me. Still, I decided to plunge in.

"You know how much we love your work, Simone. Nonetheless, I don't understand why the female characters in your novels are so negative. Liberty and action seem to be male prerogatives. Sure, the women try to have access to independence but they attain it with great difficulty. At times they are totally incapable of it and slip into madness."

Without saying a word, Simone got up and went over to the refrigerator. She took out a bottle of vodka. In spite of my aversion to alcohol, I wet my lips with the contents of the glass she handed me. She began to speak with great assurance:

"I want to describe women the way they are! I don't like positive heroines. I don't want to set my writing in a feminist framework. . . . In the work people send me, which I read very carefully, I often notice that the greatest weakness lies in the moralizing and didactic tone they take. And more than anything else, I dread falling into the stereotypes that Communist literature has inflicted on us."

Impassioned, she then explained to me that her books were not intended to be reassuring but aimed rather at reflecting the ambiguity of human relationships. I noted to what extent our age difference—forty-two years—divided us. Simone gave as an example the women of her circle, women who had no promise of a career or any focus of interest. According to her, they dramatized their lives in order to fill their interior void. I answered:

"Many women, with or without a career, show real courage and have many resources. Their life is often a long chain of trials and tribulations, and yet they manage to pull through."

"That's not what I see around me, and it's not what I read in the mail I receive."

I was quiet for a few moments and wondered. Simone had frequently criticized creative women and artists, both in *The Second Sex* and in her novels. She ridiculed women who tried to write. Why such furious tenacity? She reacted vehemently:

"It's a long drawn-out job, a discipline that requires years of effort. You don't call yourself a writer because you have some free time and your heart is aching. I've read too many manuscripts written on the run and without any literary value. Writing is a serious activity, a profession. Not a pastime."

Her words made me think, even if I found them simplistic. As I was listening to her, I recalled the Sundays we had spent together trying to change the world. She would evaluate our suggestions and achievements most of all by how serious they were. And it didn't prevent her from appreciating our bursts of laughter. But in her novels, her male heroes were plagued by fewer doubts and exemplified truly free human beings. The sense of alienation and anguish was reserved for her female characters.

I worried—had I hurt her feelings with all my questions? I was so afraid of letting her down. Simone got up and to my great surprise pulled me over to her little desk. The table was strewn with sheets of cross-ruled paper filled with her slanted writing. A pile of manuscripts was stacked up beneath them.

"Do you see these documents?"

"Yes. . . ."

"They are theses on my work, sent to me from all over the world. Not one of them has to do with your dissertation subject. Mostly they are philosophical works. But if they are of interest to you, take any that might be helpful."

I examined them one by one. Most of them were of no use to me, for my topic focused on her feminist commitment. At the time, this theme was barely mentioned in the universities. Still, to please her, I chose two copies that dealt with death and existentialism. At the door, blushing again, Simone smiled and said:

"Thank you, Claudine. . . ."

"For what?"

"For devoting so much time to my work. . . ."

In her eyes I glimpsed the tears she was trying to hold back. Then I, too, was overcome with emotion and added these awkward but heartfelt words:

"It is we, Simone, who thank you for everything you do for us."

Relieved and happy, I left her building.

■   ■   ■

I knew how much Simone loved food. She would devour her favorite dishes as she discussed the day's events or her writing. Her clipped delivery wouldn't falter. But she wasn't alone in this—all of us of the MLF had a good appetite. We often said that in order to struggle effectively feminists should be well fed! That particular day, I had invited Simone together with Anne Zelensky and Annie S., two of the founders of the MLF, to my apartment. Not wanting to count on my cooking, I had made other arrangements. When Simone discovered Hélène behind the stove, unaware until that moment that her younger sister was even in Paris, her usual reserve vanished. She hugged her tightly, kissed her, and laughed:

"What a lovely surprise!"

I was thrilled to see them together, so alike and yet so different. Simone suddenly said:

"I'd really like a double whiskey."

"I was planning to serve you your favorite champagne. . . ."

"That doesn't mean. . . ."

The few glasses of the Roulet family's favorite Bordeaux were not enough for Simone. She had to have whiskey before lunch and whiskey before dinner. Sometimes she might force herself to have some tea in the afternoon. It was obvious she had passed the limits of reasonable alcohol consumption long ago. I knew that the housekeeper in Goxwiller would often find a glass of whiskey next to her bed. One night Simone had such a heavy nosebleed there that the carpet had to be washed down. "Too much alcohol," Hélène decided with a sigh. Still, like everyone faced with this problem, we hesitated to refuse her a drink. I gave Simone the whiskey, which she drank down almost in one gulp. We opened the champagne. My other two guests didn't drink at all. Simone turned to me:

"You, Claudine, will surely have some champagne with Poupette and myself?"

"Of course."

I had answered in a tone that was meant to be confident, but I was worried I wouldn't be able to keep up.

After the smoked salmon and a few drinks, the conversation turned to feminism. Sitting to the right of her sister, Hélène told the story of her experience with the home for battered women in Strasbourg. She avowed her enthusiasm and pleasure at participating in the battle. Anne Zelensky spoke of the need for raising women's consciousness about the facts of abuse. Hélène then opened her mouth to reply.

"Shut up!" Simone ordered her curtly.

We were stunned. Hélène huddled in a corner of the sofa. Silence fell. Abashed, Anne finally began to speak again. Soon the discussion digressed to the subject of psychoanalysis and liberty. Since analysis frees the spoken word, it should also contribute to women's liberation. Simone sat up and declared acrimoniously:

"That Lacan is a misogynist. I met him at the end of the war. His writing is not clear and it denigrates women. I cannot take him seriously. We should be wary of him."

"Psychoanalysis is not restricted to Lacan," I came back.

Through the speaking cure, Freud and Jung had brought relief to certain patients. Simone was fidgeting on the couch and asked Hélène to pour her some more champagne.

"Are the girls of the MLF interested in psychoanalysis?"

"Yes, Simone."

We had answered as one. She emptied her glass again and in a decisive tone cut in:

"Once you start with analysis you never stop. It's a drug. . . ."

At that moment her hand hit the corner of the table and the glass broke. The alcohol was beginning to have its effect. She went on:

"After the war, bourgeois American women who had money, who were in the house and didn't work, began to suffer from depression. The psychoanalysts convinced them that their boring, uninteresting lives were actually enough to make them happy. That is not what we want! We want women to be able to choose their own profession, including the ones that until now have been reserved for men."

We understood what she was saying. There was still so much to do. Women had just obtained the right to have a personal checking account. This revolution had aroused the wrath of its detractors. In *The Second Sex* Simone had already written pages critical of Freud and psychoanalysis, and she was prepared to defend her point of view until the end. The fact that her close champions were interested in psychoanalysis worried her. She continued:

"Psychoanalysis refers to the nature of woman as wife and mother. You know very well that these are the two arguments that for centuries have confined women to the kitchen and to subordinate roles. Don't trust the insidious undercurrents of this practice, for there is a real danger that it will support a return to this so-called feminine nature."

I took a sip of champagne. Simone's intensity no longer surprised me. At sixty-eight, she was still as quick-witted as ever in her reply. For better or for worse, I tried to respond to her in the same tone:

"We are just as mistrustful of this backlash as you are. But psychoanalysis does liberate through the speaking cure. Perhaps in some of its aspects it could help women find their way to liberation."

Simone shrugged her shoulders and sulked. Her beautiful blue eyes looked at me with disapproval.

"You know very well that at the present moment most analysts are men and they are misogynists. They want to restrict women to their function as mothers. You should be very careful."

Sending me desperate signals, Hélène buried herself deeper into the cushions. I, for one, felt like defending my position, which the other guests shared.

"As far as motherhood is concerned," I said with a tiny smile, "you know my views. If only non-feminist women have children, we're heading for a catastrophe!"

Silence fell for a few moments. Was Simone going to get angry? She sighed, settled back in the cushions and responded more gently:

"I agree with you that we need more feminist mothers. It would contribute enormously to changing the world. But be careful! Our detractors are many and are only waiting for one little ambiguous sentence from our end to withdraw our rights. We must show ourselves to be on the offensive and always be clear."

She leaned over to me, asked for another helping of cherry clafoutis, and concluded:

"I've said this to you before and I shall say it again. The few women's rights that we have managed to extract by struggling long and hard these past few years are fragile. Very fragile. All it takes is another economic, political, or religious crisis for them to be challenged. All of you, Anne, Annie, and you, Claudine: as long as you live you will have to watch that society and the politicians don't cunningly nibble away at these rights. You'll have to be on your guard, don't ever forget that."

Hélène sat up again. She knew her sister had relaxed a little and that, in the end, she had confidence in us. I watched them, so close, each in her way so beautiful. Hélène was the only married woman at this dinner. She was smiling at me now, discreetly, reassured that the discussion had reached some common ground. How else could it have gone? We were the daughters of *The Second Sex*.

Soon after, Simone checked her watch, her face tense. The hour of her meeting with Sartre was approaching. I called a taxi for her, and as she hurried down the stairs, I followed. The effect of the alcohol was no longer noticeable. I went back up to my apartment where Hélène and the others were waiting for me. At last, the younger sister could breathe freely again and we continued the discussion in a distinctly mellower atmosphere.

▮   ▮   ▮

The years went by. Simone welcomed us with a glass of vodka in hand. It was barely noon. In 1979, Sartre was at his worst and Simone was trying to fight her anxiety with large quantities of alcohol. Hélène sat down and right away began to talk very excitedly:

"Lionel, Claudine, and I are going to America!"

Amused, Simone listened to her sister. After Japan, where Hélène had gone not long after her sister, the artist was going to have the pleasure of discovering a new continent.

"Oh, we won't be visiting the bars of Chicago. We're going to the heartland of America, and to visit the feminists!"

She went on about the various stopovers that were planned: Oklahoma, Las Vegas, California and the women's clinics, New York for the opening of one of her exhibits, and finally Princeton, in the footsteps of Einstein and his colleagues. Simone was startled—what were we doing going to Oklahoma? Vast plains where herds of buffalo roamed, flat Indian territories, and oil wells hardly seemed to fit in with a journey of intellectuals! I had to justify our stop in the Midwest, tell her about my friends, my meetings with Native Americans who were working with a linguist friend of mine.

After Oklahoma, we would go to Los Angeles to observe the difficulties of the feminists there firsthand. Hélène would be the guest of honor in clinics where Simone had never gone. I thought of the film on women's anatomy during which Simone had closed her eyes. I had told Hélène the anecdote but had her promise me to keep it secret. As I feared, she couldn't resist provoking her older sister.

"You know, I'll be visiting the clinic where the movie on women and their bodies was made. I do believe you saw that, didn't you?"

I lowered my head and examined the carpet. Simone answered persuasively:

"Yes, a very good film, too. Those women do excellent work. . . ."

"They're arranging for a screening for me in Los Angeles. I'm eager to see it."

Simone turned to me, her eyes wide with disbelief:

"But you're not planning on inviting Lionel to that screening, are you?"

I reassured her. She sighed with relief and made Hélène promise to keep her up-to-date.

"How lucky you are to be going to the United States!"

There was nostalgia in her voice. Sartre's slow physical decline prevented her from traveling much anymore and forced her to curtail her movements between their two favorite cities—Rome in the summer and Paris the rest of the year. The philosopher's blindness was growing worse. His steps were more hesitant, he was increasingly short of breath, and his morale was lower than ever. His thinking, once so clear and caustic, was becoming hazy. He was heavily under the influence of his secretary, who badgered Simone with his arrogance and insolence.

Her happy memories of America with Nelson Algren seemed very distant. Added to that was the disgrace we all recalled but didn't dare mention—the scathing article that her former lover, now a destitute alcoholic, had published in an American magazine in 1972. He had exposed his private life with Simone in the most offensive and malicious terms. He compared Simone to a camel and, adding insult to injury, accused her of being stingy although he had benefited from her generosity for years.[3] In addition, the magazine had thought it necessary to print a caricature of Simone with her eternal turban, on a camel in the desert, between two photographs of nude women.

"It hurt her deeply," Hélène had told me at the time. "I think she still loves Algren. . . ."

We at the MLF were mortified. How, under those conditions, could she possibly have gone back to the land of her great love? When she closed the door, it was obvious that she was envious of our freedom and of the discoveries awaiting us.

■　■　■

"All right, if you insist, we'll go to Las Vegas."

In an air-conditioned car we were passing through the last suburbs of Los Angeles before reaching the desert. Lionel had answered my request in a furious tone. His painful memories came rushing back:

"Gambling horrifies me. It was the reason my parents squandered their fortune and ruined us."

Suddenly, in the middle of nowhere, Las Vegas appeared. Thousands of lights—pink, ochre, turquoise blue, yellow—illuminated the Strip, the famous avenue of gigantic casinos with their rows upon rows of slot machines. Lionel observed this world with overt mistrust. Once we had checked into our hotel, we went to the slot halls, armed with our nickels, quarters, and dimes. Lionel, too, took a small coin and threw it into one of the brightly lit slot machines. He seemed taken aback by his own audacity. Hélène and I lovingly observed him confront the monster of his youth. He lost. He instantly abandoned it, preferring instead to watch us having fun like little kids. We lost one coin after the other. Finally, Lionel could hold out no longer. He put one of our last quarters into a one-armed bandit. With deafening noise, the dollars came cascading down and fell all over the floor. He had won a small jackpot!

"Well, that's enough! I'm taking you out for dinner and we're not going to play anymore!"

Lionel dragged us to a restaurant where the pasteboard décor tried to imitate the gleaming splendor of an Egyptian palace. He ordered French wine. Tasting the Bordeaux, Hélène said:

"Well, Lionel, admit it—I do believe you actually had a good time!"

He put down his glass. His eyes glittering with mischief, he said:

"Yes, Hélène, I admit it! But I didn't gamble away our house in Goxwiller! And you can still continue to buy your canvas. Be that as it may, I don't want to spend any more time here. We're leaving for Oklahoma tomorrow!" And with that he paid the check with the money he had won.

■   ■   ■

Why Oklahoma? Simone's confusion before our departure had delighted Hélène. It was her turn to discover the heart of America. The plane landed in Oklahoma City. The road from the airport ran across long plains. The silent pumping of the oil drilling machines digging tirelessly into the soil to extract black gold was in evidence everywhere. Nobody paid any attention to it here; oil simply was part of the landscape.

Between 1834 and 1889, Oklahoma—in Choctaw the word means "the red people"—was Indian Territory. White people had chased off the indigenous population from many regions in America, exiling some of them to this land; it was not yet known that it was brimming with oil. The Native Americans were forcibly marched over thousands of miles of dusty, tortuous roads, which came to be known as the Trail of Tears. Without any resources, lost and desperate, many of them died before ever reaching Oklahoma.

Cecelia, a friend from my university days in the States, welcomed us at the door of her wooden house, surrounded by cactuses. Her companion, a Midwestern man in a cowboy hat, taught at the university and was developing a lexicon of the Delaware language with the help of a group of elders from the tribe. Since theirs was not a written language, the young people spoke English better than the language of their ancestors.

When grandparents died a culture vanished with them. Passionate about the history of civilizations, Lionel listened intently to Cecelia as she described our plans.

"Sunday, we will take you to a Native American celebration we've been invited to. There'll be no tourists there. It shows they trust us."

Hélène was enthralled with the prospect of this adventure in ancestral America. How Simone would have liked that! Oklahoma with its oil reserves didn't resemble the wasteland she had imagined when she was in Europe. We sat down on the verandah to savor the immense landscape and the quiet of nature. Soon the conversation moved on to art and notably to an American painter by the name of Glenda Green, who had managed to create an original and well-recognized body of work. Her paintings were reminiscent of some of the Surrealists, Salvador Dalí in particular, and were reproduced all over the country.

"American women painters are lucky," Hélène noted. "Their work is seen, they have exhibitions!"

"Yes," Cecelia answered. "American women have been fighting for several years to have creative work by women recognized in all areas of art. It's an important and essential battle. What are you in the MLF doing?"

I was forced to admit that we had focused on emergency action. Art wasn't on our list of priorities. I thought of the exhibitions Hélène already had held all over the world. This trip, too, was to end with a retrospective of her work at the Ward Nasse Gallery near Washington Square in New York. She had been very successful there before, in 1974. This time she was going to show her feminist and ecological canvases. New York, Tokyo, Brussels, Lausanne, Rome, Milan, Amsterdam, Boston, Mexico, The Hague, Strasbourg, Prague, Paris in 1978—in the past ten years, Hélène's career had confirmed her international scope, yet, for all that, it hadn't fulfilled her completely.

Sitting in an armchair with Cecelia's cats on her lap, Hélène pursued the topic that was so dear to her heart.

"Look at the fame Georgia O'Keeffe managed to gain in the United States! She deserves all of it, for her work is magnificent. But she had the benefit of a reputable and daring New York gallery owner who pushed her into the ranks of internationally recognized artists. For the dozens of museums that are dedicated to men, how many museums are there for women artists? Think of the museums for Picasso, Matisse, Chagall, and so many others: is there a single one in France devoted to the work of a woman? Berthe Morisot, Rosa Bonheur, Mary Cassatt, and Elisabeth Vigée-Lebrun don't have their private museums. Their paintings merit it, but nobody gives it any thought! They've been relegated to a corner somewhere, crushed beneath the piles of compositions by men."

"In the United States," Cecelia said, "American feminists have been criticizing this situation for some time. I am sure things will improve."

At the time we didn't know that Georgia O'Keeffe, many of whose paintings reflect the American Southwest, would have a museum in Santa Fe that was to bear her name. Similarly, in Washington, D.C., a museum was opened, dedicated entirely to art created by women and another one was under construction in San Francisco. At the beginning of the twenty-first century in France, not a single woman has yet been the object of a similar tribute. With her eight hundred paintings, many of them masterpieces, Elisabeth Vigée-Lebrun is still in the shadows; the Rodin Museum, which also holds very beautiful sculptures by Camille Claudel, only carries Rodin's name. Not only was Claudel locked away in an insane asylum for the second half of her life so as not to disturb her community, concerned with its respectability, but even today there's no thought of renaming the place, which after all could simply be called the "Rodin-Claudel Museum."[4]

"What is so dramatic," Hélène exclaimed, "is how the situation is trivialized. If we mention the injustice it looks like we're jealous of male success. And there's always some sensible art critic around to state in the press that these women's work doesn't quite live up to the emotional and technical quality of that of men. Statements such as these are unbearably condescending—I, for one, believe we shouldn't accept it any longer, and that goes for women composers and sculptors as well."

The following Sunday, accompanied by Cecelia and her partner, we went to the celebration. After a long trek on a dusty road, we came to a field that formed a sort of basin in the middle of a windswept plain beneath a blue sky. Native Americans dressed in jeans and boots were arriving by car, as were we.

Slowly edging forward, the dancers moved one behind the other to the beat of drums and the sound of a chorus. They sang this way for hours. Being part of the chorus was an honor. The entire ceremony revolved around reciprocal gifts and esteem. Women offered shawls as tokens of respect and friendship that they had embellished with long fringe that swayed as they danced. Cecelia received one.

We were about to leave the gathering when an old man called to us. His left eye was covered with a bandage. His right arm was bent, resting in a sling made from a scarf. He asked us gently:

"Are you French?"

He held out his good arm to us and whispered with moist eyes:

"I'm one of the American soldiers who liberated France."

We were amazed and very moved. He told us of his memories, the battles with the Germans, the joy of the Liberation, and most of all about the French women who had given him flowers and blown him kisses.

"The liberation of your country was one of the most beautiful days of my life. People were so warm to me, I've never forgotten that."

Native Americans were of great service in the U.S. Air Force because of their excellent vision and their exceptional composure. Others were employed in the navy as coastal lookouts, alone for months in the jungles of the Pacific. Some of them, because of the uniqueness and complexity of their language, served as radio operators to protect the exchange of information between land and navy units. Still others, such as the man before us, had fought in the Ardennes during the German counterattack of December 1944. Here in Oklahoma, he had brought us back to France.

■   ■   ■

The blinds were closed in the small meeting room overlooking Crenshaw Boulevard in Los Angeles. Hélène sat down in the front row next to Carol Downer. I was behind her while Lionel, who was not allowed into the screening, sat in the waiting room. He chatted with the employees, asked questions about the way the clinic functioned, went into raptures over their common sense and resourcefulness when they had so few means. He was enjoying every moment.

"It's a good experience for him," Hélène told me. "This way he'll understand my support for the feminists better!" For a man of his generation, the "brother-in-law" and "bourgeois" so maligned by Sartre and Simone, showed an exceptional comprehension and openness to the women's cause.

At the end of the screening, Hélène said:

"Well, I didn't close my eyes. It's a fantastic film that every woman should see once in her lifetime! I'll tell Simone that, too."

Then Carol Downer told her about her tour through the small towns of America. For several months, she had crisscrossed the United States showing the documentary to thousands of women. In all seriousness, she declared:

"We, too, have had a long march, just like Mao Tse Tung."

At the end of our stay, Hélène gave one of her paintings to the clinic in Los Angeles; it showed the naked body of a woman in pastel tones of blue and green. Carol assured her it would hang in the patients' reception room, facing the window that looked out on the boulevard so that everyone could admire it.

"Keep up the good fight," Hélène said in farewell. "Yours is an avant-garde action and women on other continents need to follow your example."

Carol told her that similar clinics had opened all across the United States but that the health center's plan for expansion had not yet been completed. If Ronald Reagan should be elected president, they expected the worst and it would be the Americans' turn to reach out for international support. Hélène promised to bring up the matter with Simone.

❚   ❚   ❚

Night was falling over New York. The skyscrapers were lit up. Ambulance sirens filled the city with their strident sounds. Near Washington Square, the Village was crammed with rumpled passersby, students and academics, penniless intellectuals, and bohemians of the Vietnam era.

The Ward Nasse Gallery was closed to the public. In an elegant, tight-fitting dress, Hélène welcomed her guests to the opening of her most recent painting exhibit. For her second exhibition in America, feminists from all over the East Coast had come to greet her. They commented on every painting, some of which denounced the oppression of women.

"We didn't know painting like this existed in Europe. It's an awe-inspiring testimony, and by Simone's sister. This gives it even more prestige and radiance!"

Standing among the guests, Lionel courteously greeted the activists.

"You are happy for Hélène, aren't you?"

"Happy and proud," he said with his warm smile.

He knew how much his wife had suffered from her older sister's fame. That evening, Hélène received the artistic and political approval of the same feminists who generally reserved such admiration for Simone. The photographers' bulbs flashed. I could feel how thrilled Hélène was that she, too, was at last being recognized for her commitment.

The few phone calls the sisters exchanged did not bode well: Simone and Sartre were spending their vacation in Rome and the philosopher's health continued to decline. But that evening in New York, the champagne sparkled in the glasses and the guests were buying paintings. Even if Sartre was living out his final days and Simone was in great anguish, for the time being, Hélène intended to enjoy life and her success.

▌　▌　▌

After the opening, Hélène and Lionel came with me to Princeton, the region of my youth. Nestled among trees, lawns, and ponds forty miles south of New York, this little green town with its old houses and their columns recalled the charming cities of the American South. Princeton is home to the prestigious Institute for Advanced Studies. In earlier days the Institute was under the direction of Robert Oppenheimer, the father of the American atom bomb. The world of scientists, and especially that of mathematicians, intrigued Hélène and Lionel. Sartre and Simone had wanted little to do with it.

"And yet," Hélène told me more than once, "Simone really is interested in your family, and she respects them. Mathematicians are creators."

"Yes, but creators whose books one cannot read. It's very strange and frustrating not to be able to understand the books my father has published. There isn't any dictionary to help me with it either—I'll die without having grasped a single word of his work."

Albert Einstein's shadow hovered above the place; the street where I had lived when I was young was named after him. It was a few hundred yards from his former home on Mercer Street. Einstein didn't want it to become a museum, so there was not even a plaque mentioning its illustrious resident. Hélène and Lionel wanted me to show them the environment that was so different from the literary one they knew.

"Simone has given lectures and met intellectuals in many American universities, but not the ones who are the source of this century's science and technology. We are eager for you to show us the world of your younger years."

I did, actually, feel at home here. We entered the faculty lounge of the Institute. The mathematician Armand Borel and his wife Gaby were waiting for us. This cultivated and refined man of Swiss origin had started his scientific career at the same time as my father. They had published theorems and had both been members of the Bourbaki group.

Hélène was dying to ask him a question:

"Are there any women mathematicians?"

"Very few," Borel responded, "I don't really know many names. But since 1968, we are seeing more and more women in the international colloquia. So it is a situation that should develop favorably."[5]

"There is much work left to be done," Hélène remarked.

"Yes, but we are making progress. It needs more time."

"Hélène, when I see the inroads we have made in France in just a few years, I feel really hopeful. Sure, American women are ahead of us in the area of creativity and art. But their example in this sector can only help us, and sooner or later will have repercussions in Europe."

"Yes, but the situation is still blocked. I'm thinking of your mother, who is a chemist, and the obstacles she ran into after the war to be accepted in the world of science. She had to fight just to hold a position of some responsibility. I'm not young anymore, and I'd like to see women mathematicians and artists recognized while I'm still alive."

▮   ▮   ▮

The sun streamed into the studio as I sat down in a chair opposite the yellow sofas and the Egyptian mask. Simone asked me to pour us some vodka. It was noon and I had absolutely no desire for a drink, but I knew she'd appreciate having company; in resignation, I sipped the harsh, translucent liquor. Simone drank it in one gulp. She instantly became lively again.

"Poupette has told me all about your trip to the United States. The feminists who work in the clinics in California are very brave."

"Yes, Simone, they really are. They're living under the constant threat of assassination attempts or physical assault. Many of them are afraid for their children. Hélène's visit renewed their energy. They were very impressed with her stamina."

"It's true. My sister came back very enthusiastic, which I'm happy about. But. . . ."

Simone motioned me to fill her glass. I did.

"But . . . ?"

Her voice became less certain.

"It's hard, you know, to be the sister of someone famous. You are the butt of so much humiliation and jealousy. Relationships with others can sometimes be marred by ambiguity. Poupette is more fragile than she looks. Sometimes I worry about her. Of course, Lionel is there, but Poupette needs someone to take care of her, to protect her."

She sighed.

"One day, I'll be gone. . . ."

I lowered my eyes and mumbled what seemed obvious to me:

"But I'll be there, Simone."

I slowly raised my head and caught her glance. Her eyes were filled with tears. The silence that lasted just moments seemed interminable. Then, almost inaudibly, she changed the subject.

"So, now tell me about the work these women do. . . ."

I was upset when I left Simone that day. The words I had just pronounced in front of her resonated inside me like a vow.

█   █   █

Simone was crying on the phone.

"It's scandalous!" Hélène kept saying furiously. Like all of us, she felt helpless in the face of the betrayal Sartre was suffering.

In April 1980, Pierre Victor, his secretary, had published an interview in *Le Nouvel Observateur* in which he had induced the philosopher to deny the principles of existentialism. At the end of his strength, Sartre was nothing but a blind and weak old man. Once so alert, his mind was confused. Pushed around and exploited by this self-assured young man, Sartre disavowed his theory of freedom in favor of a doctrine tinged with spirituality and religious influence. Without realizing it, Sartre had betrayed Sartre. It was intellectual suicide.

Simone tried to prevent the article from being printed. In vain. The intellectual world in France and internationally was astounded to read his words. The secretary's light tone shocked people: he used the informal *tu* with Sartre, though the philosopher had always used *vous* even with those closest to him, including his dear Castor. The girls of the MLF were sick with rage. When I showed my support to Simone, she burst into tears in front of me. I took her in my arms and told her how much we loved her and how appalled we all were. She could not stop crying. Finally, still sobbing, she said to me:

"Wait until we die, Claudine. What they will write about us will be even worse."

That day I promised myself I would defend Simone's memory as long as I lived.

█   █   █

Night had fallen in Goxwiller. Hélène ran to the phone and heard her sister's broken voice. Simone couldn't catch her breath. Her delivery was even faster than normal:

"Sartre is in the hospital, this is the end!" And she began to sob. The following day, Hélène came to stay with me for six weeks. Together we would face bereavement and trials that would bond us forever. April 1980 would remain engraved in our memories as the end of an era, an era of hope for a better world.

The final years of Valéry Giscard d'Estaing's seven-year term as president of France had been difficult. *Libération* was crumbling under libel convictions. Simone was helping Sartre financially, and some of his former and present mistresses received a monthly stipend. Hélène confirmed the rumor that Simone actually handled his expenditures indirectly and that, at the end of each month, these amounted to huge sums of money.

When I commented somewhat cynically that this was a sad development, Hélène invariably replied:

"Simone loves Sartre so much! She can't do without him. I've sometimes wished they would leave this life together, but," she added sadly, "that will undoubtedly not be the case."

A few hundred yards from my apartment, the little man was fighting death in a room at the Broussais Hospital. His pulmonary edema had worsened. Without lowering their guard, Simone and Arlette—the young woman he had adopted and who had become his companion of long standing—took turns staying with him. In the MLF, we were on Simone's side—fifty years of love, writing, complicity, and struggle for liberty couldn't just be swept away with a stroke of the pen. Simone's grief became ours. Hélène told me about the bullying and sarcastic remarks Sartre's entourage inflicted upon her sister. Many of them wanted her to feel she was nothing but an "old woman." In the past, Simone had been critical of the sad lot of the aged. Now a peculiar and ironic turn of destiny caused her to experience this dismal condition herself.

On the morning of April 16, 1980, Simone entered her companion's overheated room. Sitting in a chair, Sartre was choking. He took her hand and murmured:

"I love you very much, my dear Castor. . . ."[6]

Simone knew he was saying goodbye to her. She leaned over and kissed him on the mouth. Then she heard footsteps in the hallway and understood. It was time to let her rival take over. Arlette had arrived. She would have loved to stay close to him, to watch him live a few moments longer. She would be denied even that. After a last glance, she left the hospital without a word and returned home.

The walk seemed endless. From her apartment, she watched the sun go down over Paris. The telephone rang. Sartre would not see the light again. He had died as soon as she left him. Simone would not be the one to close his eyes. She dissolved in tears. It was time to go back and keep watch over him. Sylvie, Claude Lanzmann, and a few friends from *Les Temps modernes* went with her. Soon the whole world would hear the news.

The next morning, Hélène turned on the radio: "He was a great philosopher. . . ." She collapsed in my arms:

"My whole life long I've been afraid I'd hear of either Simone or Sartre's death on the radio." Her eyes red, she added:

"Why didn't she call me? Why?"

■   ▓   ▊

All along the Avenue du Général-Leclerc, the headlines in the windows of the newsstands repeated the news. Hugging me closely, Hélène kept murmuring "Poor Simone, poor Simone. . . ." We finally arrived at her building. Photographers moved toward Hélène who ignored them. We rang. No one opened. Hélène began to sob.

"Where can she be?"

With the journalists watching, we went to the Place Denfert-Rochereau. It was painful to see the now seventy-year-old Hélène in her black suit and stockings. Devastated with grief, she slid into a telephone booth and managed to find Claude Lanzmann. He told her that Simone had sought refuge at his house.

"May I come and see her?"

"She's sleeping; she sat in vigil by Sartre all night long, better let her sleep."

"Yes, of course. . . ."

Then in a thin voice, hesitant with sorrow, she begged:

"When she wakes up would you please ask her to call me at Claudine's?"

"Yes, Hélène. . . ."

All we could do was go back home. The same avenue, the same news-stands, the same papers. On Rue d'Alésia, we listened to the radio again. Everywhere, the same symphony of praises and saccharine statements. Suddenly, those who for years on end had spoken words laden only with hatred against Sartre were now changing their tone. In spite of her sorrow, Hélène burst out angrily:

"It's incredible, listen to these people! They're the ones who heaped him with abuse and slander in their vitriolic articles when he was alive! Just listen to them!"

It was, indeed, shocking. Fortunately, Hélène's friends and some MLF women called to comfort her as much as they were able. Then she heard Simone's voice at last:

"Why didn't you call me?" she asked.

"I did, I had your number on me, but there was no answer. . . ."

Inside, I thought that Simone probably preferred to be with the clan that she had chosen and established for herself over the course of the years. Away from Paris for three decades, Hélène had a separate place in her circle of nearest and dearest. The younger sister saw Simone's friends as her own, and her feelings toward them were selfless, I had no doubt. On the other hand, I wasn't so sure that her fondness for them was reciprocated.

The sisters decided to meet at Simone's apartment. Claude Lanzmann, Jacques-Laurent Bost, a former student of Sartre who became a great friend to both Simone and Sartre, and Sartre's adopted daughter were arranging the details of the funeral. Hélène asked me to join her at her sister's to work out the issue of the procession and crowd control. On the way, I imagined the enormity of Simone's bereavement. I knew she had feared this moment throughout her life. I couldn't think of a single thing to say. I rang the bell.

The door opened. For the first time ever, it was not Simone who let me in but Hélène. I found Simone on her yellow sofa. Large circles under her eyes showed she had wept, but her features seemed relaxed. Piles of telegrams and mail from all over the world lay by her side. With a wan smile, she asked me to sit down in the heavy mauve armchair across from her, as always. She didn't say much. Her voice had softened, no doubt as the result of tranquilizers, Hélène told me later. But her gaze was direct.

"Have you arranged for any police protection for the funeral?"

"I refused the prefecture's offer," Simone answered. "It would be a provocation to put policemen along the route of the procession. I was ready to accept their offer for the cemetery, but they told me it had to be for the whole funeral or nothing at all."

Hélène and I were aghast. This meant there might be droves of people pushing and the risk of skirmishes and suffocation. I reminded Simone that there would be a sizable crowd. We had to think about her safety and make sure that Sartre would have a solemn and dignified burial. Hélène let me talk without saying a word, merely nodding her head. Was she afraid of her older sister's reaction? I was insistent.

"If you agree, the girls of the MLF will stay around the hearse. We have to protect you, Simone, you never know what may happen."

"Fine, if you think that's helpful."

I was worried about the funeral. Would the crowd, whose predicted size grew with every passing day, behave itself? The tense relationship with the power structure suggested the worst. Simone would also have to confront Arlette, who from then on represented the Sartre family. Even if the messages that came from around the world were addressed to Simone, as Sartre's true companion, this face-to-face would be painful. Simone would ride in the hearse with Arlette, Sylvie, and Hélène. Thus, two loyal women would be by her side to protect and comfort her. I disappeared so that the sisters could have some time alone together.

Another question remained. Would Lionel attend the funeral? Sartre's former student spent part of his free time taking art-loving tourists to Greece and could in this way share his passion for the history of civilization. His decision from Delphi was final. He couldn't just abandon his group for the burial. I saw Hélène turn pale when she heard his response. Over the phone, Lionel asked me later to take care of his wife. In addition to crowd control and the throng, now I had something new to worry about. It was a short and uneasy night.

"Will Simone bear up under it all?" Hélène asked me when she turned out the light. I answered affirmatively. Simone had always been brave. But in the half-dark I wasn't so sure.

■   ■   ■

In front of the Broussais Hospital, the crowd blocked our passage. After a few attempts, Hélène finally managed to make her way to the entrance of the building. In the silence of the room where the coffin stood, the two clans ignored each other. Arlette and Pierre Victor, the young generation that had caused Simone so much pain and suffering, faced us. The philosopher had died a few days after the so-called interview that had distorted his ideas and betrayed the very meaning of his life.

Hélène went over to her sister. Sitting on a chair, her eyes red and her back stooped, she clutched a handkerchief in her hand. Hélène kissed her, put her hand on her shoulder, then took her in her arms. Two gigantic bouquets of flowers, from the daily paper *Libération* and from the Gallimard publishing house, framed the coffin. I left to join the girls of the Movement. Hundreds of people were gathering, men and women of all ages and backgrounds, and journalists from all over the world. Floral wreaths were piling up. Suddenly the door opened to an indescribable uproar. The funeral cortege appeared. In just a few seconds we had surrounded the hearse. University students came to lend us a hand. A human chain formed to prevent trouble.

In the back of the car, photographers flashing away, Simone sat between Sylvie and Hélène, who had placed herself between Arlette and her sister to make sure Simone wouldn't have to be next to her young rival. Hélène put her hand on her sister's arm. The car was almost immediately submerged in the crowd. Every generation was present—men who had fought in the Algerian War, those who were present in May of 1968, and also veterans of World War II. The cortege left for the Montparnasse Cemetery. Sartre and Simone's apartments looked out over it. In a way, all the philosopher did that day was cross the street.

Simone watched the sites parade past, happy witnesses of her life: the apartment on the Boulevard Raspail, the cafés of their younger years, the Rotonde above which she and Poupette had been born, the Dôme, and finally La Coupole, where they had so often had lunch. As they passed, waiters and maître d's came out of the restaurant and formed a guard of honor, white napkins folded over their left arms. With tears in her eyes, Simone watched them emotionally:

"It's exactly the funeral Sartre would have liked," she said to her sister.

The MLF girls formed a barrier around the hearse, but they were having trouble withstanding the pressure of the ever growing crowd. Through the glass I glimpsed Simone and Hélène in the half-light of the car. The dismay on their faces when they saw the frenzy of the photographers renewed our resolve. Then a cry went up. The cemetery entrance was blocked. The cortege stopped, then managed to advance to the grave amid an indescribable tide of humanity. Journalists and curious onlookers were perched on tombstones, besieging the lanes, climbing the walls.

Amid the confusion, Simone, Hélène, Sylvie, and Arlette got out of the car. Trampled by the photographers, I felt like screaming more than once. Two of them struck me in the sides, on the shoulders, and in the chest with their cameras. I couldn't breathe. Around me, the same thing was happening to some of my friends. It was a terrifying spectacle—Claude Lanzmann, protecting Simone with his right arm, was dealing punches with his left to make a path for her.

Having reached the grave, Simone discovered a man who had fallen into the pit. They needed to get him out. In spite of the requests of the funeral director, nobody had the decency to keep quiet. In the turmoil of all the pushing and shoving, an ashen and exhausted Simone threw a rose on the coffin of her companion. All around me men and women wept silently. As for me, short of breath as I was, I no longer had the strength to unleash my emotions. Only one question plagued me: how to get Simone and Hélène out of this mess alive.

The photographers wouldn't stop and increased their pressure. When Lanzmann helped Simone out of the cemetery, the chaos was at its peak. They were literally trampling us. Simone was choking, and Hélène was about to pass out as well. In the media rush, all respect for those in mourning was shattered. Blows rained down on the approaching guard. Screams, shouting, insults, cameras wielded as clubs: we were surrounded. Lanzmann succeeded at last in bringing Simone to a car that belonged to the district city hall. Slowly, she left the grounds, while a worn-out Hélène looked for me amid the commotion. We finally found each other and returned to my place. Later I heard that during the burial the MLF girls had made it a point to criticize loudly in front of the media Sartre's last secretary, whose disgraceful behavior disgusted us.

In the evening, Hélène met Simone, Lanzmann, and a few people close to the couple at the Brasserie Zeyer, on the corner of Rue d'Alésia.

"It's Sartre's treat!" Simone declared. She drank even more than usual, as her sister watched and worried.

■   ■   ■

Simone was not allowed to return to her companion's apartment. She wanted to retrieve the collections of stage plays she had inherited from her father and given to Sartre.

"You remember how Father made us laugh when he would read us these plays?" Simone asked her sister.

"Of course!"

"The heiress won't give them back."[7]

Simone had no claim whatsoever on these vestiges of their childhood. She wasn't able to rescue what belonged to her and only received the chair she used to sit in during her almost daily work sessions with Sartre. She was also allowed to keep a small lamp.

These sordid details shocked us. Hélène was by far the most philosophical of us all.

"You'll see, Claudine, soon the names of these mediocrities won't even be remembered."

Two days went by. Overtired from the ordeal of the funeral, Hélène wasn't ready yet to return to Goxwiller. Lionel was still traveling in Greece. Then Sylvie and Lanzmann found Simone lying on the floor. They took her to Cochin Hospital. Her health was so poor that they began to fear for her life. I accompanied Hélène to visit her sister and to meet with the doctor who headed the department. He took the younger sister aside and informed her that Simone was suffering from circulatory problems due to excessive alcohol consumption. He was hoping to save her but it was essential that she go to a detoxification center. Whatever she did, the doctor felt her life expectancy would be limited; he gave her about four years. Visits were restricted to half an hour a day. As we left the hospital, Hélène was shattered.

Lionel returned from Greece, tanned and relaxed. His archeological lectures had provided him with some precious moments of rest and freedom. Sitting in an easy chair in my apartment, he listened to Hélène recount every detail of the exhausting days we had just lived through.

"Neither Sartre's nor Simone's group talks to me anymore."

"Maybe that's just as well. . . ." Lionel answered pensively.

He was not sorry he had been able to distance himself from the little Parisian world he remembered all too well from his adolescence. He went to Cochin the next day with Hélène. That evening over dinner, he turned to me and said:

"Since you take such good care of Hélène, you won't need me, so I'm going back to Goxwiller."

We were dumbfounded and couldn't speak. His presence had been a comfort to us and there he was, abandoning us!

"In any case, I'm expected back at the European Council, I can't stay away and be on vacation forever. . . ."

Speechless, Hélène lowered her eyes. I, on the other hand, was wondering about her husband's indifference. Of the three of us he was the first one to have met Sartre. But the secondary school pupil of Le Havre had put distance between himself and his former teacher. Lionel was bent on leading his life according to his own criteria, even if that meant not conforming to the revolutionary ideals of his in-laws.

The next day, Lionel took the train for Strasbourg.

"How much longer will this go on?" I wondered in horror.

Hélène was losing weight, we were at the end of our rope. The prospect of having to meet up with antagonistic people made us nervous.

A few days later, Simone was finally able to return home. She, too, had lost weight, was very weak, and was beginning a life without Sartre. This new solitude compelled her to go back to writing. She alone could talk about the final years of her companion. In order to counteract the hideous article published in *Le Nouvel Observateur*, she was going to write some irrefutable pages and prove to the world that Sartre had been faithful to his ideas. A literary undertaking such as this would take long days of hard work and a great deal of energy, but she was determined. To achieve this labor of love and mourning, she was going to fight again and make Sartre's spirit live once more.

Then Simone announced to her sister that she wanted to legally adopt her friend Sylvie to whom she was so close. Since Sylvie was still young and held an *agrégation* degree in philosophy, she would be able to deal with Simone's work after her death. As Hélène was her sister's designated heir, Simone needed her agreement.

"I'm prepared to compensate you," she told her.

"Let's not even mention that," Hélène answered. "If this is what you want, I agree."

Hélène, now disinherited, returned to my place that evening looking distraught. Was she thinking of Sartre and Simone's wariness regarding Lionel? Be that as it may, she did her best to make a good impression and not reveal how betrayed she felt by Simone's decision.

"Simone has protected me all my life, and I'm no longer of an age where I could handle her work. Sylvie has the advantage of being young. I hope it will all work out."

Then, looking gloomy, she began to get her things together in preparation for her return to Strasbourg.

■   ■   ■

The years passed. Simone gradually recovered from the death of her companion. I visited her often. Hélène made frequent trips to Paris and stayed with me. In June 1984, four years after Sartre's death, we went to Simone's apartment together.

"It's not possible!"

Comfortably settled on her sofa, Simone burst out laughing. The story Hélène and I told her was fantastic. I had just recounted the incident that had brightened up the defense of my dissertation on her work and her commitment to women's rights. I had not wanted her to attend—knowing her incisive personality and her thorough habits as a teacher, she would undoubtedly have intervened. She had read and approved my work, even if she challenged my criticism concerning her female characters. And so I had done the defense in a stuffy atmosphere; the committee consisted of two professors of philosophy, two of literature, and two of history. During the debate, the chairman of the committee had made an astounding error as he read his notes, which undoubtedly contained the initials of Simone de Beauvoir.

"Now then," he stated, "*Salle de Bains*"—bathroom—"writes in *The Second Sex* that woman . . ."

He didn't even have time to finish his sentence, for audience and committee exploded in laughter. From then on the atmosphere lightened up somewhat.

In her apartment, Simone caught her breath.

"I've been called just about every name before, but never *bathroom*! What a pity Sartre isn't here. That would have really entertained him. . . ."

I looked at her. She had become more slender, younger. On her doctor's advice she had decreased her alcohol intake. She had also rid herself of Sartre's entourage and the young women who sponged off him.

"I no longer have anything to do with those widows," she was glad to announce. She had published her testimony on the final years with Sartre, six hundred pages, three hundred of which consisted of a fascinating unpublished dialogue between the two celebrities. *Adieux: A Farewell to Sartre* had incensed some people, who reproached her for having the audacity to describe the philosopher's physical decline. Nevertheless, the book was enormously successful both in France and abroad.

She addressed her last love letter to the man who had shared her life for fifty years. Sartre's secretary was cast in an arrogant light. She countered the fifteen pages he had published in *Le Nouvel Observateur* in April 1980 with a dialogue that was infinitely more credible.

"Simone has some of her vitality back!" I said to Hélène.

"Yes, but she has more and more difficulty walking."

Hélène was thinking of the doctor's warning after Sartre's death. Simone would survive him by at most four years. In spite of her concern, Hélène began to hope again—what if the medical world were wrong?

In July 1983, Simone returned to the United States. With Sylvie, she took the Concorde to New York. Nelson Algren would not be waiting for her, but with time her pain had lessened. Upon her return, Simone told us about her trip.

"You were right, the condition of women has regressed under Ronald Reagan."

"Yes," I agreed, "and one by one the women's clinics are being forced to close. Too may assassination attempts and threats against the patients."

"On the other hand, Women's Studies Departments are being started in American universities."

"That is good, Simone, even if it's less dangerous than keeping the clinics open. Those departments are very useful and the history of women, so long forgotten and neglected across the centuries, can now finally be studied."

Simone readily agreed. Since 1975, the year that the UN had designated as the International Year of Women, the number of our supporters had increased. By breaking the law of silence on taboo subjects such as abortion, rape, incest, battered women, and so on, we had changed society's outlook. These days the public was aware of us.

"Now," I said to Simone, "we have become respectable."

"Certainly, but look at what is happening with abortion in the United States. In the seventies they were ahead of France. Now it's the other way around. Women's rights are never definitively won. We must stay vigilant."

At seventy-six, she certainly practiced what she preached. Simone actively supported the feminist Yvette Roudy, Minister of Women's Rights under François Mitterrand,[8] who had become a friend of hers, as she worked to change laws and improve the lives of women in France. Simone had also established the League of Women's Rights with Anne Zelensky in 1974, and played a very active role in it. It was a subject very dear to her heart.

Sitting next to me, Hélène had followed the conversation without saying a word. Her sister would hardly let her intervene. Even though the younger Beauvoir testified in trials in Strasbourg and was continually active in defending women's rights, she was always asked to be quiet. Hélène didn't bear her any grudge. Back at my place, she admitted she was gratified that Simone was coming to the country regularly with Sylvie. Sartre had despised all that was green and had deprived her of it for years. Still, every time we saw her, we noticed that she was having greater difficulty moving around. Gradually her legs became numb and she was in pain. Her enthusiasm and lively spirit remained intact but her physical being was growing weaker.

■ ■ ■

"Is that really sensible?"

Sitting on her yellow sofa, Simone reacted with her usual candor. My next trip to the United States worried her. Since the ultraconservatives had returned to the White House, the pressure groups hostile to voluntary termination of pregnancy were intervening more and more and with increasing violence. Men and women were chaining themselves together in front of the clinics to get the public's attention. The full names of the physicians who were "guilty" of practicing abortion were listed on the signs they carried. Sometimes, in an upsurge of violence, the demonstrators entered the sites by forcing open doors, broke equipment, and terrorized the patients, who ran out screaming. Whether by conscious decision or coincidence, the police were usually slow to come. The clinics were destroyed and the employees terrified. Women in distress no longer knew where to go, once again traveling hundreds of miles in search of an establishment willing to give them the help they needed.

In the Los Angeles facility, as in the other women's clinics, the tension was at its height. Death threats, bomb scares, accusations—the extremists shrank from nothing. Carol Downer, director of the Federation of the Women's Health Centers, and Rebecca Chalker, both authors of remarkable texts on women's health, had invited me to the annual conference of representatives of the different clinics to give a report on the condition of women in Europe and feminist struggles in other parts of the world. In spite of the danger, I had accepted. Hélène had phoned me immediately from Goxwiller.

"Yes, Hélène, this trip may be a little dangerous, but under the circumstances, these women need our support more than ever. Otherwise they will feel the international community is abandoning them and then worse things could happen."

Simone understood my attitude, but insisted that I keep both her and Hélène apprised of any incident, no matter how small.

"If necessary, I'll intervene immediately. I'll make a statement to the press the moment you think that would be helpful."

I thanked her and left for California, reassured by her support. Simone had always kept her word. I myself had gone to the post office with her on many occasions to send telegrams to feminists in trouble. Her reaction could be scathing and eminently effective. Everywhere in the world, radio and television stations would vie to be the first to broadcast her words.

At the Los Angeles airport, Carol and Rebecca were waiting for me with drawn faces.

"We've had several bomb scares this month alone; our teams are working seventy hours a week in a state of enormous anxiety. Sometimes the electricity goes off and we don't know why. Demonstrators are screaming in front of our clinic doors every Saturday and keeping patients from coming in. I don't know how much longer we can hang on!"

What a contrast with 1974, when these clinics were opening. Back then it was in France that the situation was delicate. Abortion was still a crime there at the time, and California was a small island of liberty and tolerance. Now we were driving to Crenshaw Boulevard with our hearts in our mouths. In spite of the pleasure of seeing everyone again, a palpable atmosphere of dread hung over the building. Hélène's painting hanging in the reception room was a reminder that somewhere in Europe we were thinking of them and were in solidarity with their struggle. Chicanas and African-American women from Watts waited with their kids for a medical consultation or procedure. Some of them, pregnant and wretchedly poor, wanted an abortion. Babies slept in their strollers. I had a hard time containing my feelings. How could anyone attack human beings who were this defenseless?

That evening, I slept like a log, worn out from the flight and the time change. At five A.M., Carol woke me, all upset. In San Diego, more than a hundred miles south of Los Angeles near the Mexican border, one of the clinics had been bombed. Miraculously, no one had been sleeping there that night. The force of the explosion broke windows in the neighboring houses. We drove down immediately.

San Diego and its famous exotic Balboa Park; San Diego and its marina; San Diego and its millionaire retirees—these clichés seemed so far from our reality. The clinic buildings were for the most part destroyed; glass was strewn across the floor, women's portraits in the entry hall had been torn to shreds, and the furniture was reduced to rubble. All that was left of the children's nursery were some pieces of stuffed animals on the sidewalk among the shattered chairs and tables. The police bustled about in the chaos. Their politeness couldn't conceal their chilly attitude.

"We're in Republican territory here," Carol Downer said to me. "These guys forget that someday their own wives might have health problems and come knocking on our doors."

One by one, the female residents of the neighborhood paraded by. As I took in the enormity of the disaster, France seemed like an oasis of civilization to me. I told Hélène by phone about the climate that prevailed on the shores of the Pacific.

"Don't stay there, come home."

"That's out of the question."

Hélène spoke at length with Carol to give her encouragement. She told me repeatedly, until the day she died, that next to Simone, Carol was the woman who most impressed her. Completely exhausted and haggard, Carol listened to the voice from France. She hung up and said to me:

"Hélène is going to alert her sister. They will send us a telegram of support. You have no idea how much that will help to keep us going. We feel so isolated!"

We left San Diego for the High Sierras, north of Los Angeles. The telegram arrived from France. In the meantime, new bomb scares had taken place. In Tallahassee, Florida, and Atlanta, Georgia, the demonstrations were growing more intense in their virulence. In these southern towns it was even more difficult than in California to protect the anonymity of those who practiced abortion. Threats against the clinics' staff were more personalized, with activists putting signs in front of the private homes of doctors who performed the operations. They pasted flyers with the physicians' photos in public places, treating them as murderers. The atmosphere encouraged informers and, insidiously, incited lynching. A climate of hatred was spreading. Before I boarded the plane, Carol and Rebecca asked me:

"Are you sure you want to go to Atlanta?"

Carol shivered. There were dark circles under her eyes, her pale pink complexion and blond hair were faded. Her youngest children, who had come to say goodbye to me at the Los Angeles airport, kissed me. I hugged them tightly. What if something were to happen to them? The telegram from France had raised the teams' morale but went almost unnoticed in the media; the press showed no interest in the attacks. After all, nobody had been killed. I assured Carol and Rebecca that I really did want to go to Atlanta and had to catch this plane; I had taken it upon myself to come and bear witness from the perspective of our own struggle in Europe. It was important to me to proclaim Simone and Hélène's support, which wouldn't change the situation, but at least would give the women doing battle the sense of being less alone.

At the clinic in Atlanta, I had a shock. By the front door inside, uniformed men were camped out, guns in hand. They were members of the FBI and had been put in charge of protecting the people who worked here. In the hall where I was supposed to speak, women with babies and children waited patiently. Some of them were sitting on the floor chatting, unconcerned, about the risks they ran. The agents paced up and down, checking through the windows for the least little sign of hostility outside.

"They're afraid grenades might be thrown at us. They're quite worried."

"And these women came with their children?"

"Yes, they want to show the cops that we will not be intimidated."

In my speech, I relayed the message from Simone, Hélène, and the other feminists. After the debate, some of them came to take my hand; they were deeply moved.

"Your hand has shaken the hand of Simone de Beauvoir. Tell her that reading *The Second Sex* changed our lives. Promise us that you will!"

I hugged them and promised. Their eyes expressed both gratitude and deep distress. Simone was right to urge us never to give up, under any pretext whatsoever. I sensed the need for that more than ever before. Hélène phoned me:

"This time you really have to come home."

I consented and returned via New York and Princeton, where people seemed unaware of the shouts of hatred and noise of bombs, which hadn't reached that far north. Here, my testimony received no more than a polite, even indifferent, hearing, and I was discouraged when I got home. Once back in Paris, all that was left for me to do was tell the two sisters and the girls of the MLF about the ghastly power struggle being played out on the other side of the Atlantic.

The surge of 1968 had receded, and Ronald Reagan still had many years in power ahead of him. One by one, clinics continued to be bombed. Some of the doctors abandoned the fight. Women continued their struggle at the cost of personal attacks. In California and Florida, physicians became the targets. One of them was killed, then a second one, then others.

■   ■   ■

In April 1986, in one of the rooms of La Salpêtrière Hospital, Hélène was helping Lionel drink his tea. He had undergone an operation on his right ear, which had been causing him pain and dizziness for some time. The rounds of doctor's visits had started all over again, reminding him of his nightmarish tuberculosis years in Berk, before the war. Simone's health, too, was deteriorating. Two months earlier, Yvette Roudy, who had been so active in promoting women's rights through her dynamic work in the Mitterrand government, had prepared a huge retrospective of Hélène's work at the Ministry of Women's Rights. Simone had visited the exhibition, supported by her sister and the minister, but walking was becoming increasingly difficult for her. Women from several countries and the old guard of the MLF attended, as we all wanted to pay homage to both sisters and their lifelong efforts. It was the last time we saw her upright.

Hélène took Lionel home to Goxwiller to recuperate. He seemed to be improving. Reassured, Hélène feverishly began to prepare for her trip to the west coast of the United States. Yolanda Astarita Patterson,[9] a professor at California State University, Hayward, was devoting an exhibit to her work. The telephone rang; it was Sylvie.

"Hélène, Simone has just been hospitalized. She was vomiting all day yesterday; they're afraid it's appendicitis."

Hélène immediately returned to Paris and went to Cochin Hospital. She found Simone in bed, her face very pale. In spite of her own weak state, Simone asked after Lionel's health right away; then she was worried about the cost of the plane fare to America. In her mind, Hélène saw their mother's hospitalization again—could this appendicitis business be hiding another cancer? The nurses reassured her the next day, but still Hélène was hesitant to leave. Like Simone, I urged her to cross the Atlantic.

"You'll only be gone for two weeks," I told her, "and I will call you every day to keep you posted."

A few days later, she phoned and described how successful the exhibit had been. The faculty had given her flowers to thunderous applause. Everyone loved her new paintings. In spite of jet lag and anxiety about being far away from her sister and Lionel, she treasured her trip. The following day I had to tell her that Simone was once again in intensive care. She had caught pneumonia. She was released and brought home two days later.

"Is this the end?" Hélène asked me.

I tried to reassure her but was worried myself. Two days later, on April 14, 1986, Hélène received a call from Sylvie. Simone had died at four o'clock in the afternoon. The daily paper *Le Monde* then contacted me; they suggested I write an article that night on Simone's work on behalf of women. How can you write about someone so dear to you whom you have just lost? I spent the night amid tears and rough drafts I was constantly crossing out. At six in the morning, I wrote the final line of the piece: "After having changed the universe of her contemporaries and met the insolent girls of 1968, Simone de Beauvoir remained faifthful to the idea that women had one task to accomplish: to live."[10]

■   ■   ■

Hélène managed to catch a plane in San Francisco. Although still convalescing, Lionel came immediately. Listening to the radio together, we waited for Hélène. It was not the symphony of hypocritical praises sung at Sartre's death. For Simone the tone was more critical, almost reserved. The author of *The Second Sex* had still not been forgiven for having condemned the oppression of women. She had been refused the Nobel Prize in Literature, although she was one of the most widely read French writers in the world. At my house the phone never stopped ringing. Women from Canada, Africa, Australia, and Asia were calling. They wanted to express their sorrow, their emotion, and their gratitude to the one who had shown them the way to freedom. At last Hélène arrived.

"I don't know if I'm up to attending Simone's funeral. . . ."

"You have to go, Hélène."

Her tears came twice as fast. At seventy-six, her courage was faltering. We tried to calm her down, but I had serious misgivings—what would the funeral be like? Sartre's burial still haunted me. It was also Hélène's first question. Would Simone be honored in a way that was worthy of her? She was afraid the crowd at the cemetery wouldn't give her any breathing room. While Lanzmann and Sylvie arranged the funeral, I spoke with one of Mitterrand's advisors. According to him, many socialists would be out of town that weekend and wouldn't be able to attend the funeral. I leapt from my seat. Had the President forgotten that, unlike Sartre, Simone had always called on people to vote for him? He might very well not have been elected without the women's vote. My worry grew as the hours went by—what if there were only a handful of us the next day?

At breakfast, Lionel announced that he wouldn't be able to escort Hélène to the funeral.

"I'm still too weak. I get dizzy. You'll take care of her. . . ."

It didn't surprise me; he was still recuperating from his surgery and wasn't strong.

The following day, we made sure to leave early. Even so, we had great difficulties making our way through to the temporary mortuary of Cochin Hospital. Journalists from all over the world and large numbers of women, arms filled with flowers, were obstructing the entrance. The crowd kept growing.

Entering the dark room, we were shocked. Lying in her coffin, Simone seemed tiny. So imposing when she was alive, she suddenly looked very frail. She was dressed in a pretty silk shirt and a pair of pants and had her headband on. On her left hand she had a watch with flower motifs and the Mexican ring that Nelson Algren had given her. In spite of the hurt, in spite of the insulting article and the American writer's wish to sell Simone's letters, she had kept on her finger this token of their passion. For the sixteen years that I had known her, she had always worn it.

On the other side of the coffin, Sylvie was crying. Hélène collapsed. I held her up as best I could until Lanzmann came over and took her in his arms. He, too, found himself unable to stop weeping. He had loved Simone, had been her last lover and then her best friend. In the past there had been some tension between Hélène and him, but on that day he was able to bring her comfort. Between fits of sobbing, Hélène kept repeating:

"She protected me for seventy-six years, what will become of me now?"

I tried to reassure her, reminding her that Lionel and I would be there to take care of her. Sylvie and Lanzmann chose to walk behind the hearse. Hélène got into the back seat with two cousins, Madeleine de Bishop and Jeanne, née de Beauvoir; Gégé Pardo, a friend of both sisters, followed. I sat next to the driver.

The cortege started off amid total disorder. On Rue Saint-Jacques, the crowd barred the way. Finally, the car reached the neighborhood where Simone had spent her entire life: Avenue Denfert-Rochereau, Boulevard Raspail, Boulevard Montparnasse. In front of La Coupole, there was silence, and Hélène held back a sob. Just as for Sartre, the waiters were standing outside on the sidewalk, their napkins over their left arms, forming an honor guard. Almost every day for forty years, Simone had lunched there with Sartre.

Near us, young *lycée* students marched with roses in hand. Now aged, the group of 1968 was there, acting like well-behaved children. A few politicians, Lionel Jospin and Michel Rocard among them, participated in the march. They slipped in among the crowd and avoided the photographers. Their circumspection pleased Hélène who, in the back, was reminiscing about her childhood. The Beauvoir cousins answered her, laughing at times. Sitting in front of them, I realized that the blood ties that Simone had wanted to ignore at all costs had not completely vanished from her life.

Suddenly the crowd became very dense. I could see some pushing and shoving ahead of us. My heart contracted. In a few moments, we would have to confront the final ordeal. Hélène leaned forward toward me and whispered:

"We've arrived, haven't we?"

I confirmed that we had. She put a nervous hand on my shoulder.

We remembered the panic that had reigned at Sartre's funeral, the violence of the journalists, the blows, Simone's fainting attacks, Lanzmann's fearlessness. There was no doubt, the same nightmare was about to begin again. The gates of the Montparnasse Cemetery opened slightly. Curious bystanders were amassing behind the barriers. City Hall had taken proper measures to protect the cortege. I helped Hélène and her cousins out of the car. In front of the grave, Lanzmann took out one of Simone's books and read a few lines. In a low voice, together with the women of the Movement and those close to us, I recited the refrain of the MLF, whose words Simone had loved so much:

> We who have no past,
> Women,
> We who have no history
> Since the dawn of time,
> Women,
> We are the black continent!
> Arise, women enslaved
> Let us break our shackles!
> Arise! Arise!

With the reporters' cameras flashing, Hélène sent her sister a final kiss, then broke down in tears in my arms. After the ceremony, she whispered to me:

"Did you notice Sylvie's attitude? She never even looked at me. If it hadn't been for me, she wouldn't be Simone's adopted daughter. . . . What harm did I ever do her?"

The friction that had poisoned the atmosphere at Sartre's death surged up again. Simone had suffered the humiliation of being unable to have a few moments to herself in Sartre's apartment and forbidden to retrieve her father's books. No longer Simone's heir, Hélène was not permitted to go to Simone's home to say goodbye to the place her sister had cherished. While Simone had received a chair and a pair of shoes as her only inheritance, Hélène only got an old coat that had belonged to her sister. Concerned about his wife, Lionel said with his usual wisdom:

"Hélène, we have nothing else to do in Paris. Let's go home."

■   ■   ■

"This is the painting of my grieving," Hélène told me a few weeks later in Goxwiller. I was speechless. *Portrait of Simone in a Red Jacket* brought back so many memories. Simone looked at peace; her face bore no traces of pain. She was strangely familiar, leaning back in her cushions, the way I had so often seen her.

"I'm going to put this painting in my room, facing the bed," Hélène said to me. "That way I can see my sister as I fall asleep and as I wake up."

I took her in my arms.

"And Sartre? Did you ever paint him?"

"No, I didn't dare. I wouldn't have wanted to show his ugliness, and it would have been difficult to make him good-looking."

Standing in front of Simone's portrait, I asked:

"You will continue painting, won't you?"

"Of course, it's what keeps me alive."

Then I remembered what Hélène so often said about her sister to new visitors:

"It's not just by chance that two sisters who are so different in temperament share a similar attitude toward life. Simone and I both desperately wanted a life that would be unlike that of our mother, our aunts, and all those virtuous and resigned women who only speak of duty. We wanted happiness, life; we wanted to create."[11]

Letters arrived in Goxwiller from every continent. Simone continued to be present from beyond the grave. Readers, academics, and activists all wanted to meet Simone's sister. Gradually, Hélène began to enjoy this new role; she was becoming the center of attention and answering researchers' questions. Through her Simone survived. Surrounded by her cats, with her sister's portrait in front of her, Hélène offered her visitors tea. In the Louis XVI chair she had inherited from her parents, she told anecdotes about the woman who had been such an influence on her throughout her life. In August of that same year, she granted an interview to *Elle* magazine, titled "My Sister, Simone."

With Simone gone, with the help of Marcelle Routier Hélène wrote her memoirs, which were published in 1987. Her adventures with Simone and Lionel, and the trips abroad she so enjoyed recounting to her friends, now became public knowledge. The book received critical acclaim but did not become popular. It was a disappointment to her, but she didn't show it. She was happier when, in 1991, a book devoted to her painting was published by Côté-Femmes. Little by little, Hélène regained strength and found renewed hope. A new life seemed to be opening up for her. However, after all the pain and sorrow, a new ordeal awaited her.

CHAPTER SIX

Goxwiller

D espite her seventy-six years, Hélène continued painting in her studio for hours on end. Lionel, on the other hand, although three years her junior, seemed tired. Hélène watched her husband hunched over his desk in the library, his face twisted in pain. With his right hand he was covering his ear.

"Lionel, what's going on?"

"I'm dizzy. I don't feel well."

"I'm calling the doctor."

Hélène was living through another nightmare at home. She was still recovering from her sister's death a few months before, and now her husband was falling ill. Now retired from the European Council, Lionel continued to organize cultural trips to archeological sites in Greece and Turkey. But gradually he had had to restrict his activities and abandon journeys that were too long and exhausting.

"Hélène, do you think I'll be able to take those trips again some day?"

"Of course, Lionel, and soon, too, but first you should get some rest."

The doctors couldn't figure out the exact cause of his dizzy spells, other than the problems with his inner ear and weakness due to old age and his earlier tuberculosis. On the days when he felt better, Hélène took him on walks in the Vosges. They would choose one of their familiar paths and walk until they were weary. Then Lionel felt that his legs were fine and that his once so tormented spine remained healthy. He put his arms around Hélène and murmured:

"You're right, I'm still in good shape."

They would then return home to some hot tea and their two cats. On days like that, Hélène didn't have the energy to go back to her studio but, in the gentle dusk, her husband's smile was a solace to her. Sadly, the intervals never lasted very long. Doctors, medications, blood tests, x-rays, dizzy spells, and pain now regulated the couple's life. Finally, Lionel had to be hospitalized again at La Salpêtrière in Paris for an indefinite period of time. Hélène came with him and stayed with me.

"I feel I'm reliving the last days of my mother all over again. Lionel is in pain. And I can't do anything for him. . . . I don't want him to endure what the doctors made my poor mother go through. She suffered for more than a month, and with Lionel it keeps going on and on, with ups and downs."

I tried to console her but couldn't. I decided to take her to the movies with a friend to see *The Music Master*. In an easy chair at dinner she spoke of the years they had spent in Milan, the happiest years of her life, of evenings when she had dined with Maria Callas who was giving a recital at La Scala. Her voice still trembled at the memory, and she lamented that a "woman with so many reasons to be entitled to some happiness had been so unhappy." She was grumbling about Jacqueline Kennedy who, as she put it, had achieved nothing very remarkable in life other than marrying millionaires. At the time we didn't yet know about the letters Simone had sent to Nelson Algren in which she voiced some acerbic criticism of John Kennedy's widow. As evening fell over Paris, Hélène returned to memories of Françoise de Beauvoir.

"When our mother became sick, Simone and I took turns by her bedside. We were there for each other. This is the first time I'm going through a family drama like this all by myself."

I reassured her. No, she was not alone. Sandro, Lionel's adopted son, Sandro's mother Monique, his sister Chantal, and I were there for her.

Simone and Hélène.

Hélène in her studio.
© Victor Koshkin-Youritzin

Lionel in his office with
part of a painting by
Hélène behind him.
© Sandro Agenor

The author at an abortion march in 1971.
© Catherine Deudon

Hélène and Lionel in
Oklahoma in 1979.
© Claudine Monteil

Simone, Hélène, and Yvette Roudy, then minister of women's rights, at the opening of Hélène's exhibit at the Ministry of Women's Rights, three months before Simone's death in 1986.

Hélène and the author at Simone's funeral.

Hélène and the author in Nice on the day that the author presented her thesis on Simone at the university in 1984.

The author, Hélène, and friend in a Paris restaurant in 1995.

The author, Hélène, and Carol Downer in the
painter's studio in front of her feminist painting
Les Femmes Souffrent, Les Hommes Jugent (Women Suffer,
Men Judge).

The author in front of a painting of Simone done by Hélène in 1936.

Of course, we couldn't possibly replace her beloved sister, but we could at least support her with our love. She sighed, then added in the heat of the conversation:

"It's hard living without Simone. On Sunday mornings I expect her to phone me. She doesn't. Sometimes I feel like dialing her number and then I stop. Do you understand?"

I remembered the nights of insomnia after Sartre's death, Simone's illness, the months of grieving and the crying spells. I knew Hélène would soon know more sorrow. At last, Lionel was able to leave the hospital and go back to Goxwiller. Two days later Hélène phoned me. In a broken, gasping voice she said:

"The doctor told me that Lionel shouldn't stay in the bedroom anymore. We have to set up a hospital bed that is wider and more comfortable for him here at the house. I'm in the process of moving the dining table into my room. Lionel will be better off this way, but the house will look like a nursing home."

She was sobbing:

"I want him to end his days at home."

In his bed, Lionel continued reading. He took notes from humanities and history books "for his upcoming trips." We encouraged him. Hélène no longer went out other than to go to her studio in the back of the garden. Their house in Trebiano was closed up. I went to Goxwiller frequently, now staying in Lionel's old room.

In December 1989, for New Year's Eve, we set the table with an embroidered tablecloth and crystal glasses. Wearing a gray lace dress, her hair pulled back, and with light makeup, Hélène did not look her seventy-nine years. She wore an old silver necklace, inherited from her mother, which enhanced her elegance. A glass of champagne in her hand, she was no longer able to hide her distress.

It was a sad evening. In the former dining room, which was now the sickroom, Lionel dined alone, as he couldn't sit at the table. Pillows supported his back. His oxygen tank was within reach, and he needed it often. In addition to his earaches and dizzy spells, he now also had moments when he could hardly breathe. Confined to the house, barely able to wander as far as the library, he had no energy left. His body was gone. Lionel had nothing further to expect from life and he knew it.

A few months later, with his beloved by his side, Lionel left this life. This time, we had to cross the river to the Right Bank and climb up the paths of Père-Lachaise Cemetery to bring him to his final resting place in the Roulet family vault. Supported by Sandro, Hélène walked behind the coffin, in a black suit and gloves, a lace handkerchief in her hand. Only friends who had come to be with her attended—Gégé Pardo, and her son Frédéric, who was Sartre's godson and a painter as well. Hélène was now the only one left of her generation; with Lionel, the last witness to her youth had disappeared. As she had done for Simone, she threw a few roses into the grave and blew some kisses to the man who had made her happy for more than fifty years.

That evening we had dinner in a restaurant close to my apartment with Sandro, Gégé, Lionel's sister, and a few other friends. The Montparnasse neighborhood was changing. New buildings were replacing the old town houses and artist studios. I accompanied Hélène to La Rotonde and La Closerie des Lilas, two of Simone's favorite restaurants, after going by the cemetery first. Even if she didn't believe in the hereafter, she wanted to "tell" Simone that she, too, had now lost her partner. Then I took her back to the station:

"Come back to Paris, Hélène, you must."

She managed to smile at me, got into the train and, turning around, added:

"Fortunately, I still have my studio. Come and see me soon. I'll certainly have some new paintings to show you."

As the train moved off into the mist, I felt renewed hope. The creative work of the Beauvoir sisters sprang from an inexhaustible well, and Hélène's was far from being depleted.

▮   ▮   ▮

Four years had gone by since Simone's death and a few months had passed since Lionel's. Climbing the stone staircase in Goxwiller, I found Hélène looking pale, exhausted, and with circles under her eyes. Usually so sparkling and warm, her glance seemed lifeless. In a shaky voice she whispered:

"Come in, quickly."

In the living room, surrounded by her cats, she poured tea and we drank in silence. Finally, I ventured:

"What is going on?"

Open on the table lay the first volume of Simone's letters to Sartre. Hélène put her cup down wearily.

"I thought I'd already experienced the greatest pain of my life. But," she added in one breath, "I was wrong. All Simone does in these letters is disparage me! And I thought she loved me! Listen to this: 'Dreary session at the Salon de Mai with my sister and Roulet. It was a question of proving to myself that the other painters her age are as bad as she is—and it's almost true'!"[1]

She burst into tears. I took her into my arms and held her close.

"Hélène, these words are meaningless. They may have been written in a moment of passing irritation, as so often happens. It didn't prevent her from loving you and being happy when she was with you. I saw her with you. She really loved you, do you hear me?"

How could she hear me? At eighty years of age, it was a brutal revelation and one she had difficulty accepting. She had admired her sister since her early childhood, had confided in her, had supported her during hard times, and ceaselessly proven her affection for Simone. Now, in these letters, Simone was critical of the official posts held by Lionel, whom she couldn't forgive for having become part "of the system." She ridiculed her sister's painting, which in her view was worthless. I thought of Marcel Proust's words on the aberrations of the heart. If the older sister's judgments were sometimes biting and uncompromising, this didn't mean that she had not loved Hélène. Besides, she wasn't the only one to be mistreated: Simone and Sartre's closest friends, their freely chosen "family," were victims of her caustic pen as well.

"Simone and Lionel were the two great loves of my life," Hélène went on. "How could anyone have allowed these pages to be published while I am still here? What did I do to deserve this?"

That evening, she spent a long time wondering about Sylvie's course of action—had Hélène herself not agreed to it, she could never have been adopted. She had welcomed her as her own niece. Once the formalities had been taken care of, Sylvie had talked to her only twice, to tell her about Simone's hospitalization and then about her death. Hélène began to wonder if perhaps adopted families are jealous of those who are connected by blood. In any event, she didn't understand the antagonism against her. I myself was crushed by it. For sixteen years, I had watched Simone protect her sister, even if she occasionally bullied her as well. I had been on good terms with Sylvie for many years, and her actions left me speechless.

Hélène wept bitterly, her face in her handkerchief. Sartre hadn't spared the younger sister either. In his letters to Simone, the philosopher had also used cruel humor at Poupette's expense.[2]

These revelations were extremely cruel, coming at a time when Hélène could no longer turn to her sister to question her. She caught her breath and remembered her sister's warm words in the various volumes of her memoirs.

"Look," she said to me as she opened the dresser drawer, "read the letters she wrote me. Look at those sweet words, those are signs of love!"

I recognized Simone's broad and slanted handwriting on the yellowed paper. Full of loving comments and funny anecdotes, they had such a different tone from the one she used when writing to Sartre! Here there was no disdain at all, just warm, protective, entertaining words. Hélène showed me more than eighty letters from Simone, all of them loving and complicit. Later on, Hélène tried to have them published but she needed Sylvie Le Bon–de Beauvoir's permission for that, which the latter did not grant her. And yet publication of those letters would have confirmed a different reality.

Among the correspondence I also found a text that Sartre had written for the catalogue of the Brest exhibition in April 1975:

"The work shown by Hélène de Beauvoir today is the culmination of lengthy research. She discovered early on that by producing illusory work one fails to expect things: still, she loves nature—forests, gardens, lagoons, plants, animals, and the human body—too much to forsake their inspiration. Between the vain restrictions of imitation and the aridity of the purely abstract, she has created her own path. Loathing trompe l'oeil, she has deliberately rediscovered the naïveté of the primitives who set their universe down on flat surfaces; but in this imaginary space, freed from the laws of perspective, the outline of a flower, a horse, a bird or a woman evokes reality. In *Alice in Wonderland*, a cat disappears leaving only a smile for the astonished onlooker; it is the same in the paintings of Hélène de Beauvoir, where joy and anguish emanate with gripping evidence from images whose outlines have not been traced. There is nothing gratuitous in these compositions, where form and background, inventions and evocations intermingle at their own dictates. Nevertheless, a blissful exuberance shines through the rigor. Beyond her collective inventions, the painter loses herself without reserve in the pleasure of painting, and that is why her work seduces us."[3]

Hélène reread the article with a gloomy look in her eye, put it down again, and pondered the volume of letters.

"For me, what she wrote is dreadful. I will never get over it. Simone and Lionel are gone. And now these letters. . . . I've lost everything. Everything."

I was appalled. Mail from all over the world sent by women—often academics and activists—who had admired Simone, was piling up on the table. As her sister used to do, Hélène would answer every one of them:

"That way I feel Simone is still near me," she often said. What would happen from here on in? Added to her loss was the stab of betrayal that called into question many of her happy memories.

Hélène chose to condemn the publication of Simone's letters to Sartre in the daily newspaper *Les Dernières Nouvelles d'Alsace*. She didn't understand why it had been permitted to print such abomination about someone who was still alive. But the sentences that were insulting to her were not the only reason for her pain. She was upset to see that her sister's love affairs with young girls were displayed in the bright light of day.

Hélène felt great solidarity with the struggle for gay rights. She was to show this when she agreed to an interview about her painting with a homosexual feminist publication, *Lesbia Magazine*.[4] She was aware of Simone's penchant for affairs with women but hadn't thought it very important. Not just Olga but several other female students had surrendered to the charm of her older sister while they were still minors.[5] Did this betray a lack of perception on Hélène's part? Doubt tormented her. She looked at me questioningly.

"You know, Hélène, we weren't aware of Simone's bisexuality either."

"Simone was always very discreet about that. For years I thought that the Department of National Education had mistreated her by firing her during the war." Simone had been readmitted after the war, but had resigned to concentrate on her writing. "Now I know I was wrong. My sister should never have wooed her students. Today I understand why the parents of those girls lodged a complaint against her."

I thought of our Sunday meetings. Simone froze when anyone tried to question her about her attraction to her students. She denied and denied and denied it. She was undoubtedly worried about the damage it could do to her family and her reputation. Yet she had never taken the necessary precautions to spare those close to her from discovering after her death what she had so carefully hidden from them while she was alive.

Later, Hélène read Bianca Lamblain's[6] account. A Jewish girl, she had been courted by Simone under the Occupation, then pushed into Sartre's arms to form the trio so dear to the author of *Being and Nothingness*. Then, at the height of the war and heedless of the consequences, Simone and Sartre abandoned her. When their correspondence was published, Bianca, too, discovered passages concerning her. In these sections Simone, whom she had loved so much, expressed profound disdain for her. In retaliation, with rage in her heart, she wrote her version of their affair. It was a damning version for the two mandarins. Hélène began to wonder, furthermore, whether that particular episode had not been the real reason for Sartre's adopting Arlette. Since she was Jewish as well, perhaps it had allowed Sartre to ease his guilt for his cowardice and foolhardiness during the war.

"After reading her testimony, I immediately wrote to Bianca," Hélène told me. "I wanted her to know that I knew how much she had suffered. And she did answer me. The publication of those letters destroyed both of us."

I covered Hélène's hand with mine.

"Simone loved you, Hélène, I know it, I can vouch for that. In those very closed literary circles, they all criticized each other and sneered at those who weren't part of their group. That didn't stop your sister from being very fond of you."

The younger one nodded her head. She knew my arguments by heart.

And yet she needed to hear them over and over again, like the refrain of a familiar piece of music. Reassured for a moment, she would listen to me, and then doubt would regain the upper hand. She'd raise her head and the leitmotiv began again:

"But still, how could they possibly have published these letters? How?"

■ ■ ■

Alone at home now with her cats, Hélène painted with desperate energy. In *Le Grand Paquebot* (*The Great Ocean Liner*), a ship moves away from the shore. The paper streamers that had linked it to the wharf are broken, and on the pier a woman is gathering up bits of paper.

"I am that woman," Hélène told me. "Lionel and I used to love that custom, throwing streamers to the passengers who were heading for the open sea."

"You haven't done a new portrait of him?"

"No. I didn't have the courage. And besides, I already have one close by me, done when he was still young. My beloved dead are here, in paint."

My visits were not enough to alleviate her solitude. I urged her to come to Paris and go out. She accepted, met some new people, had a show in Brussels. She helped prepare a book on her work.[7] After the publication of her memoirs in 1987, this book brought her a measure of comfort and reassurance:

"You see, Claudine, my work as an artist is recognized."

"Of course it is, and it will be even more so in the future, you'll have other exhibits. And your book is going to be translated into German."

"Yes, and I'm delighted about that. My paintings have always sold well on the other side of the Rhine. No doubt because of the ecological themes—and my defense of women."

I felt comforted. Hélène had plenty of projects.

"I met a charming couple who are wild about my work. They want to make a famous painter of me. They do not understand why, with my talent, my friends haven't already helped me to become known all over the world. They have a few ideas for exhibits and are coming to Goxwiller to pick up some paintings and have them shown."

These words caught my attention. She had thrown herself into a whirlwind of activity but it had not managed to hide her heartache. At almost eighty-five, Hélène was still vulnerable.

"I'm convinced that some fine years are waiting for me," she said to me over dinner. I wanted to believe her but inside I wasn't so sure. Her sudden infatuation with unlikely exhibitions all over the planet made me cautious.

Hélène's health was deteriorating. A few months later she was diagnosed with a heart murmur. She would have to undergo open-heart surgery. Nevertheless, she was still climbing Mount Sainte-Odile and the Champ du Feu, and hiking in the Vosges every week. Those of us close to her all had the same concern: perhaps the operation might leave her worse off than she was.

"I am going downhill physically," she confided to me. "No doubt it is my age, and then the accumulation of all the hard times. Simone's death, Lionel's death, and the publication of those letters have really worn me out. But I'd rather have the surgery, they're very skilled at this operation now, I'm told."

For her own survival, she immersed herself in her work. In spite of her arthritis, which made her hands very rigid, Hélène painted from morning to night in her light-filled studio, with the voice of Callas resounding. The artist wouldn't let herself be imprisoned by sadness.

"Despite everything, life is beautiful," she repeated to me with what seemed overstated conviction. The operation was postponed for a few weeks. Before it took place Hélène wanted to take a trip to revisit the shores of her youth. A friend from Portugal had come to visit her in Goxwiller, and in the studio, behind dusty partitions, he had found paintings done during the war in Alvaro, Oporto, and Lisbon. The painter wouldn't show them. She was only interested in her current work and that of recent years, while the canvases from before were soon forgotten. However, the idea of a pilgrimage, a return to the source, had roused her interest:

"I haven't been back to Portugal since the war, when I married Lionel," she told me emotionally. "Fifty years have gone by. Please come with me!"

I accepted. Monique would also join us. In spite of her shows during World War II, Portugal had not paid any attention to Hélène for half a century, which gave our journey a special significance. This time, she had been officially invited by the University of Aveiro, in southern Portugal, for the opening of three exhibits devoted to all her paintings from her Portuguese period.

The president of the republic at that time, Mario Soares, was supposed to be present but broke his arm the day before and had to cancel his visit. The Minister of Culture came to represent him. Inside one of the ultramodern university buildings, Hélène gave a lecture on women and creativity, a subject crucial to the understanding of her work and about which people had asked Simone's advice many times without bothering to ask her. It was time for Hélène to expound loud and clear on the injustice done to women artists. She knew the agony of their path all too well.

"All you need to see is the misogyny that governs the French museums," she would say to me. "The locations of the work of Suzanne Valadon leave much to be desired. Few of the paintings of Sonia Delaunay are exhibited in comparison to the number of her husband's, although she was a very fine painter. He himself recognized that it was she who gave him the enthusiasm for painting.[8] And Viera da Silva has just one small painting in the hallway."

I understood her frustration.

"The creative work of a woman isn't taken seriously," Hélène would say again. "I wish creative women would receive the same recognition as their male colleagues, that is to say, be seen as professionals."

The television cameras and photographers' lenses were not focused on Simone anymore. It was her sister who now received unexpected attention and glory. Hélène recited the damning history of women artists who had been forgotten throughout the centuries. To those who heard her, the subject seemed inexhaustible and the obstacles still huge.

Large in number and tightly compressed, the audience listened silently. The new Portuguese generation preferred English, and in the last fifty years the French language had lost its standing as the international language of choice. Still, academics, painters, writers, and female politicians had come from Oporto and from Lisbon, too. They were amazed and excited when they saw the paintings showing the life of peasants, farmers, and workers in the Portugal of the forties.

"This Portugal no longer exists!" they told her. "Today your work belongs to the national heritage of Portugal!"

Hélène assented. Her painting paid luminous homage to the people who worked so hard. Scenes in the fields and hunched-over women working in the salt marshes revealed a critical view of social life. At the time, when the artist was thirty years old, she had relinquished intimist scenes in favor of a harder and more truthful reality.

This time, she held her own. She didn't hear a single allusion to her sister. At the end of the day, she donated her paintings to the University of Aveiro for the creation of a museum that would bear her name. She felt at peace with herself. Returning to the source had brought her unanticipated energy. I was dumbfounded and thrilled.[9]

The day before our return to Paris, we visited a wine cellar in Porto. The owner, who had been alerted to Hélène's arrival, brought her three glasses of old port on a silver tray:

"Taste this, Madame!"

Hélène forgot her fatigue and, smiling, drank all three glasses. In the evening, she listened to *fado* music until two A.M. We were exhausted, but Hélène was caught up in an unbelievable whirlwind:

"In one more week I'm having surgery. I want to take advantage of these last few moments!" she cried out as she let the music sway her. How well I understood. Her heart murmur didn't seem to bother her. And yet her days and hours were numbered. She knew it herself. At the airport, Hélène kissed me goodbye, cheerful and delighted with her trip.

"See you next week at the hospital!"

■　■　■

The months went by. Back home, after heart surgery and a lengthy convalescence in a rehabilitation center, Hélène spent her time reading mail, newspapers, and books. She wandered through the house at a slow pace. The days followed one another without a single visit to her studio, without any painting. Near her on the large couch, the telephone was her only connection with the outside world. But the calm did not last. Some weekends, the couple whom she had befriended returned. The house filled with cries and laughter, bawdy jokes told loudly for all to hear. Madame Marie, the housekeeper, was ousted from the kitchen. These people wanted to take care of everything. They went to the bank and generously settled Madame Marie's salary and the bills through Hélène's account.

"I'm very happy with these new friends," Hélène kept repeating to me. "Thanks to them, I shall soon be really famous."

Hope sprouted in her, a hope that reinvigorated her after all these years of grief and desolation. I understood. However, jewelry disappeared and silver started to go missing. At the same time, a young woman came to help Hélène with the housekeeping. She pushed Madame Marie around in the kitchen:

"Move over, you are too old! Just let me do it! Come on now, let go!" She could hear the yelling. At eighty-five, Madame Marie continued to be loyal to the woman for whom she had worked for years. Still, because of problems with her back, she couldn't climb stairs any longer. Like Hélène, Madame Marie was born in 1910. She had known Alsace under the German Occupation. She had worked as a maid in Paris before returning to her own region and getting married. A handicapped child was born from this marriage. She started working for the Roulets at the age of sixty, and also worked on a farm and delivered newspapers early in the morning. She watched over Hélène and those close to her unobtrusively. But those days were over. Hélène, in her much weakened state, listened to the household staff argue with each other.

"I will not go back to Madame de Roulet," Madame Marie told me one time when I was visiting, "it hurts too much."

Thereafter, the house was often handed over to the couple who intended to lead Hélène on to glory. One day, a van arrived from Paris to pick up numerous paintings and about a hundred engravings, the most beautiful of them all. In the village, the neighbors were upset. Not long after this, I mentioned the sudden removal and asked:

"Where will they be exhibited?"

"I don't know the exact place yet, but there will be one or two large shows."

"You didn't find out first what the names of the galleries are?"

"Of course, not. I trust them. It's important in life to trust your friends."

On my next visit, I noticed her car had disappeared.

"The new housekeeper who helps me out suggested she should buy it from me, so I sold it to her."

"Did she pay you?"

"No."

"But she did give you a down payment, of course?"

"No, she doesn't have much money, you see. But don't worry, she will settle up with me as soon as she can."

The inhabitants of the village, perplexed, watched a young woman drive around at the wheel of the car that belonged to the woman they considered their chatelaine. Hélène was very much loved in Goxwiller: for years she had spent evenings correcting the homework of many children who came knocking on her door. She would make hot chocolate or lemonade for them and gently reread their compositions or have them repeat their multiplication tables. She greeted her neighbors, and sometimes they gave her a head of lettuce, a few tomatoes, or flowers from their garden. Rumors had been spreading ever since the couple had appeared. The house wasn't the same anymore. Strange things were happening there. How would all this end? They were sad for her, but what could they do? And then the farmers would go on their way, sighing about the passage time and the distressing loneliness of the aged.

The paintings and engravings were not returned. Unexpected expenditures emerged on a regular basis and the "new friends" didn't have a nickel—they needed financial help. Hélène hoped in vain for the great exhibitions that were supposed to bring her the recognition she had dreamed of for so long. Against this backdrop, a telephone call came that made us realize something was wrong. The bank phoned and requested that money be deposited in Madame de Roulet's account, which was vastly overdrawn. Hélène was no longer able to travel, she wasn't spending money on painting anymore, and her only entertaining consisted of visits from her friends. Lionel had left her with a comfortable widow's pension and a portfolio of stocks, so she shouldn't have had any financial concerns whatsoever. However, the bank was quite businesslike. Hélène owed money; what Lionel had saved all his life had melted away in two years' time. Almost every week, Madame de Roulet had signed checks for several thousand francs[10] to pay the expenses of her "friends." At the age of eighty-seven she found herself ruined. It was a catastrophe, in addition to which many of her paintings had vanished. If the disbursements continued, she would soon have to mortgage her house.

Hélène did not seem to be aware of the danger she was in. She kept repeating happily:

"I don't need much to live."

It was true. After the surgery, she had not regained her strength, and all she could do was read. The studio remained locked. When I brought up her financial situation she would invariably tell me that it didn't matter and avert her eyes. One evening, she admitted that she felt lost. She looked over at Simone's and Lionel's portraits on the wall. She took my hand and added:

"It's hard to be alone with one's dead."

During the following months, Hélène agreed to have her legal affairs taken in charge. A first guardianship was established under the control of an agent from Strasbourg. A second one, a year later, came under the control of the French state. Not a single person from her close circle was in any way connected to this guardianship. We insisted that the latter be executed without any ambiguity and in complete confidence. Hélène no longer had any checks at her disposal and soon her bank account returned to normal. The couple planned to visit her house in Trebiano to collect paintings that were essential for the great exhibitions in the making. An old friend of Lionel and Hélène exclaimed on the phone:

"Let them come, I'll be waiting with a rifle!"

The "friends," no longer able to obtain any money, slowly stopped coming. They no longer came to sit by Hélène's bedside. Occasionally, a phone call reminded her of their existence. In six years she did not receive a single visit from them, nor did the money for the paintings they had supposedly sold ever arrive. The canvases and engravings were never returned. Perhaps they will emerge one day in an auction room. As for the international exhibits, they never took place.

■ ■ ■

Thereafter, Hélène was preoccupied with other matters—she wanted to stay in her house until her death. She made us all promise—Sandro, his sister Chantal, me, and her cousin Catherine—that she wouldn't end her life in a nursing home. We gave her our word. It was not an easy thing. December 1995 was the first Christmas Hélène spent lying in bed. She had great difficulty moving from one room to another.

"Wake me during the night if you need to get up."

"Yes, I promise."

She got up by herself, missed a step, and crumpled to the ground in the entryway, screaming. I jumped out of bed. Hélène was on the floor, moaning in excruciating pain. I called an ambulance. It was Christmas night, and snow was falling over the Alsatian countryside. We drove to the hospital in Strasbourg. Lying on the stretcher, Hélène was weeping:

"Take me home, right now."

"No, Hélène, first they have to take an x-ray and have a doctor examine you."

"But I'm fine."

The nurse protested: "No, Madame, you have been hurt."

At the hospital they discovered she had broken her hip. I thought of Simone and my promise to her that I would take care of her younger sister. I hadn't been able to avoid the worst. For Hélène, the past year had been one long bout of pain and hospital stays. I didn't dare hope any longer that her health would improve. And yet a few weeks later the younger Beauvoir sister was back home with her paintings and her cats.

"I have always been sad to lose my cats," she told me. "They don't live as long as we do, and then we miss them."

On her couch, her two new companions, Artemise the Siamese and Agathe, a European female, were huddled against her legs. They wouldn't leave her.

In the spring, leaning on a cane and helped by a home nurse, Hélène was able to go down to the garden; she watched the goldfish in their ponds and admired the new flowers. Passing by the studio, she gave it a rapid glance as if she didn't want to reopen an old wound.

"I'm still too tired to stand up and paint, but this coming summer I should be able to go back to my brushes."

I agreed with her. She sank down into an armchair and contemplated Goxwiller, her world. Her pension was barely enough to cover the expense of round-the-clock nursing care. The women who watched over her were mostly psychology students and brought a breath of youth to the house. Their presence helped me realize how many years had passed—May 1968, the struggles for women's rights with the Beauvoir sisters — it all seemed so long ago. When I mentioned these times to them, they would answer:

"Madame, we weren't born yet. It's history for us."

I then realized how much older I myself had grown. I was in the skin of a veteran now, nostalgic for the past. That same spring, Hélène had some good news. A couple of Germans who owned a gallery had managed to sell several of her paintings. She received the fruit of her labor from them and said to me:

"Every now and then I still earn my living with my artwork. Simone would have been pleased, don't you think?"

For a few moments she smiled her old smile, the one that had seduced Jean Giraudoux and Lionel, then very quickly immersed herself in her reading again, although it was hard to know whether her concentration on the book was real or make-believe.

Hélène gradually recovered from her fall. She would have lunch at the dining table, with some difficulty but always cheerfully. Her strength slowly and quietly returned. She was growing more serene again.

█   █   █

I picked up the telephone. The voice on the other end of the line was terribly upset. Hélène's home nurse had lost her composure:

"Madame de Roulet had visitors this afternoon. They were friends from Strasbourg who brought her the *Letters to Nelson Algren* written by her sister. They were just published. She started reading them but then fell asleep. What should I do?"

I shivered. I was convinced that another shock would be fatal for Hélène. The publication of Simone's letters to Sartre had already caused a wound that wouldn't heal. *Letters to Nelson Algren* contained unbelievably condescending words about Poupette. If she read them, she would suffer enormously and end her days in despair. I caught my breath and answered firmly:

"Hide the book!"

"But what should I tell her when she wakes up?"

"Tell her she finished the book."

"She won't believe me."

"Try it anyway. And make sure the book disappears."

Shaking, I hung up. What Simone had written to her lover about Hélène and Lionel would have absolutely destroyed her drained and fragile younger sister. Why make her suffer more than she already had? How could she have understood Simone's lack of compassion for Lionel when he lost his job in 1948? On January 26 of that year, Simone wrote to her lover in Chicago:

"My brother-in-law arrived yesterday. I had lunch with him and my mother, and all they did was quarrel, both of them wrong, both of them equally petty. . . . Of course, he's having a hard time since he just lost his job (in the wake of a general layoff of state functionaries) and has no roof over his head. A month from now my sister will return from Yugoslavia, they are broke and don't know what to do. . . . He thinks he has the <u>right</u> [underlinings are Simone de Beauvoir's] to get help from everyone, and I hate people who think they have the slightest right over <u>anyone at all</u>. . . . Furthermore, he was moaning because my sister is having another exhibition in June, when she will be showing her paintings in a gallery, and he claims that <u>I ought</u> to be there. . . . Well, I won't and you know the reason why. How can I give her any talent when she doesn't have any? . . . What she should do is make good paintings, and if she can't, let her quit. I cannot convince the public of her genius if she doesn't have any, just because I am her sister. . . ."[11]

The passage bewildered me. The small world of existentialists in

Saint-Germain-des-Prés right after the war was two-faced. The affection-ate face that was there for, and concerned about, the family, was the world I had known and seen with my own eyes—Simone attentive to Hélène, wor-ried about her, asking me questions about her well-being. I had experienced these signs of affection. I could still hear their laughter on the phone when they would be like two young girls in cahoots with each other. But then there was this intimate, private correspondence so entirely different in tone.

A few minutes after she awoke, Hélène looked for the book, but the nurse stuck to her guns. From her bed, Simone's sister cast a reproachful look at the woman, who was only trying to protect her. The following week, some other unthinking friends brought her as a present these "mar-velous" letters by Simone. The scene was repeated. When the third volume vanished, Hélène did not protest anymore. The letters to Nelson Algren re-tained their secret.

■   ■   ■

The twentieth century was coming to an end. On New Year's Eve, we managed to help Hélène to get up and sit at the dinner table. Madame de Roulet was no more than a ghost. She no longer fixed her light blue eyes on us with the same intensity. Huddled in an armchair, supported by pillows, she barely had the strength to drink a glass of Bordeaux and nibble on a piece of dark chocolate.

In the face of her silence and her difficulty eating, I felt a boundless nos-talgia. The happy dinners with Lionel, the cheese soufflés and chocolate mousses and ebullient conversations, that whole world peacefully observed by the cats from the Louis XVI chairs had disappeared forever. The house seemed inhabited by ghosts, and Hélène was its last phantom. Her hands trembled. I took a fork and helped her eat. Her frailty overwhelmed me. Over dessert, Hélène raised her head and looked for a long time at her por-trait of Simone in a red silk tunic, then at the one of Lionel as a young man:

"I like being here. I can look at my paintings. That's all I have left. I am with them."

Hélène signaled to me that she wanted to go back to bed. We gently placed her in the chair right next to her bed. I was alone with her now and helped her slip into a nightgown. Every motion was hard for her. Suddenly, she smiled at me:

"Claudine…"

"Yes, Hélène…"

She looked at me fixedly:

"I think I'm going to die soon."

The nightgown almost fell from my hands. My heart went wild. I had to collect my wits very quickly. I smiled back and made my voice firm:

"But of course not, Hélène, you're doing so much better than last year! Much, much better!"

Hope filled her voice:

"Do you think so? It's true, last year I was very tired. Tell me, do you think of Lionel? Remember, we were a good match, weren't we?"

"Yes, Hélène. Not only did you make him happy for fifty years but more important, you saved his life! Without your love, without your support he might never have recuperated from his tuberculosis. He might have remained paralyzed."

In just a few moments she seemed just as alert as in the old days. Her voice shaking, she asked:

"Tell me, do you believe my work will last?"

"Of course, Hélène!"

"Do they still mention my name in Paris?"

"They certainly do, Hélène, you are known and recognized! There is absolutely no need for you to worry."

Her emaciated little hands grasped mine and she gave me a look that was more like a plea:

"And it has nothing to do with the name of my sister, does it?"

"Nothing at all, Hélène. I assure you. You are known for your own work!"

"Ah, that makes me so happy. I miss Simone and Lionel so much. They loved my painting. Soon I'll be going back to my studio, won't I?"

"Yes, Hélène, but you'll have to wait a few days. It's still too cold now."

I put her to bed, then closed the window. The north wind had increased, and with it came an icy cold. She fell asleep in minutes, her features relaxed. Her lips showed something like a smile. We had talked about her painting and about the dead who were so much alive inside her. I had exaggerated her fame but felt no discomfiture about it. If her work was not listed with art dealers in France, it was still selling very well in Germany and Japan. In her bed, curled up under the sheets, Hélène seemed reassured.

■   ■   ■

Soon thereafter, she began to spend all her days and nights sleeping. Between naps, she read the newspaper or a review, such as *Les Temps modernes*,[12] to which she subscribed. It became automatic, a habit. Her attention dwindled after a few minutes, and then she'd fall back into her indolence.

Sometimes she'd call me and discuss things with a surprising presence of mind, just as she used to before her operation. Those moments of grace would fill me with joy and emotion. These lively, intelligent, funny conversations reminded me of the past. I'd think that Hélène, whom I loved so much, was coming back to life. But the next day she wouldn't remember that we had spoken at all.

On the morning of June 9, 2000, I went to Goxwiller filled with apprehension. The evening before, I had been alerted to the fact that Hélène was feeling very weak and was slipping into sleep and a state of melancholy. Her birthday was approaching: she would celebrate her ninetieth year, and her cousin Catherine, my partner, and I were determined to be with her on that particular day.

Around Verdun, I phoned Goxwiller. What if Hélène was not awake yet? To my surprise, it was not the nurse who picked up. Hélène herself answered and said in a rejuvenated, happy voice:

"My dear Claudine, there are flowers everywhere! It's a marvelous birthday! I can't wait to see you! We're really going to celebrate!"

She was waiting for us with makeup on, all dressed up. Her cheekbones and blue eyes reminded us how beautiful she had been. We put her in her favorite armchair. In the dining room Hélène watched everything:

"No, not those glasses, the fluted ones over there will be nicer. So, when are we having our champagne?"

Visitors and friends poured in. Catherine had come from Strasbourg. The neighbor, Madame Grucker, brought roses from her garden. The mayor and his assistant gave her a plant. Finally, the champagne was served. I brought in the birthday cake—a coffee-mocha cake—and she blew out the candles.

The house livened up. Hélène recounted her memories during the two-hour party. Simone's portrait on the wall seemed especially striking, and the bright oil colors made her seem even more present. In a corner above the bed in the small room, Lionel observed us with that enigmatic look of his, lips tightly closed. We listened intently to Hélène, the way one savors rare moments with a cherished person. In my mind I went back over the twenty-five years of our friendship and affinity. They were etched in my memory forever.

Before dinner, Hélène started to weaken and then slept for twenty-four hours straight. I had to wake her up to kiss her goodbye the next day before going home to Paris. She started, mumbling a few confused words. She had forgotten yesterday's party.

From that day on, her health continued to decline. Catherine would stop in on her several times a week. We all wanted to surround her with our loving presence, and visits from people close to her followed one after another in close succession. Telephone conversations became shorter, for Hélène had trouble catching her breath and in the earpiece I would hear her choking. One autumn evening she called me. She had just finished reading my biography of Sartre and Simone, *Les Amants de la liberté* (*The Lovers of Freedom*):

"I have just been reliving some happy moments," she told me with emotion. "And since neither Simone nor Sartre nor Lionel is here anymore, I was sad. I wanted to tell you, since you knew them, that I feel sad and a little lonely. You understand, don't you?"

I didn't know what to say to her. What could I possibly add? Then her voice filled with tears. Before hanging up, she added:

"It's done me so much good to hear your voice."

New Year's Eve 2001 was sad. Hélène had not retrieved the fleeting energy of June 9 again. When I said goodbye on January 2, her eyes welled up. Her smile had faded. So frail in her blue robe, she stared at me intensely, her gaze full of sadness.

"I'll see you very soon, Hélène," I told her, a little too loudly.

■   ■   ■

"What are you talking about?"

She startled me. Lying on the couch of the main room with Agathe, the cat, beside her, Hélène had awakened. The subject I had mentioned concerned her directly: it had to do with the sale of Simone's apartment. Anne Zelensky and I were trying to persuade the French government to buy it and turn it into a museum. It proved to be a difficult task.

Hélène tried to get up, but in vain. In one breath she muttered:

"That isn't possible! Simone would so have liked for her home to be turned into a museum or a women's shelter! The place is filled with history. You can't give up!"

Her hands were shaking.

"And what about the foundation project?"

"The one Anne proposed? That was abandoned a long time ago."

Hélène asked me to come closer. I leaned over the couch, as her voice was almost inaudible.

"So, there won't be any foundation or museum, and the apartment will be sold, is that it?"

"That's what it looks like, Hélène."

She closed her eyes, breathed again, and added:

"What a waste!"

I stayed by her side for a long time, her small hand in mine. As she rested, I was immensely sad. The apartment on Rue Schoelcher had stood guard over Simone during the most intense years of her life: her love affair with Claude Lanzmann, her evenings with Sartre and the team from *Les Temps modernes*, the Sundays when we prepared our battles for women's rights in France amid such good cheer. I tried hard not to cry.

The government didn't have time to study the file. A few weeks later there was a buyer for the apartment. Since then, we feminists have avoided Rue Schoelcher.

■　■　■

In May 2001, the guardianship could no longer find a nurse to watch over Hélène day and night. For three weeks she had to be hospitalized in Obernai. The nurses took very good care of her; they invariably answered our questions about her health by saying, "We put Madame de Roulet in front of the television, but she sleeps a lot."

Finally, by the end of May, she was able to go home. There was a wound on her right foot, and bedsores caused her tremendous pain, but the Beauvoir sisters had been taught not to complain about pain. After five years of physical ordeals and melancholy, Hélène wept only when her visitors left.

Every morning the nurse changed her bandages. Her moans came through the partition:

"My foot, I beg you, don't touch my foot."

Medications didn't help. The flesh on the underside of the foot had been slowly eaten away, and she couldn't walk anymore. She slept in the former dining room, transformed into a sickroom when Lionel's health had gone downhill. The love of her life had taken his last breath in the bed where she now lay. The only things that brightened up the room were a poster of a colloquium in which Simone had participated, a few photos of Lionel, and an engraving by Hélène, testimony of her work. The paintings, and particularly those of the people she loved, decorated other rooms in the house. We didn't dare move them. She would have understood that there was no hope.

Hélène wanted to leave the room that reminded her of too many sad events. She asked to be in her living/dining room, from which she could see the street, the neighbor's houses, the town's inhabitants, and the children on their way to school. The architecture of the house made it complicated to move her, as it consisted of two Alsatian houses connected to each other on several levels. You had to go up or down steps to get to the kitchen and living room. One nurse alone couldn't carry her from room to room. The only solution would have been a wheelchair, which Hélène refused.

Early in June we were all hoping that her foot would heal. Her birthday was approaching. We wanted to re-create the festive atmosphere of the year before when she had turned ninety. From Paris I phoned the mayor of Goxwiller, who was a warm, kind woman, and asked her to join us for tea. On June 9, Catherine and her husband met me at the Strasbourg train station.

"Hélène is worse, but she does remember that today is her birthday."

I ordered the same mocha cake in Obernai. Monique and the nurse had managed to carry Hélène to her favorite room, where she awaited us. A few bouquets of flowers brightened the living room. The mayor brought champagne. I thought of last year's celebration and felt a shock. Hélène wasn't speaking anymore. Her bandaged foot, on a pillow, caused her a great deal of pain at even the smallest touch. Her mouth sagged. It seemed that life had abandoned her body. Only her gaze proved she was there. One by one, we told her our funniest memories, hoping to pull her out of her torpor. She would nod her head, smile in spite of her visible exhaustion. I reminded her of our trip to the American West Coast. She muttered:

"I remember that very well," but so faintly that I had to read her lips.

She held out for two hours, then fell asleep. We laid her down on the couch. She spoke no more for the rest of our stay. In the evening, Monique and I helped her eat. The happy home had become a sanctuary. We didn't feel much like talking ourselves. I cut her food, held her fork, handed her a glass of Bordeaux. I needed to be there, to hold her hand, and to protect her. I knew that we had just shared her farewell tea and that this was her last birthday.

■   ■   ■

The next day I left for Paris with Monique. As at every other departure, she lay in her bed, head against her pillow, her face tense, turned toward the windows looking out over her garden. We leaned over to kiss her goodbye. She turned around and then closed her eyes. We left the house quietly.

The wound on her right foot grew larger over the next few days. The flesh was stripped, as if eaten away from the inside out. Antibiotics no longer worked.

"It's becoming more and more painful to change the bandages," her favorite nurse informed me, very upset. By mid-June, Hélène could hardly feed herself anymore. The wound continued to grow. Staphylococci were gnawing away at her bedsores and eating the flesh; they were afraid of septicemia. When Sandro contacted the doctor, he was told that Hélène's right leg should be amputated. He was startled. How could they think of doing such a serious operation on a lady her age? Emaciated as she was, she weighed less than a hundred pounds. It wasn't certain that she would even be able to withstand general anesthesia.

The few people close to Hélène, myself included, shared Sandro's feelings. It seemed madness to take such a risk when the end results were so precarious. We urged her to resist. Nevertheless, Hélène was taken out of bed to go to Strasbourg by ambulance to see a surgeon. Lying on a stretcher, all she could say was:

"I want to go home."

"Do you know what that means? We won't be able to guarantee anything where your health is concerned."

"Just let me die."

The ambulance took her home. A day later, the general practitioner returned to ask Hélène whether she was willing to let them operate. In the presence of the guardian, the nurse, and Sandro, who had come from Paris in a panic, she opened her eyes:

"I want to stay home."

"Madame de Roulet, are you aware of the consequences of this decision?"

"Leave me alone. Just let me die."

Hélène had made her decision. Despite her extremely feeble physical state, she was lucid; it was the same lucidity that was at the basis of her older sister's strength. Nobody could override her decision.

The doctor gave her no more than a few days, two weeks at the most. We all had the same desire: that Hélène not die in pain. On June 29, 2001, the doctors began to give her palliatives, doses of morphine to ease the pain. She no longer moaned when her bandages were changed, but the wound spread and consumed her flesh. The foot was black, with oozing pus. On June 30, Hélène stopped eating. She seemed to have sunk into a coma and we didn't know if she would come out of it. In Paris, I was frantic. For professional and family reasons I wasn't able to be by her bedside. On July 1, Catherine was with her. We phoned each other every two hours.

At ten after seven in the evening, Catherine went over to Hélène and said with a forced smile:

"Claudine just called, she sends a big kiss! You see, everyone is thinking of you!"

Poupette opened her eyes slightly. Did she understand these final words? A minute later, her cousin closed her eyes.

■   ■   ■

When I heard she was gone, I was speechless. I felt numb but not shattered.

"Hélène's suffering has come to an end," I thought. "She is at peace." I felt both the immense shock of bereavement and a certain sense of relief. Sandro and Catherine made arrangements for the funeral. I contacted the women's groups that had known her or been inspired by the two sisters. Phone calls and messages of support came pouring in. The reactions of the former MLF girls were similar to mine and to those of so many others:

"It's a little bit as if Simone has died a second time," they said, "but a warmer and more cheerful Simone."

Once again we were mourning a Beauvoir. Hélène's death was the death of the last witness of a generation that had changed the condition of women. It was with that in mind that we published the announcement of her death in *Le Monde*. The feminist groups that Simone had established, the Simone de Beauvoir Institute in Nantes, as well as forty associations, Yvette Roudy, and I paid a last tribute to the painter and feminist. It was best that way. Hélène had told me many times how much she wanted for Simone's friends to escort her to her final resting place.

On Thursday, July 5 at eleven A.M., we were in Père-Lachaise Cemetery. The two sisters were going to be separated forever. It was Simone's privilege not to have to leave the neighborhood of their childhood and to remain with her companion in the Montparnasse Cemetery. It was Hélène's destiny, as behooves a wife, to be interred beside her husband in the Roulet family vault. Hélène de Beauvoir became Madame Lionel de Roulet again, for all eternity.

There were just a few of us at the main entrance to the cemetery—nothing like the massive crowds at Sartre and Simone's funerals—with Sandro, Monique, close friends, and Lionel's sister Chantal with her son Ariel. Feminists and representatives of the various associations had left.

Behind Sandro and Catherine, we followed the cortege up the hills of the cemetery. It was drizzling and the walk seemed interminable. We slipped on the wet cobblestones. In my mind I heard Hélène's voice, her encouraging words. Tirelessly, joyfully, as if the words were fresh each time, "Be happy!" she had always said to me. Sandro read a text in which he described Hélène through the eyes of the little boy he once had been. Yolanda Astarita Patterson, president of the Simone de Beauvoir Literary Society, spoke of her memories of being with Hélène. I said a few words about her painting and her commitment to politics and feminism. Then we threw roses into the grave, her favorite flowers. Hand in hand, we walked back down the hill.

As we moved away, I kept thinking of the life force and energy that Simone and Hélène had bequeathed me. The moments of happiness we had shared resurfaced. Even before I left the cemetery, I knew what it was I had to do. With Simone and Hélène gone, I needed to bring them back to life.

At dawn the next morning, I started to write.

ENDNOTES

Prologue

[1] In the eighties, some women legally registered the acronym MLF (Mouvement de Libération des Femmes). As a result, they are the only ones who can lawfully claim membership in the MLF. However, in 1970, when the movement was created, and during the years in which the events described in these pages took place, the MLF was not meant to be either a party or a structure or a hierarchy. Besides, none of the women mentioned in this book who participated in the meetings at Simone de Beauvoir's house, felt that these legal steps applied to her.

[2] *Le Nouvel Observateur* is a very popular French left liberal weekly political magazine.

Two Dutiful Daughters

[1] Hélène de Beauvoir. *Souvenirs*. Remarks collected by Marcelle Routier. (Paris: Librairie Séguier, Garamond/Archambaud, 1987), p. 57.

[2] Ibid., p. 58.

[3] Simone de Beauvoir. *Tout Compte fait* (Paris: Gallimard, 1972), p. 15. [The book appeared in English under the title *All Said and Done*. However, as all

the passages quoted in this book were put into English by the translator of *The Beauvoir Sisters*, no page numbers are provided for the published English translations, unless otherwise indicated. Trans.]

4 Simone de Beauvoir. *Mémoires d'une jeune fille rangée* (Paris: Gallimard, 1958), pp. 63-64. (*Memoirs of a Dutiful Daughter*)

5 Ibid., p. 125.

6 Ibid., p. 130.

7 The *lycée* is the French secondary school, but rather more academic than the average American high school. It offers the only diploma that provides entry to the university.

8 Ibid., p. 109.

9 Ibid., pp. 190–192.

10 Ibid., p. 208.

Freedom

1 Ibid., p. 289.

2 Hélène de Beauvoir. *Souvenirs*, p. 289.

3 Ibid.

4 Ibid., p. 43.

5 Simone de Beauvoir. *Mémoires*, p. 331.

6 Hélène de Beauvoir. *Souvenirs*, p. 77.

7 Simone de Beauvoir. *Mémoires*, p. 433.

8 Ibid., p. 452.

9 Saint-Germain-les-Belles: literally "Saint-Germain the beautiful women."

10 Ibid., p. 456.

11 Ibid., p. 502.

12 Ibid., p. 503.

13 Jean Giraudoux was a well-known French writer and career diplomat.

14 The Jockey is a very popular bar in Montparnasse.

15 Simone de Beauvoir. *La Force de l'âge* (Paris: Gallimard, 1960), p. 28. (*The Prime of Life*)

16 Hélène de Beauvoir. *Souvenirs*, p. 127.

17 Ibid. The articles were published in February 1936.

18 The Cité Universitaire is the compound of combined student residence halls in Paris.

19 Hélène de Beauvoir. *Souvenirs*, p. 135.

20 Once it had dried, the painting was put in a corner of the studio and forgotten. Transported more than once when Hène de Beauvoir moved, it was found only fifty years later by a gallery owner. It now belongs to the

author.

21 The Front Populaire was a coalition of leftist parties that governed France from May 1936 until April 1938.

22 Simone de Beauvoir. *La Force de l'âge*, p. 384.

23 Ibid., p. 409.

24 *Les Chemins de la liberté* is the overall title of a trilogy consisting of *L'Age de raison*, *Le Sursis*, and *Morts sans sépultureI*. (*The Age of Reason*, *The Reprieve*, and *Troubled Sleep*)

25 Simone de Beauvoir. *Une Mort très douce* (Paris: Gallimard, 1964), p. 149. (*A Very Easy Death*)

26 During the war, there were two French Institutes in Lisbon, one supporting Pétain, the other De Gaulle.

27 Simone de Beauvoir. *L'Invitée* (Paris: Gallimard, 1943), p. 82.

28 The Prix Goncourt is the most prestigious annual literary prize in France.

29 Hélène de Beauvoir. *Souvenirs*, p. 164.

Achievement

1 Hélène de Beauvoir. *Souvenirs*, p. 186.

2 Simone de Beauvoir. *La Force des choses* (Paris: Gallimard, 1963), p. 346. (*Force of Circumstance*)

3 In 1898, Emile Zola wrote "J'Accuse" (I Accuse), an open letter to the President of the Republic that appeared in the newspaper *L'Aurore*, in which Zola criticizes the irregularities committed in the courtroom against Alfred Dreyfus, a Jew, in a scandal known as the Dreyfus Affair.

4 Simone de Beauvoir, *The Second Sex*, trans. H. M. Parshley (New York: Vintage Books, 1989), pp. 704-707.

5 Ibid., p. 707.

6 Simone de Beauvoir. *Un Amour transatlantique, Lettres à Nelson Algren* (Paris: Gallimard, 1997), p. 320, letter no. 150, 22 November 1949.

7 As recounted by Hélène de Beauvoir. Cf. also *Souvenirs*, p. 229.

8 *Arts*, 26 June 1954 and *Le Monde*, 28 May 1957.

9 *Simone de Beauvoir: un film*. Script by Josée Dayan and Malka Ribowska (Paris: Gallimard, 1979).

10 Simone de Beauvoir. *La Force des choses*, vol. II, p. 45.

11 The OAS (the *Organisation de l'armée secrète*) was an illegal military organization supporting French rule in Algeria in the sixties.

12 A drink made with champagne and peach juice, a Venetian specialty.

13 Hélène de Beauvoir. *Souvenirs*, p. 233.

[14] Ibid.

[15] Front de Libération Nationale: the organization struggling for Algeria's independence.

[16] The Evian Agreement between France and Algeria recognized Algerians' right to independence. Algeria became a sovereign nation as a result of this agreement.

[17] *Simone de Beauvoir: un film*, p. 34.

[18] Simone de Beauvoir. *Une Mort très douce*, p. 11.

[19] Hélène de Beauvoir. *Souvenirs*, p. 32.

[20] Simone de Beauvoir. *Une Mort très douce*, p. 148.

[21] As told to the author by Catherine C.

[22] Simone de Beauvoir. *Une Mort très douce*, p. 114.

[23] Ibid., p. 113.

[24] Ibid., p. 109.

[25] Interview with Hélène de Beauvoir.

[26] Simone de Beauvoir. *Une Mort très douce*, p. 126.

The Women's Cause

[1] Xavière Gonthier, ed. *Les Ecrits de Simone de Beauvoir*, textes inédits ou retrouvés (Paris: Gallimard, 1979), p. 463. (*The Writings of Simone de Beauvoir*, unpublished or rediscovered texts)

[2] Bernard Pivot, a longtime literary critic and commentator whose literary and cultural TV broadcasts *Apostrophes* and later *Bouillon de culture* were extremely popular cultural programs in France.

[3] Three leaders of the May 1968 student revolutionary movement.

[4] After four weeks of a general strike in which both factory workers and students had paralyzed France, Jacques Chirac, (later President of France), led the government negotiations with the leaders of the workers' unions. To end the strikes, the French government allowed the largest wage increase ever, and by mid-June 1968, the workers returned to work and the riots stopped.

[5] Jacques Prévert was a very popular poet whose poems were taught to schoolchildren.

[6] Hélène de Beauvoir. *Souvenirs*, p. 253.

[7] "A travers les galeries," in Courrier des Arts, *Le Monde*, 20 November 1969.

[8] Hélène de Beauvoir. *Souvenirs*, p. 255.

[9] Ibid.

[10] Boris Vian: a well-known French author of the late twentieth century.

[11] *Filles* in French, which also means her "daughters."

[12] During the Algerian War, Simone and the French lawyer Gisèle Halimi wrote a book telling the story of an Algerian young woman Djamila Boupacha. Beauvoir and Halimi denounced the fact that French soldiers had tortured Djamila Boupacha. The publication of the book created an uproar in France.

[13] Lorraine Rothman was a biology teacher and a feminist active in the area of women's health. She was one of the founders of the Feminist Women's Health Centers with Carol Downer.

[14] The Elysée Palace is the French presidential abode.

[15] SOS Battered Women stands for "Help battered women."

[16] The Légion d'Honneur is one of the highest medals of honor in France, established by Napoleon in 1802.

[17] All four of these were among the great twentieth-century writers of France.

[18] Monique is a very dear friend of both Hélène and Lionel.

The Twilight of the Mandarins

[1] Catalogue of the exhibition of paintings and engravings by Hélène de Beauvoir, Palais des Arts et de la Culture, April-May 1975.

[2] Though it was hard on me, as a woman and as a feminist, not to intervene and defend this woman.

[3] This was an extremely unfair accusation. As mentioned in other parts of the book, Simone was always very generous to her sister, Nelson Algren, her friends, Sartre, and numerous women in difficult economic situations.

[4] "In 1914, in an exchange of letters between Mathias Morhandt (first biographer of Camille Claudel, in 1898) and Auguste Rodin, the latter agreed in principle to take a few of Camille Claudel's sculptures. 'A few structures will need to be added, for her as well as for me. But whatever the proportion and if the thing is finished (sic) it will have its place.' In 1916, Rodin donated his work and his property to the state. He suffered another stroke. As he had not written this wish down in his will, the Rodin Museum opened its doors in 1918 after the artist's death without his wish being observed. Not until 1984, with the great retrospective of the work of Camille Claudel, organized by the Rodin Museum in 1984, would a room be permanently devoted to the artist." From Jacques Cassar, *Dossier Camille Claudel* (Paris: Maisonneuve et

Larose, 1997) pp. 252-253. Referred to the author through the kind cooperation of Jeanne Fayard.

5 Armand Borel always did recognize the professional qualities of his female colleagues. Yet prejudice remained strong in this milieu—women still could not become mathematicians, even after the war. In the last thirty years the situation has improved considerably, and more women mathematicians teach in universities and hold prestigious positions. Perhaps in the twenty-first century great women mathematicians will become famous. Thus far, however, not one of them has been awarded the Fields Medal or the Abel prize, both considered equivalents of the Nobel Prize in mathematics.

6 Simone de Beauvoir. *La Cérémonie des adieux* (Paris: Gallimard, 1981), p. 155. (*Adieux: A Farewell to Sartre*)

7 As told to the author by Hélène de Beauvoir after Sartre's death.

8 Yvette Roudy, one of the key figures in the history of French feminism, along with Simone de Beauvoir, made the greatest contributions to changing the laws in favor of French women's rights. A longtime French and European Congresswoman, and mayor of the town of Lisieux, Roudy was Minister of Women's Rights under François Mitterrand from 1981 to 1986. She continued to play an active role in promoting women's rights in France and in the European Union and became one of the leaders of the Socialist Party in France (the country's second largest political party).

9 Professor Yolanda Astarita Patterson founded and is the president of the international literary organization known as the Simone de Beauvoir Society. She has written a well-known book about Beauvoir and organizes an annual worldwide colloquium on Simone de Beauvoir. Professor Patterson knew Simone personally, and she and her husband became close friends of Hélène and Lionel. See bibliography for her contact information.

10 "Simone de Beauvoir, l'engagement d'une œuvre et d'une vie." Obituary of Simone de Beauvoir in *Le Monde*, 20 April 1986.

11 Patricia Niedzwiecki. *Hélène de Beauvoir, peintre* (Paris: Côté-Femmes, 1991). An art book containing many reproductions of the paintings. (Front flap of dust cover)

Goxwiller

1 Sylvie Le Bon–Beauvoir, ed. *Lettres à Sartre*, vol. II, 1940-1963 (Paris: Gallimard, 1990). Letter no. 312, late May 1954, p. 424. (*Letters to Sartre*)

² A viewing of these letters in the Department of Manuscripts at the Bibliothèque Nationale (microfilm 8658 and 8659) confirms that Simone de Beauvoir had rescinded the less complimentary passages (which are bracketed in the manuscript) concerning her sister. Usage requires that they not be quoted. Research performed by Anne Strasser-Weinhard for her doctoral dissertation, "Les figures féminines dans les autobiographies de Simone de Beauvoir," University of Nancy-II, 2001. ("Female Figures in Simone de Beauvoir's Autobiographies")

³ Catalogue of the exhibition of Hélène de Beauvoir's paintings at the Museum of Brest, April 1975.

⁴ *Lesbia Magazine* 105, May 1992, pp. 24-28. A lesbian feminist magazine very active in promoting women artists.

⁵ At the time, majority was reached at the age of twenty-one.

⁶ Bianca Lamblain. *Mémoires d'une jeune fille dérangée* (Paris: Balland, 1993). (*Memoirs of a Disrespectful Daughter*)

⁷ Patricia Niedzwiecki. *Hélène de Beauvoir, peintre.*

⁸ Thanks to the dynamism of the (female) director of the Paris Museum of Modern Art over the last twenty years, women artists are beginning to be recognized. But there is still a long way to go.

⁹ The museum has not been established yet, but in one of the buildings of the University of Aveiro a room displaying works of art was named after Hélène de Beauvoir.

¹⁰ This amounted to a sum of around 700 to 800 hundred dollars every week.

¹¹ Simone de Beauvoir. *Lettres à Nelson Algren*, Letter no. 66, 26 January 1948, p. 157.

¹² *Les Temps modernes* is the prestigious philosophical, sociological, and literary review founded by Sartre and Simone de Beauvoir in 1945. It was first directed by Sartre, then after his death by Simone de Beauvoir, and later by Claude Lanzmann.

Bibliography of
Simone de Beauvoir

All French editions published by Gallimard, Paris.

Novels:	**English Titles:**
L'Invitée, 1943.	*She Came to Stay*. New York: W. W. Norton & Co., 1945. Tr. Yvonne Moyse & Roger Senhouse.
Le Sang des autres, 1945	*The Blood of Others*. New York: Penguin, 1948. Tr. Yvonne Moyse & Roger Senhouse.
Tous les Hommes sont mortels, 1946.	*All Men Are Mortal*. New York: W. W. Norton & Co., 1955. Tr. Leonard M. Friedman.
Les Mandarins, 1954.	*The Mandarins*. New York: W. W. Norton & Co., 1956. Tr. Leonard M. Friedman.

Les Belles Images, 1966.	*Les Belles Images.* New York: French & European Publications, 1968. Tr. Patrick O'Brian.
Quand Prime le Spirituel, 1979.	*When Things of the Spirit Come First.* New York: Pantheon, 1982. Tr. Patrick O'Brian.

Narrative:

Une Mort très douce, 1964.	*A Very Easy Death*. New York: Pantheon, 1966. Tr. Patrick O'Brian.

Short Stories:

La Femme rompue, 1968.	*The Woman Destroyed*. New York: Pantheon, 1969. Tr. Patrick O'Brian.

Theater

Les Bouches inutiles, 1945.	——————————————

Literary Essays:

Pyrrhus et Cinéas, 1944.	——————————————
Pour une morale de l'ambiguïté, 1947.	——————————————
L'Amérique au jour le jour, 1948.	*America Day by Day*. Berkeley: University of California Press, 1953. Tr. Patrick Dudley.
Le Deuxième Sexe, I and II, 1949.	*The Second Sex*, 2 vols. New York: Vintage Books, 1952/1989. Tr. H. M. Parshley.

La Longue Marche	*The Long March*. London: Phoenix Press, 1958.
Mémoires d'une jeune fille rangée, 1958.	*Memoirs of a Dutiful Daughter*. New York: Perennial, 1959. Tr. James Kirkup.
La Force de l'âge, 1960.	*The Prime of Life*. New York: Marlowe & Co., 1994. Tr. Peter Green
La Force des choses, 1963.	*Hard Times: Force of Circumstance*. New York: Marlowe & Co., 1994. Tr. Richard Howard.
La Vieillesse, 1970.	*Coming of Age*. New York: W. W. Norton & Co., 1996. Tr. Patrick O'Brian
Tout Compte fait, 1972.	*All Said and Done*. New York: W. W. Norton & Co., 1974. Tr. Patrick O'Brian.
Les écrits de Simone de Beauvoir, Edited by Claude Francis and Fernande Gontier, 1979.	———————————
La Cérémonie des adieux, plus *Entretiens avec Jean-Paul Sartre*, 1981.	*Adieux: A Farewell to Sartre*. New York: Pantheon, 1984. Tr. Patrick O'Brian.
Lettres à Sartre, vol. I, 1930-1939; vol. II, 1940-1963. Introduced, edited, and annotated by Sylvie Le Bon--Beauvoir, 1990.	*Letters to Sartre*. London: Random House UK, 2000. Tr. Quintin Hoare.
Un amour transatlantique, *lettres à Nelson Algren*,	*A Transatlantic Love Affair: Letters to Nelson Algren*, 1947–1964. New York: New Press, 1998.

Testimony

Djamila Boupacha, in collaboration   *Djamila Boupacha*. Gallimard, 1962.
with Gisèle Halimi, 1962.

Film Script:

Simone de Beauvoir, by Josée Dayan and Malka Ribowska,
directed by Josée Dayan, Paris, 1979.

General Bibliography

Books

Bair, Deirdre. *Simone de Beauvoir, a Biography*. New York: Touchstone, 1991.

Beauvoir, Hélène de. *Souvenirs*. Memories collected by Marcelle Routier. Paris: Librairie Seguier, Garamont/Archimbaud, 1987.

Brownmiller, Susan. *In Our Time: Memoir of a Revolution*. El Dorado, AR: Delta Press, 2000.

Chalker, Rebecca. *The Clitoral Truth: The Secret World at Your Fingertips*. New York: Seven Stories Press, 2000.

——————— with Carol Downer. *A Woman's Book of Choices: Abortion, Menstrual Extraction, RU 486*. New York: Seven Stories Press, 1996.

——————— *The Complete Cervical Cap Guide*. New York: Harper Collins, 1987.

Federation of Feminist Women's Health Centers with Carol Downer and Rebecca Chalker. *A New View of a Woman's Body*. Feminist Health Press, 1991.

——————— *How to Stay out of the Gynecologist's Office*. Feminist Health Press, 1991.

Firestone, Shulamith. *The Dialectic of Sex: The Case for Feminist Revolution*. New York: Farrar, Straus & Giroux, 2003.

Greer, Germaine. *The Obstacle Race: The Fortunes of Women Painters and Their Work*. New York: Farrar, Straus & Giroux, 1982.

Millet, Kate. *Sexual Politics*. New York: Doubleday, 1969.

Moberg, Åsa. *Simone and I: Thinking about Simone de Beauvoir*. Stockholm: Norstedts, 1996.

Moi, Toril. *Simone de Beauvoir: The Making of an Intellectual Woman*. Malden, MA: Blackwell, 1994.

Monteil, Claudine. "Une femme en mouvement," (interview by Michel Braudeau on Simone de Beauvoir and May 1968), in *Le Monde*, 23 May 1998.

——————— "Simone de Beauvoir and the Women's Movement in France: An EyeWitness Account," in *Simone de Beauvoir Studies*, No. 14, 1997.

Niedzwiecki, Patricia. *Hélène de Beauvoir, peintre*. Paris: Côté-Femmes, 1991.

Patterson, Yolanda Astarita. *Simone de Beauvoir and the Demystification of Motherhood*. Rochester, NY: University of Rochester Press, 1989.

Roudy, Yvette. *A Cause d'elles* (memoirs). Preface by Simone de Beauvoir. Paris: Albin Michel, 1985.

Schwarzer, Alice. *Simone de Beauvoir Today: Conversations, 1972–1982*. New York: Vintage, 1984.

Serre, Claudine. *L'Évolution du féminisme à travers l'œuvre et la vie de Simone de Beauvoir*. Nice: Université de Nice, 1984.

——————————————— "Les Beauvoir," an interview with Hélène de Beauvoir in *Le Monde*, 20–21 April 1986.

——————————————— "L'engagement d'une œuvre et d'une vie" (Obituary of Simone de Beauvoir) in *Le Monde*, 20–21 April 1986.

Reviews and Magazines

Simone de Beauvoir Studies (ISSN 1063-2042). A bilingual English-French literary review published by the Simone de Beauvoir Society (20 volumes).

DVD

Escal, Emmanuelle. *Simone de Beauvoir*.

Feminist Associations and Organizations

Société Simone de Beauvoir (bilingual literary society). President: Yolanda Astarita Patterson (guyyopat@aol.com); Secretary General: Liliane Lazar (lillazar@aol.com).

About the Author

An active feminist in France since 1970, Claudine Monteil befriended Simone and Hélène de Beauvoir and Jean-Paul Sartre early on as they fought together for women's rights. She has published several books, which have been translated into several languages, including a biography on Sartre and Beauvoir, and today lectures regularly at conferences both in France and abroad. She lives in Paris and travels frequently to the United States. To contact her, please email her at claudincmonteil@hotmail.com.